ROUTLEDGE LIBRARY EDITIONS:
ORGANIZATIONS: THEORY & BEHAVIOUR

ORGANIZATION IN BUSINESS MANAGEMENT

ORGANIZATION IN BUSINESS MANAGEMENT

A guide for managers and potential managers

WALTER PUCKEY

Volume 24

LONDON AND NEW YORK

First published in 1963
Second revised edition 1970

This edition first published in 2013
by Routledge
2 Park Square, Milton Park, Abingdon, Oxon, OX14 4RN

Simultaneously published in the USA and Canada
by Routledge
711 Third Avenue, New York, NY 10017

Routledge is an imprint of the Taylor & Francis Group, an informa business

British Library Cataloguing in Publication Data
A catalogue record for this book is available from the British Library

ISBN: 978-0-415-65793-8 (Set)
eISBN: 978-0-203-38369-8 (Set)
ISBN: 978-0-415-82492-7 (Volume 24)
eISBN: 978-0-203-38385-8 (Volume 24)

Publisher's Note
The publisher has gone to great lengths to ensure the quality of this reprint but
points out that some imperfections in the original copies may be apparent.

Disclaimer
The publisher has made every effort to trace copyright holders and would
welcome correspondence from those they have been unable to trace.

 MIX
Paper from
responsible sources
FSC
www.fsc.org   FSC® C013604   Printed and bound by CPI Group (UK) Ltd, Croydon, CR0 4YY

ORGANIZATION

IN BUSINESS MANAGEMENT

A guide for managers and potential managers

SIR WALTER PUCKEY

HUTCHINSON OF LONDON

HUTCHINSON & CO. (*Publishers*) LTD
178–202 Great Portland Street, London, W.1

London Melbourne Sydney
Auckland Bombay Toronto
Johannesburg New York

First published 1963
Second (revised) edition 1970

Printed in Great Britain by litho on smooth wove paper
by Anchor Press, and bound by Wm. Brendon,
both of Tiptree, Essex
09 103890 1 (cased)
09 103891 X (paper)

Acknowledgements

The author wishes to acknowledge with thanks permission to make quotations from the following:

Management and Organization by Louis A. Allen, Copyright 1958, published by McGraw-Hill Book Company Inc.; *Principles of Self Organization* by Dr. W. Ross Ashby (Editors Von Foerster and Zopf) Pergamon Press Ltd.; *Concept of the Social Organization* by E. Wight Bakke, John Wiley & Sons Inc.; *Principles of Social and Political Theory* by Sir Ernest Barker, The Clarendon Press; *Remembering* by Sir Frederick C. Bartlett, Cambridge University Press; *The Hinge of Fate* by Sir Winston Churchill, Cassell & Co. Ltd.; *Organization and Mangement* by R. C. Davis, Harper & Row Ltd.; *Organization Engineering* by Henry Dennison, McGraw-Hill Book Company, Inc.; *The Anatomy of Work* by Georges Friedmann, Heinemann Educational Books Ltd.; *Organization as a Moral Problem* by Robert T. Golembiewski, printed in Public Administration Review by permission of the American Society for Public Administration; *Are the Colleges killing Education?* from an article by Oscar Handlin published in The Atlantic Monthly; *The Quality of Leadership*, a paper by Cameron Hawley at the A.M.A. Midwinter Personnel Conference in 1960; *Autonomous Group Functioning* by P. G. Herbst, Tavistock Publications; *Eugenics in Evolutionary Perspective* by Sir Julian Huxley from The Galton Lecture published in The Eugenics Review; *Organization Structure and the Performance and Job Satisfaction of Physiologists* by Meltzer and Salter, American Sociological

Review; *Onward Industry* by Mooney and Reilley, Harper and Row Ltd.; *A Methectic Theory of Social Organization* from a paper by Dr. T. T. Paterson; *Listening with Both Ears* by Dr. A. Rapoport, Research for Industry, Vol. 14, No. 5, Stanford Research Institute; *Personnel Selection and Vocational Guidance* by Rodger and Cavanagh, from *Society*, Routledge and Kegan Paul Ltd.; *The Battle for the Mind* by William Sargant, William Heinemann Ltd.; *On Growth and Form* by Sir D'Arcy W. Thompson, Cambridge University Press; *20th Century Leadership* by L. Urwick, Isaac Pitman & Son Ltd.; *The Making of Scientific Management* by Urwick and Brech, Isaac Pitman & Son Ltd.; *The Living Brain* by Dr. Grey Walter, Gerald Duckworth & Co. Ltd.; *The Limits of Business Administration and Responsibility* by G. Prys Williams, The Pall Mall Press Ltd.; *Management and Technology* by Joan Woodward, H.M. Stationery Office, Code No. 47-203-3.

Permission has also been gratefully received to use extracts from the following publications:

Management Report dated August 30th, 1962, of the Research Institute of America; *The Economist* of December 23rd, 1961; *The Manager* (Viscount Slim's Elbourne Memorial Lecture); *Financial Times* of November 10th, 1962.

The author wishes to make special reference to *Understanding Organizational Behavior* by Chris Argyris, Tavistock Publications; *Organization, The Framework of Management* by E. F. L. Brech, Longmans, Green & Co.; *The Study of Groups* by Josephine Klein, Routledge & Kegan Paul Ltd.; *Modern Organization Theory* edited by Mason Haire, John Wiley & Sons Inc.; these books have given him a great deal of valuable information.

Contents

Foreword to Second Edition

SINCE THIS book was originally written, the significance of management has become even greater, and the number of young managers even larger. What is not so apparent is a wider understanding of management itself, and a corresponding ability to bring the many courses of study available in line with modern, national requirements.

The proliferation of courses has continued unabated, and the number of institutions catering for managers has grown greatly in recent years, ranging from universities and business schools to those many commercial bodies which organize instruction. An examination of their syllabuses and subjects causes one to wonder whether an adequate amount of co-ordination and simplification has been applied. Management today has so many facets that it is in danger of losing its ability to produce light.

Of one thing I am sure. Organization, as an essential management skill, is even more important today than when I originally wrote this book, and current industrial, economic and social trends all underline the need to consider even more fully and skilfully the relationships between groups and individuals with which this book is primarily concerned.

A Personal Introduction

THIS BOOK is written primarily for the young manager and all who are concerned with his development. Those who set out to read it are entitled to an explanation of my own managerial development and how I came to hold my present views.

Have you ever made a list of those people, ideas or events who or which have played an unusually significant part in your life? I once read a paper at a graduate conference on 'the men in my life', who ranged from a small and insignificant-looking foreman during my apprenticeship to a professor of mathematics in one of my educational periods. Such men had an ability to teach and to inspire far beyond normal, and I remember them all with gratitude.

What *managerial* marks has my past made upon me? They are few in number but significant in character. The first was a sudden realization that I should be more concerned with men than machines. I was trained as an engineer and having risen to junior management I became more involved in discussions and decisions about people, which convinced me that it is one thing to take part in personal discussions in the home, or in some other social setting, but the problems become more complicated when one's working life is involved. There are, for instance, greater organizational and economic pressures applied to the individual within his business, and there is, too, the added pressure of *external*

9

forces, such as those exerted by unions, government and competitors.

I had, I suppose, the usual opportunities of a young man to live a family life and to mix in various social and educational groups. But not until I became immersed in technology and machines during my earlier working career did I suddenly realize how important were people. Perhaps this was because I was fortunate in my friends and advisers, or perhaps it was my elevation to supervisory rank which made me realize that machines could be really effective only if they were accepted by, and used wisely by, men.

I began then to see more clearly that individuals could attain real personal stature only if they were effective members of a group. From that date my interest in organization grew.

My third significant managerial milestone was a fuller understanding of management as a social as well as an industrial force. I said earlier that there are certain significant differences between a 'social' and an 'industrial' task; but increasingly over the years I have seen far more points of similarity than difference, and today I realize that woven intimately into my managerial task is a 'social' responsibility which requires me, before making almost any major internal decision, to consider its external implications. I, and my company, can exist satisfactorily only if the ambient conditions are right. We react upon each other.

The fourth managerial mark made on me was that an understanding of the 'objectives' or purpose of a group was a necessary prelude to greater personal and group efficiency. This sounds almost a truism, but while in theory we usually support such a statement, we often do not, in practice, act accordingly. Let us consider, for instance, what to me was a most significant *managerial* decision—to adopt 'joint consultation'. In the early days of World War II Ernest Bevin was appointed Minister of Labour, and set the stage for wide-spread management/labour changes. He sponsored an agreement between Ordnance factory managers and the Unions which provided for formal joint consultative committees of managers and Union representatives in each factory to advise on methods of improving efficiency. No attempt was made to impose this system on private enterprise, but the Federations and Associations of Employers did advise their own members to consider seriously the adoption of similar consultative measures.

As an active young manager during that period I remember vividly the reactions of many of my fellow managers. Joint consultation in one form or another had been practised for many years by a few managerial pioneers, but the thought of making it wide-spread and official was anathema to most managers, and in the private sector of industry, despite Union pressure, very little real joint consultation had developed, and all too often what had was something of a façade rather than a real method of creating fuller understanding as a basis for greater efficiency.

In an earlier book[1] I referred at some length to those days and attitudes. Looking back over a greater span of years has confirmed in me the belief that Ernest Bevin produced, for management generally, one of its most significant milestones, and for me, personally, something which profoundly affected my philosophy and practice. It showed me during subsequent years that top managers could rise to top status only if they recognized, and genuinely acted upon the belief, that *every* person in the group wanted to help and would work better if he knew better how he could help.

This seemed to me, logically, to follow an earlier managerial milestone, that men were more important than machines. It seemed, also, to emphasize the importance of group organization, which, in order to maximize the group's contribution, had as its purpose the creation of a full understanding among all within the group.

I will select, as a fifth mark, my changing attitude to management as a profession. It is interesting to look back over managerial

[1] *What is this Management?*

discussions during past years and to reflect how little progress has been made in defining the manager's place in the community. The term 'profession' has, despite certain doubtful usages, great honour in Britain, and we are long accustomed to giving deference (if not always high incomes) to doctors (of all types), lawyers, teachers and others who are loosely grouped as professional people. We have in this country a widely based structure of professional institutions, including The Royal Society and scores of other reputable bodies. All of them require entrance qualifications, and their activities are based primarily on *individual* membership rather than on company or commercial interests.

The British Institute of Management has had a difficult childhood among its professional partners. It was launched by the late Sir Stafford Cripps in his capacity as a Labour Government Chancellor, and was provided with a large government grant which (nearly) destroyed the independence which is a feature of all professional bodies. The development of the B.I.M. involved a take-over of the Institute of Industrial Administration, which was much nearer to professional status, at least at lower management levels.

This take-over frankly recognized the facts of economic life, which in the management field meant that not enough senior managers were willing, *individually*, to provide an income to the B.I.M. which made it independent of commercial and government interests. The inevitable result was that in order to exist, the B.I.M. had to obtain a major part of its income from government and corporate, rather than individual, sources. This, by definition, placed it more firmly in the category of Association rather than Institution, and many of its earlier difficulties can be traced to this failure to be neither one thing nor another.

Over several decades there has been much discussion, often acrimonious, on the professional status of managers. In my earlier managerial years a small core of managers, centred to some extent around the I.I.A., inclined to the view that management was a subject which should be as intensively studied from as early an educational age as any of the specialist subjects like engineering or chemistry. This involved early selection as a management trainee, and it was often considered unnecessary—in fact, undesirable—to achieve status in another specialism as a basis for managerial selection and advancement.

There were times when I had the impression that my own technological training and technically based management experience were misfortunes rather than, as I believe today, advantages. The term 'scientific management' was emerging and had little to do with any particular science, but connoted rather a scientific understanding of management, and with it, one assumed, professional status.

Looking back, one wonders why an attitude developed which at that time denigrated rather than supported a scientific or technical education as a basis for management training. We would expect a science or technological graduate to be more capable of 'thinking scientifically' than, say, an arts graduate, although there are several limitations to this argument. But there was, in earlier years, no strong inclination, when selecting management trainees, towards those with a background in science or technology, but only the view that they should be caught young and given a fairly long specialized training in 'management'. The form of training was hardly what I would have described as 'scientific'.

Several influences are changing this earlier attitude. First, the working world is increasingly conditioned by scientific and technological developments, which are best likely to be effectively controlled by those who reasonably understand them. Second, scientific management, or at least a scientific approach to management, is, many of us believe, best practised by those whose education has been subject to the 'discipline' inherent in scientific or technological studies. Third, management is not only 'top' management, and it is likely that more and better top managers will emerge from those who have successfully displayed good managerial qualities in technical fields lower down.

An earlier technological training combined with a pretty intensive engineering experience left its mark on me to the extent that I looked, and still look, at most subjects through 'scientifically' tinted glasses, and terms like 'scientific management' were lapped up with gusto. But I have already confessed that I began to realize, at a critical point in my managerial career, that men, and the organization of men into groups, were much more difficult subjects on which to practise my scientific approach and machine theories. I realized too that because there were severe limitations to scientific management there were many obstacles in the path to 'professional' management and a professional institution of managers. My own period of membership on the Council of the British Institute of Management confirmed this view.

But I must affirm my present view, which is that although I see more clearly today the difficulties of developing scientific management, I see equally clearly that a greater proportion of first-class young men are going to be 'scientifically' educated, and will provide a larger pool of potential managers. Their disciplined education and their theoretical skills can be their managerial hope, and also their downfall. It will be their hope if they challenge tradition with modern tools and a liberal outlook, their downfall if they ever forget that better management must in the end result in better men and women.

My managerial career has made at least one other significant mark on me: it is a realization that automation is not advanced mechanization but something much more significant. Its ability to provide many new mechanical machines, systems and controls is highly important to me as a manager, but much more important is its effect on control and communication, which are vital managerial tools. Mechanization provided tools which managers persuaded others to use; *automation can be directly applied by us to our own managerial tasks.* Is not management itself likely to be influenced greatly by computers, cybernetics, ergonomics, neurology, psychology, biology, communication theory? Already we see clearly enough into a misty future to realize that the Second Industrial Revolution is more revolutionary than many are prepared to admit.

The first hundred or more years of our industrial history saw a great magnification of man's muscles through the use of machines. The next few decades will witness no less an interest in machine muscle power, but a tremendously increased interest in brain or control power, designed to make managers, men and muscles even more effective. Dr. Bowden in his B.C.A.C.[1] 1962 lecture[2] gave a fascinating review of these developments, and his paper is well worth reading by those managers who doubt whether computers can play an increasingly useful part in *managerial* development. He and I have no doubts—they can.

I use the rather mundane term 'management mechanics' to illustrate these new developments, and while most of them are currently being developed in their own right, as specialist technical projects, they are likely increasingly to provide better tools for managers and may well drastically revise management education, training and practices. Let me quote only two examples. Neurological experiments have already shown us that electro-encephalography is not only capable of analysing brain rhythms in disturbed minds but *may* provide us with a means of assessing personality, which is one of the missing links in management selection. Operational research, aided by modern data-processing equipment, will not only help to provide a scientifically based solution to, say, product distribution patterns, but may also reduce the number of variable factors on which a manager has to exercise vital judgement. He can be provided with a greater volume of programmed decisions, enabling him to devote more time to the

[1] British Conference on Automation and Computation.
[2] 'Can Managers be automated?' Dr. B. V. Bowden. *B.C.A.C. Record*, 1962.

unprogrammed variety, including that important group known as 'personal difficulties'.

Perhaps all this seems to indicate that management will increasingly rely upon mechanics, which will require managers to be more skilled in scientific and technological developments over a wide field. To some extent this is true, but the wise, knowledgeable manager will realize that although his tool-kit is becoming larger, his own skill must be developed, not necessarily in designing those tools but in ascertaining their potentialities (and their dangers).

Finally, I have been impressed greatly in recent years by the reaction upon each other of the individual and his group, which underlines a comment I made earlier. Some years ago I decided that a more scientifically based method of management selection was required, which, to a considerable extent, sprang from my earlier realization that one man could make or mar a company. It has been gratifying to me and complimentary to my fellow managers that better selection methods have been so readily accepted in Britain. Yet, paradoxically, this concentrated preoccupation with the selection of individual managers has tended to confirm in me the view I expressed earlier, that however important the individual, his group is equally important. Such an attitude sounds like heresy to some (and often to me) and it is a matter of considerable philosophic interest. But its effect on my managerial outlook has been to develop in me a growing interest in the place of an individual within his group, and also in the organization of the group, to ensure maximum individual effectiveness.

This introduction has been devoted to a record of my personal development as a manager. Every book is largely a personal interpretation of events, and in writing this one I am encouraged by the knowledge that many young managers have, over the years, asked for my advice on the assumption that my experience as a manager has been wide enough in scope and intensive enough in application to be interesting.

What pattern emerges from the managerial marks that experience has made on me? Let us tabulate them:

(1) Men are more important than machines.
(2) Men are fully effective only as members of a group.
(3) Managers have a social responsibility.
(4) Good understanding among all grades is an essential prelude to greater effectiveness.
(5) Management is not in the foreseeable future a profession although it is desirable to travel hopefully and more energetically in that direction, educationally and socially.
(6) Science and technology will greatly influence management training and practice, particularly in providing better control and communication tools, and techniques.

Let us now see how we can apply these 'marks' to managerial development, or at least to that part of a manager's job which we call organization.

B

I

The Management Scene

How old is management? If we assume that it involves responsibility for the actions of more than one person (i.e. yourself) it was obviously practised by Adam (or Eve). It must have been an essential ingredient of millions of groups, including that basic group the family.

But the word *management* is relatively new, and a *widely* based study of it is even newer. Students will no doubt have studied the contributions made by management pioneers, and admirably documented by Urwick, Brech and others. My purpose will be served by confining myself to a relatively few significant points of progress which, if linked together, may allow us more accurately to extrapolate them into a managerial future.

The Trend of Management

Why is it that 'scientific management' has failed to make greater progress? Urwick and Brech, in Volume I of their admirable series *The Making of Scientific Management*, writing[1] twelve years after first publication, said: 'We are still trying to meet the results of scientific enquiry with "political" modes of thought. We are merely another decade nearer the catastrophe which is inevitable if we do so.' These are strong words, and one wonders why, if catastrophe is looming larger, we, as managers, have neither the sense nor the skill to avert it.

[1] Urwick and Brech. 1956.

Surveying the pioneering work in management one is impressed by the contributions made by those who would, one feels, like to be described as 'practical people'. In their selected list of management pioneers Urwick and Brech showed us that the majority of them not only brought new thinking to their subjects but were, generally, successful in applying this thinking to practical ends. They were people who 'walked with ideas but did not lose the common touch'.

Is this a special feature of management development, and is it good or bad? In the fields of science and technology we find that large-scale utilization of basic knowledge took place only after a sufficiently large theoretical pressure had generated. For instance, the First Industrial Revolution, while conditioned by other forces, was made possible largely by an earlier scientific revolution, where men like Descartes, Hooke, Newton and Boyle provided the sparks of genius which lit many practical fires. (Some of these earlier scientists were very 'practical' also, but their great contribution to knowledge was in the field of research, and the formulation of laws or principles.) Similarly, the Second Industrial Revolution, which we have now entered, was made possible by an organized, widely dispersed *research* programme, which was itself created largely by the pressure of two world wars.

What is scientific management? To quote again from *The Making of Scientific Management*: 'Scientific Management means thinking scientifically instead of traditionally or customarily about the processes involved in the control of social groups who co-operate in production and distribution.'

Urwick and Brech suggest that industry is more likely to produce 'a higher proportion of administrators equipped and intellectually disposed to think scientifically about problems of management, than other professions. Industrialists also are in constant contact with machines—themselves the product of applied science, and machinery in itself is apt to encourage an objective attitude of mind. No other attitude is very much use.

Neither passion nor persuasion will make an ill-adjusted machine work effectively; it is necessary to understand and to apply mechanical principles. No doubt a man with concern for machinery will be more successful than one who has no such interest, but the most ham-handed creature instinctively grasps that being subjective about it does not get him anywhere. Machinery imposes a mental discipline—a discipline in favour of thinking in facts and quantities, rather than in fancies and theories—in short, a discipline favourable to scientific thinking.'

As an industrialist I am gratified by these remarks, but they must, I believe, be taken with caution. It is true that industry has taken a growing interest in management, and is currently spending at least moderate sums in helping to support and provide facilities and students for management courses in a variety of universities, colleges and centres. It is true also that machines 'impose a mental discipline', which seems an essential requirement for those who wish to think scientifically about management.

But neither of these industrial qualities has, so far, enabled us to provide an adequate scientific foundation for better management. Research into management on a scale anything like research into 'things' has so far removed only the top layers of scientific excavation, and it is my view that management, like other wide-spread and important developments, must have a deeply dug scientific foundation before a better structure rises into common vision and use. As Professor Weiss Kofp[1] said 'every Society that wanted to be in the forefront of practical technology must be vigorously engaged in basic science'.

Let us consider the traditional sequence of research, development and production. Why (I again ask) has the term 'scientific management' failed to capture the imagination, or even the interest, of so many influential people? In recent years we have seen organized research emerge on a large scale, covering many

[1] Director General European Organization for Nuclear Research. Annual Lunch. Parliamentary and Scientific Committee. London. Feb. 1963.

subjects and specialisms. Yet management, which has an overwhelming claim to be the superior controlling and co-ordinating function among many specialisms, still lags seriously behind as a subject thought fit for large-scale research.

There are, I believe, many reasons, ranging from the traditional to the personal. We in Britain are quite happy to talk of 'leadership', but still consider management rather a non-U occupation. We have long accepted the concept and status of professionalism in medicine, law and teaching, for instance, but we are a long way from accepting management as a 'professional' occupation, or even one which requires professional standards of competence and integrity.

In Britain we are quite happy also to preserve the traditional concept of a university as a place which exists primarily to encourage students to think objectively and analytically about any subject, but (perish the thought) not too much about any one subject; it is considered an insult to suggest to some universities that they already provide 'vocational' education. As 'management education' is regarded by most universities as a vocational subject it is hardly surprising that it has taken so long to break through the crust of educational tradition.

Even in business, or in management circles, the term 'manager' is insecurely fixed in the job spectrum. When so many subordinates say 'We will see the *management* about it' they are denigrating the term 'manager', which should be personalized at every opportunity. The depth of the management team in most businesses is not a precise dimension, and the statement I have just quoted is often made by a subordinate because he is not sure whether *he* is in the management team. He may have been told that as, say, a foreman, he is a manager, but circumstances compel him to disbelieve it. The tradition of management as an upper-level activity is still too strong.

Another traditional barrier to managerial status has, if anything, become more rather than less difficult to break through in recent years. The Institute of Directors was formed in 1903 but only in the last two decades has it, under dynamic leadership, made significant progress. In a period of ten years it rose from a membership of 6,000 to 40,000 and provided itself with lush surroundings, an attractive journal and wide publicity.

To become a director has been, and is increasingly today, the ambition of many managers, but paradoxically its status may be hollow in terms of professional competence. A director of a company may be (I repeat, may be) incompetent, and may hold his position solely on grounds of nepotism, or for other non-professional reasons. His may be the most unskilled of all titles, but his position is secure. The Institute of Directors has sponsored research into the duties and responsibilities of directors, and its decision to support management research at Balliol[1] confirmed, I presume, the view that a link existed between 'director' and 'manager' tasks. It has the means, and I believe the desire, to do much more. My purpose here is, however, to draw attention to what seems to be a status gap near the top end of the promotion ladder which managers are expected (and hope) to climb. 'Why,' so many people ask, 'is it necessary to introduce higher professional standards into management when the *next* step upwards is into a realm where professional standards are too often regarded as a disadvantage, or at least have not, so far, been an essential qualification?'

Perhaps as good an answer as any is that the higher the professional status of managers generally, the higher the status of directors will become, which seems a good thing for all.

At the moment I am not optimistic about the greater acceptance of scientific management among a sufficiently large body of senior people. But we are living in a world which more than ever before requires better management, and I am convinced that there are

[1] Mr. G. MacLelland was appointed to a Fellowship in Management Studies.

many young managers able and willing to catch the mood and break down the barriers if they are given reasonable guidance and opportunity.

Rapid progress in most fields is made when substantial research produces a foundation of laws or principles, or a *widely accepted* 'body of knowledge'. Research has long been regarded as a vital, important component of university life, and some (including myself) believe that universities must enlarge greatly their *management* research work. What are the chances? Not particularly good when we compare management's chances against so many other claims. The University Grants Committee faces many demands, not only for a considerable expansion of existing facilities, but for the creation of many entirely new universities, but I understand that substantial additional provision for management research is unlikely unless it can be financed from other sources, presumably largely industrial.[1]

So much for a few of the traditional barriers to 'scientific management', or, putting it another way, higher professional management status. I suggested earlier that there were 'personal' reasons also why scientific management had failed to make adequate progress.

These reasons vary greatly but it is regrettably true that some of the supporters of scientific management have inadvertently erected their own barriers while ostensibly working to demolish them. In many spheres progress has been slowed down because the prophets have not themselves been accepted, which, in turn, reduces the acceptability of their message. In management circles there are just not enough people of influence at present to spread the gospel although I see signs of a 'revival' movement.

[1] The Council of Industry for Management Education has appealed for more funds, largely to provide the London and Manchester Business Schools with greater facilities.

If enough money is found, how then will vice-chancellors or principals set up facilities and find the right staff for this form of research? The present situation is patchy, and not particularly illuminating; for instance, one university includes management within its social-studies department, another within its economic department, yet another in its engineering department. Perhaps this is relatively unimportant in the early stages of research, when even the 'sponsoring' departments may not immediately be able to define the new subject. Even today one definition of economics is 'the study of the optimum allocation of scarce resources', and, as a critic has said, 'that might also fit psychiatry!' Management is, however, far behind economics in clarity of definition and in university activity. It is right, I believe, that varying approaches to its study should be made at this experimental stage, but it must be borne in mind that if the subject continues to be secondary, and not primary, it will not make full progress. Management is a subject of vital primary interest to the well-being of our country, and if it is to be treated scientifically on such a high level of importance it must become a primary subject at a number of British universities, and not only at Business Schools.

The Supply of Potential Managers

What sort of young men, and how many of them will become available for managerial development? Let us discuss one significant group. Much of my spare time was taken up some years ago in helping to establish the Diploma in Technology, and many thousands of students, or 'undergraduates', followed courses which lead to the award of this diploma, which although now changed in name, continues in form.

A special feature of this relatively new honours standard technological award was its insistence on the integration of theory and practice, which means that every successful candidate should at the end of his combined college/company course be able to apply more rapidly his chosen technological studies to practical ends.

Those following this sandwich form of university training are more likely to be candidates for an industrial management career, and will bring to it a background of honours standard theory which should, logically, be applied at all stages of their subsequent careers. Will these graduates later on approach the management job with the theoretical confidence developed in their technological work, or will they, when setting foot on the managerial ladder, put theory behind them on the assumption that they are now entering more fully into the realm of *people* who are not, so they have been told, susceptible to any theoretical analysis?

It is fascinating to an older manager such as I am to conject upon the impact on management of many thousands of young men educated and trained generally to a consistently higher technological order than their predecessors. Will this mean a much more intensive application of theory to management, and if so will the pendulum swing so far in that direction that we had better begin right away to plan counter action against this potentially heavy dose of 'scientific management'?

But there we might pause and reflect upon another feature which, as far as possible, was built in to the new courses. This was an insistence upon a reasonable amount of formal (and more opportunity for *informal*) guidance in liberal pursuits and attitudes. This part of the total course was found, in practice, to be most difficult to design, provide and assess, but it aims at creating a reasonable balance between technical specialism and social satisfaction, between the narrowing theories of science and the broadening requirements of life.

In what special manner will these young potential managers justify themselves? They will, we hope, carry forward into their working lives the two features which were, as far as possible, built into their education. First, an ability to understand theory and an opportunity to apply it more skilfully to practice; second, a realization that all technical progress reacts upon, and should ultimately be for the benefit of, social progress and individual satisfactions.

These abilities should be most valuable to budding managers. They will face in the next few decades a flood of technological development waiting urgently to be applied, yet never before were there so many people wanting to be assured that these things are for the benefit of social and individual progress, and not, largely, for destructive or sectional interests. .

This book is written for young managers and for those who aspire to be called by that title. It recognizes that what those of my generation call 'management' may not be the correct specification for the managers of the next generation. It assumes that more future managers will be educated to higher standards, generally, and in the *application* of theory, and that the technological and social climate will be even more complex than that of today. It assumes, too, that the organizational aspects of management are likely to become relatively far more important,[1] and that new areas of scientific and technological research are likely to influence management theory and practice greatly.

The willingness and ability of more future managers to use theory more intensively and wisely means that management, including its organizational component, can be approached, studied and applied more scientifically than we, the existing managers, have been able or willing to do.

I wonder whether I am expecting too much.

I said earlier that this book is written for young managers, and in writing it I have endeavoured to integrate my experiences, my theories and my hopes. The subject I have chosen is one which has not, so far, encouraged a widespread theoretical approach, but if future managers are more inclined, as I hope they will be, to support a more intensive theoretical approach to their careers, they must understand clearly where manage-

---

[1] For a summary of my reasons see *Management Principles*.

ment is today, and how it arrived here, before projecting it and themselves into the future. I hope this book will help to provide a launching platform, and guidance during the first stage of flight!

Management as a Post-graduate Study

It is relevant here to discuss the significance of management as a post-graduate rather than an undergraduate subject. British universities, and many technical colleges, have long accepted the need to provide post-graduate opportunities. In universities this has largely been through research, leading to higher degrees, and in colleges through special short courses. In all higher educational centres post-graduate work must surely increase greatly, not only in research but in course work. I foresee a considerable interest in the latter at various post-graduate levels, and it is quite appropriate for a department or school of management to exist in this context, which would influence under-graduate syllabuses, carry out adequate post-graduate research into management and organize substantial course work in its application.

The *Financial Times*, May 7th, 1963, suggested that management training is now on the move. If, as the leading article suggested, this is largely to be through the more active growth of 'business schools', I hope all will have read the strong criticisms recently made by Americans on their own business school situation. Reports such as that prepared by Silk show how much more needs to be done. I must repeat again that a further proliferation of courses based on present knowledge is hardly worth making. There must be much more research into the nature and structure of management, in other words a deeper foundation must be dug before we attempt to add more floors to the present unsatisfactory structure. This is primarily a university task, but how different from the usual conception of a 'business school.'

What other research bodies are, or should be, interested in management? One difficulty, when discussing management research, or indeed management practice, is to answer the question 'What is management?' Even the British Institute of Management finds it difficult to provide an answer. For instance, when we organize a conference on ergonomics is this a management conference? When the Medical Research Council organizes an exhibition or conference on applied psychology is it part of management? Again, when the N.P.L.[1] sponsors a symposium on communication theory is this managerial research? A short answer at this stage of the book is that all these examples contribute to management and one hopes that someone is constantly searching these off-beat subjects for their *management* significance. Perhaps the Ministry of Technology's Warren Spring Laboratory is keeping 'a continuous record of research in progress in the human sciences' with a special eye on its application to a better management theory?

Scientific management must by implication use a great variety of scientific knowledge and specialisms in a study of its theory and application, and perhaps the greatest difficulty in deciding to increase the content of management research is to decide on the definition and scope of management itself. It will certainly be found to be a meeting point of an increasing number of specialisms, and the danger is that those at this central meeting point might take unto themselves more responsibility and authority for the various specialisms than is good for either management or the specialist researchers. This was the state of affairs which developed in the management field after the B.I.M. was formed to act as a managerial focal point. The Baillieu Committee (1946) recommended that its functions should include:

(a) To provide a centre for the study of management and for enquiry and research into management problems bringing together by affiliation the existing functional bodies and assisting them as may be necessary to develop within their own specialized fields.

[1] National Physical Laboratory.

(b) To serve as a central body with which firms as such can be associated as corporate subscribers or members, to survey the whole field of management, to disseminate information and to encourage education and training.

(c) To provide a central Institution with which any person concerned with or interested in management may be associated, and to which individuals with appropriate qualifications may belong as full members or associates.

(d) To serve as a body to which educational authorities, technical colleges, universities and other educational agencies can look for advice and assistance in the development of courses of instruction for students at all levels, and which would encourage firms to give members of their staffs every opportunity to take advantage of post-graduate courses.

(e) To disseminate information about management practice and technique and current developments therein by arranging discussions on management questions, publishing a journal of proceedings and the results of specific studies, and by any other means which may be appropriate.

(f) To arrange directly or through affiliated bodies for groups of members to examine and study in the field particular problems of management which arise.

(g) To serve as a bureau of information, and as a link between those who are seeking help on management problems and those ready and able to give it.

(h) To maintain a library of management literature and to organize conferences on management.

(i) To maintain contact with management bodies and management practice in other countries as an aid to exercising all of the preceding functions.

Unfortunately, those responsible for the early development of the B.I.M. failed to realize that 'co-ordination' could easily be assumed by other bodies to mean 'control'.[1] Considerable resentment was caused among various specialist bodies years ago at what seemed to them to be the unwarranted 'control' activities of the B.I.M., resulting in years of progress lost to the cause of management through recriminations and misunderstandings.

More progress would have been made if it became recognized more widely that many established specialist bodies were anxious to introduce a certain amount of 'management' into their own syllabuses, qualifications and examinations. The B.I.M. should have extended its hands (as it now does) to these bodies, and acted as a link between specialist management and general management, assisting in providing a common approach to the former, and a smooth path for the specialist who aspired to the latter.

There are, I believe, five basic requirements which must exist before 'scientific management' takes a significant step forward. They are:

(1) The recognition by a greater number of influential managers and institutions (including government) that a more intensive study of management is overdue, and should be adequately sponsored without delay.

(2) A recognition by universities that scientific management is higher on the national education and research scale than has so far been recognized. This will result in the setting up of many more management departments and much more research.

(3) A definition of management, and an agreement with other specialists on the scope of 'management' research.

(4) The formulation of an 'integrated' research programme which takes full account of the manner in which other specialists and institutions can contribute to a fuller development of scientific management, and can use the results to improve their own specialisms.

[1] According to Mary Parker Follett it is!

(5) A central professional institution of high standing.

These five requirements are not necessarily in order of importance or timing, although if a fuller recognition (1) is established,
the others logically follow; the wide-spread recognition of a
need will usually provide the means.

So much, at the moment, for the research aspect of scientific
management. Until this is more securely and widely recognized
and organized in centres of higher learning, scientific management
will not take a significant step forward.

But what about the better utilization of better research? It is
here that the technical colleges should come even more fully into
their own, and justify their great advance in facilities, organization and status. In recent years the government has spent over one
hundred million pounds in expanding technological and technical educational facilities. A national structure, headed by
technological universities has been created which in practical
terms now enables us to see many large and impressive edifices
rising around the country, full of equipment many older universities might well envy, giving new and higher-paid opportunities to teaching staff, and capable of providing an increasing
number of potential managers.

What is the particular role of the technological universities in
management education? I have already said that management, if
it is to progress, must be provided with a greater research element
based, I believe, on universities. But research must be translated
into development and practice, and the technological universities,
because of their greater contacts with industry and commerce,
have a special role to play. I foresee a considerable extension of
management research activities, but I hope that this research will
be of a different nature and will concentrate more fully on research
into better means of utilizing new (and old) knowledge. There is
much need for it, and I believe the Ministry of Technology has a
major part to play in this development. It can, for instance, base

an applied research unit on every technological university so that the latter becomes a recognized base for applied research in a particular subject. This would lead to a greater use of it by industry, a more rapid development of research in it and an increase in its status.

The third and final stage of scientific management is its practice, and while this is largely a function of industry and commerce, the universities and colleges have an expanding role to play. Universities must provide more post-graduate special courses, particularly those which provide a common meeting place for research workers in the many specialisms which contribute to scientific management; colleges must provide an increasing number of courses which aim at carrying research findings more rapidly to the practitioners. Management research, even more than other research, requires many interpreters who can translate it into a common tongue.

It is difficult to put this sort of complete programme into quantitative and qualitative terms. The twenty-three million people gainfully employed in Britain are effective in direct relation to the effectiveness of the managers who control them. One is reminded here of the young man who wished to impress his shooting ability on his girl friend at a fair. Picking up a gun at the shooting gallery he potted one by one the various balls suspended on jets of water. A bystander said that *he* could do much better, and after being challenged to show how, picked up a rifle and in one shot dropped all the balls. He had shot the boy who pumped up the water!

Perhaps the moral is obvious, but the analogy is that we are becoming very clever as specialists, each absorbed by his own 'ball' of knowledge. But the manager must become more than ever concerned with *all* the specialisms and the best way of achieving overall results. His aim must be different. In an age of specialists it is important to encourage 'generalist' attitudes, and there are many ways of doing this. An American professor told me recently that his 'multiversity' comprised a number of separate faculties held together by a common grievance over parking. We should be able to find something better than a common grievance on which to build broader attitudes!

2

Organization
Focal Point of Scientific Management

Before commencing a detailed study of the elements of organization let us discuss more fully the problem of bridging the gap that exists between those two principal areas of responsibility which are the concern of every manager. In colloquial terms these are the area of 'things' and the area of people. A young manager soon finds that each 'area' has its own special problems, possibilities and even philosophies. Even today there are many people who, as in Berlin, are building a wall to separate the two areas. Too few are concerned with building a bridge to bring them together.

Why is the organizer concerned with *both* of these areas of management responsibility? Organization, as a key managerial activity, seems to stand between things and people. It is an arrangement of people to perform certain tasks or do certain things. It naturally follows that a major task of the organizer is to bridge this gap. He can help to do this in several ways. He can, for instance, help to create a common language so that a communication bridge is erected between the two areas. He can encourage bridge-building groups to design and use common building equipment and tools, and he can help to provide, at each end of the bridge, those who extend a welcome and hospitality to the stream of visitors who should be encouraged to cross and re-cross the bridge. In short, the organizer must help to achieve 'Common Market' conditions.

It is a depressing fact that during recent years we have widened the gap between the arts and sciences, between the so-called intellectual and the practical approaches to a way of life; between people and 'things'.

Science and technology have made great advances in recent decades, and every one of us (even those who profess to scorn science) uses the results to live a more comfortable and often a better life. But there still exists a scale of social values which is more complex than the 'U' or 'Non-U' categories, and which places technology, for instance, fairly low in the classification scale. Nowhere is this scale more apparent than in educational and journalistic circles, where there is, as yet, no strong conviction that science, and particularly technology, are other than *nouveau-riche* activities, which must be given a certain amount of consideration but in only a secondary capacity. Rarely are they considered 'in the round', with a recognition of their liberalizing influences, or the social contribution of many of their practitioners. This attitude is particularly applied by many people to our technological colleges.

I could give many current examples to illustrate this point, and I am tempted to do so. I must, however, adopt a more positive approach and endeavour to convince those at present unconvinced that there is a closer relationship between, let us say, science, technology and humanity than is now generally accepted. I must also endeavour to show as convincingly as possible that the scientific approach to management or organization, which at present is more likely to be made by a scientist or technologist, can embody within itself a humanistic and liberalizing attitude and influence.

From which side is this gap of misunderstanding likely to be bridged? Ideally the bridge should be commenced from both sides, with its builders meeting somewhere in the middle. Regretfully, because of Britain's sociological inertia, more progress is being made from the scientific bank, and more bridge-building done by scientists and technologists than by so-called humanists. A feature of today's scientific approach is its active concern with the possibility of liberalizing its approach to a modern life. In contrast, the 'liberalized' seem relatively less interested in endeavouring to understand more fully the contributions of science and technology.

I said earlier that climatic conditions today favour a wider appreciation of scientific and technological possibilities. For instance, Britain's frequent economic crises and her greater European possibilities surely point to the need for a higher standard of technical competence, using every new tool possible. To the virtues of the British-character, and our traditional social and educational institutions, we must add something else if we are to attain equal strength, or preferably achieve leadership among our associates.

So far in this chapter I have referred to broad terms such as the sciences, technologies and humanities. One of the most effective means of bridging a gap is to provide intermediate stepping-stones, columns, bastions or whatever appropriate name we may choose. These 'intermediaries' play a more important part than we usually realize; in fact in science and technology we often tend to denigrate the value of new specialisms rather than to regard them as possible linking devices or steps between one primary specialism and another.

Many examples could be quoted to illustrate this point. In the professional field the creation of new specialist institutions has caused the existing bodies whose interests were adjacent to the new specialisms to pull up their own socks and to become more active in these new fields. This is good for the new subjects *and* for those who previously neglected to sponsor them. In this field we are now taking the second desirable organizational step, which is to provide stronger links between the greater number of specialist bodies now existing. For instance, the British Conference on Automation and Computation was formed some years ago to encourage stronger links between two or more of over thirty institutions which in one specialist sphere or another had an interest in automation. Another recent example is the Engineering Institutions Joint Council, which provides a focal point for thirteen important specialist bodies in this field.

These and other activities are beginning to have two desirable results: first, by encouraging more collaboration among and between a variety of *technological* groups, and, second, by encouraging more collaboration between technological and sociological groups. The bridge is being built by more uncommon people who are finding more common interests.

Yet another development points encouragingly towards the same objective and possibility. In recent years there have emerged many significant new terms, some of which have developed to the status of a new institution or society catering for, as examples, Ergonomics, Materials Handling, and Operational Research. Other new technological terms have not, so far, attained institutional level, but are at least encouraging a new approach to old problems and influencing many established attitudes. They are playing their part as linking devices between primary positions.

Also in this category are many existing terms or words which take on a new significance as they become adopted by new interests and new groups. Let us consider, particularly, two words which have long been used by laymen but have now assumed a new scientific and technical significance. The words are COMMUNICATION and CONTROL.

Communication has become a managerial catch-phrase in recent years. As long as we 'communicate' everything is fine, says the management lecturer or student. It is generally taken to mean 'putting everybody in the picture', although a colleague defines a good communication as 'one which reaches him'! It is said with some truth that, all too often, even managers are not always put in the picture, and that, as in the early days of joint consultation, the intermediate managers are more likely to receive information indirectly, possibly through a shop steward, than to have it communicated through the managerial information system.

The study of communications is today a difficult subject and two examples illustrate how a communications network spreads through a single system (a human body in the examples). The first example described by the Delgados[1] shows how a physical (electrical) stimulation of brain cells in the hypothalamus, for example, may produce—among other effects—an output of adrenalin on the chemical level, contraction of blood vessels on the physiological level, fear on the psychological level, and spread of fear to others on the sociological level!

The second example deals with the communication channels which are used when a monkey is appropriately stimulated—'a pattern of light on the retina is transformed into electrical waves in the optic nerve level, into chemical substances at the synaptic level, into an image at the central nervous system level'. Communication is indeed a complex word.

The word 'control' is becoming more popular through the growth of automation and, now, cybernetics. An essential feature of automation is the control of machines by other machines, and this has led to an intensive scientific and technical investigation into the theory and practice of machine control. The simple centrifugal governor for controlling engine performance has developed into the control mechanisms for regulating scores of variable conditions in a large plant; the single electronic control has developed into a system which can automatically control the performance of a rocket thousands of miles away. The word 'control' will take on an even greater significance as cybernetics becomes more widely studied, because cybernetics means, approximately, control.

---

[1] *An Objective Approach to Measurement of Behavior.* R. R. Delgado and J. M. R. Delgado.

It is appropriate here to discuss briefly the contribution that cybernetics will make to a scientific study of organization. So far it has been difficult for laymen, and many managers, to understand exactly what cybernetics is, and how, for instance, it differs from automation. Quoting its modern pioneer, Wiener, 'Cybernetics is the science of communication and control'. In his book *The Human Use of Human Beings* he explains this definition more fully in the following statement: 'It is the thesis of this book that society can only be understood through a study of the messages and the communication facilities which belong to it; and that in the future development of these messages and communication facilities, messages between men and machines, between machines and man, and between machines and machines, are destined to play an ever-increasing part.'

Wiener here brings out clearly the wider concept of communication and control which will become such a strong feature of the next decade. By implication he supports openly the possibility of a closer relationship between men and machines, a concept which has so far been unpopular among many sociologists and indeed among many management students and teachers. Many philosophers, social scientists and managers believe that never the twain shall meet, at least on the philosophical level, even if close relationships have to be accepted as inevitable on the industrial working level. Even those who ostensibly support the definition and possibilities of cybernetics may appear, paradoxically, to reject this basic concept. For instance, in a paper read at the 1960 B.I.M. Northern Conference, V. W. Oubridge said: 'It is through cybernetics theory that we can appreciate the possibilities of building machines for taking over the brain work of man as well as his physical work. These possibilities far exceed anything so far seen in our electronic computers and automated plant.' But he also said this: 'Because it is important not to arouse unnecessary emotional antagonism I want to make clear that I am not sugesting that men, singly or in groups, can be likened in any way to machines. I say only that the very special technical definitions which cybernetics gives to its concept of a machine enables men and groups of men to be included within this definition for certain purposes.'

Surely these are mutually antagonistic statements? Even his limitation—'for certain purposes'—does not alter his counter-arguments, because his paper is devoted to organizational forms, which he claims, and in this I support him, will make much progress through cybernetic development. Let me admit the dangers inherent in the man/machine relationship. I have met too many scientists to be complacent about the end results of science applied too narrowly to men and women. It is all too easy to support a programme of research which starts by attempting to analyse a brain cell, and which can, unless carefully controlled, end up in the application of brain-washing techniques. We should, however, recognize the possibilities of cybernetics, and appreciate the need and possibilities of more intensive scientific investigations into man, his environment and his relationships. But is is equally necessary to recognize the dangers and limitations.

Let us return from the cybernetical future to the present. I said earlier that the two words 'communication' and 'control' are today assuming a new significance, even if their definitions are unchanged. The *Oxford Dictionary* gives us the following definitions:

Communication: Act of imparting; information given; road, rail, telegraph or other connection between places.
Control: Power of directing, command; standards of comparison for checking inferences deduced from experiments; various devices used to control direction, speed, etc.

Immediately we see from these definitions that the two words have wider meanings than those normally associated with them. They can be used in a *personal* sense, such as a person-to-person flow of information, or a command; they can be used in a *technical* sense, such as the *communication* of a message from a teletyper to a teleprinter some distance away, or the *control* of a machine tool, and its automatic adjustment (i.e. feed-back).

They can also be used in a personal/technical or a technical/personal sense; that is, communication and control between a person and a machine, or a machine and a person. We can show these uses in a simple tabular form on the opposite page.

These examples are deliberately few and elementary; hundreds of others could be chosen to show how we have willingly committed ourselves to science, technology and machine power in many ways. If, as I suggest, we are now in the process of using a greater number of new scientific tools and techniques in human communications and controls, their use will not necessarily denigrate man to a machine level; they are the logical development of a trend which started many years ago, and I cannot see man in other than full control of his environment, at least, that is, if he spends enough time anticipating the problems as well as the possibilities. An example of this sort of problem is the recent case of a man who wished to order coke from a Gas Board. He found that he had to order it 'through a machine', which in the circumstances caused him great frustration. The resultant publicity showed our unwillingness to put up with 'machine autocracy'. It also revealed, however, that a considerable number of these ordering machines were in satisfactory use, and were improving service to consumers. In this example we see the logical and desirable development of machines, but also the need for vigilance and publicity when things go wrong. We see this need also when we consider the full implications of a statement made by Delgado in an interesting monograph on electronic commands which he has applied to the fascinating study of control of behaviour among animals. He said, 'these electronic instruments can control functions of the same organ that invented them, closing, we could say, a circle of direct relation between intellectual and material worlds'.

COMMUNICATION

Possibility	Form of Communication	Examples
1.	Person to person (People to people)	A letter Advertising literature
2.	Machine to machine (Machines to machines)	Television transmitter(s) to TV receiver(s)
3.	Person to machine (People to machines)	Speaking into a telephone Discussions into 'mike'
4.	Machine to person (Machines to persons)	Telephone ear-piece message to listener Loudspeaker to listeners

CONTROL

Possibility	Form of Communication	Examples
1.	Person over person (Person over people)	Foreman over worker(s)
2.	Machine over machine (Machines over machines)	Thermostat over electric fire(s)
3.	Person over machine (Person over machines)	Switching on or off an electric fire(s)
4.	Machine over person (Machine over people)	Starting gate over jockey(s)

Can the products of man be greater than man himself? It depends on the sort of product, and the answer is 'Yes' in certain circumstances. It is probable that a space vehicle and the Jodrell Bank Observatory can be relied upon to do their own jobs more consistently than their designers can control themselves. If we take the chain, Moon Rocket—Jodrell Bank—Observer, the latter is the weak link in the chain, requiring more time off, more subjective consideration by his chief and colleagues. His margin of error in observing and reporting data is in some ways greater than that of the technical equipment he 'controls'. His personal success will be increased by the success with which his weaknesses can be overcome, and his strengths emphasized, by machines and organization.

The old term 'a chain is as strong as its weakest link' has even wider implications today. Years ago production engineers concentrated upon the machine tools of industry and didn't bother about what happened between the machines. They used the term 'floor to floor' literally to mean that their responsibility was to take a component off the floor, machine it and place it back again on the floor. Automation was born when the link between one machine and the next was discovered, and better communication and control established over the complete chain of production. Door-to-door superseded floor-to-floor. Recent years have seen many developments in linking mechanisms, whether they be institutions, conveyors between machines or radar links between a rocket and Jodrell Bank. But *human* terminal points remain, in some ways, the weakest links in the complete chain, and future *technical* achievements, which are inevitable, will only accentuate these human weaknesses unless we are willing and able to use science and technology more intensively in our study of men.

If, as I said earlier, the two key technological words are 'communication' and 'control', how are scientists and technologists developing these words? Today the technological emphasis is on 'systems', and on the ever-more-precise control of the variable factors, or elements, of that system. Let us take a simple example. The automatic pilot of an aircraft is designed, when switched in, to take over flying control of the whole aircraft (i.e. system). The aircraft system comprises many elements, such as rudder, ailerons, gyros, motors, compasses, all having an individual and integrating effect upon the others and the system as a whole. This system can be called the organizational structure, that is, the whole piece of mechanism, with each element precisely related to the others. Looked at in this way, there is a close analogy between a complete mechanical (obviously this includes electrical, hydraulic, etc.) system or structure and a complete organizational system or structure. Both structures also require life to be breathed into them by being put to work to achieve a human objective.

What has the automatic pilot achieved? The following seem the most important:

(1) For a large part of the flying time a considerable relief from monotonous tasks and unnecessary strain.
(2) A degree of control which is likely, *normally*, to be greater than any one or more human beings could achieve. This greater control is achieved by
  (a) mechanisms which are more reliable than human beings for long routine tasks, and
  (b) a more rapid method of communication between the various elements in the system than could be attained by humans. The more rapid the communication over the system, the more control over the variables and the greater the stability.

The type of technical achievement exemplified by the automatic pilot, by feed-back automation, by integrated control over many variables in, say, a chemical process, gives many clues to the possibility of similar progress in human systems, whether we are talking of individual men or groups. Whether we can restate Pope by saying that 'the proper study of man is the machine' is another matter, but I am convinced, in face of many sceptics, that the words 'communication' and 'control', the technical developments surrounding them and the research behind them must be a required study for those interested in managerial development, and, in particular, the development of organization.

Let me at this stage, offer yet another piece of evidence which shows how machine theory is making apparent the great need for closer understanding between specialists. At the Integrated Data Processing conference in Amsterdam, June 1962, the following extracts appear from a report:

'Two issues emerged from the conference. First the urgent need for fundamental research on I.D.P. ·The second is the confusion caused by the fact that different sciences and arts, which our educational system so far kept separated, have been thrown together because they use the same information processing machine.

'This meant that delegates had a variety of education, background, sphere of work and objectives. 'The "accounting group" dominated at this conference; others were management and applied mathematics. But all agreed that 'balanced integration of these specialists around the gravity centre of information processing still has to be reached, for which purpose a suitable vehicle has to be made.'

Let us come back to the building of our bridge. Have I been emphasizing that there is largely one-way movement, from machine-theory to man-theory? I certainly have suggested that research into management, organization and social theories is more likely at present to be made by so-called narrowly based scientists than by liberal-minded 'arts' men. My hope is that the bridge will be built from both 'sides', meeting as near to the middle of the gap as possible. Scientists and technologists, including myself, need a constant reminder that whatever the theoretical strength of an organizational structure it will need constantly, in its working life, tolerance, friendliness, thought-fulness, wisdom, compassion, initiative, management by men for men, all of them qualities it is difficult to feed into a computer. We need, too, a reminder that the word 'control' has been studied deeply by social scientists, and one in particular, Mary Parker Follett, made a notable contribution to organizational theory when she discussed the relationship between the two words 'control' and 'co-ordination'. I shall return to this discussion later. Our so-called liberal thinkers will also need their reminders, in particular that science and technology must be understood more fully, and that there are many technological means of helping us to achieve a fuller life.

Perhaps I should pause here. I am tempted to discuss other ways and means of achieving this greater understanding between science and art. Our educational and training programmes are being re-organized with this objective in mind; some of our scientific and social workers are breaking down inter-specialist barriers. The bridge is being designed. Let us in the remaining chapters attempt to forecast how it will be securely built, and how organization can play an important part in bringing the two 'sides' together.

What is Organization?

Readers may already regard organization as a key activity, and in a previous book, *Management Principles,* I gave reasons why in my view it is likely to become of greater importance to managers.

It is desirable at this stage to agree on a definition, as I have found the word 'organization' used more loosely than most functional terms. It is, for instance, quite common for young managers or management trainees to claim that they are good organizers without even having made a disciplined study of the word and its implications. Many definitions exist, and as they vary greatly in content and scope I will quote, later, a representative selection. First, however, I will give you my own definitions:

(1) The 'organizational structure' is the framework within which the people act.
(2) The organization of a business is the arrangement of the people in it so that they act as one body.
(3) 'To organize' is 'to arrange the parts so that the whole shall act as one body'.

A newcomer to organization, particularly if he is technically educated, will be struck by the use of terms which sound 'mechanical'. For instance, words like 'structure', 'framework', 'the parts' and 'act as one body' are quite likely to be found in technical documents. Is this an advantage or disadvantage? I believe that the use of analogies is of growing importance in the study of almost any subject. Let us remember, particularly, that a rapidly growing proportion of young potential managers will approach the subject of organization from their own technical base, and are likely to assimilate managerial ideas and subjects if these are explained in terms already known and understood.

Let us remember, too, that many non-technologists can be encouraged to use technically based analogies in order to improve their communication links with technologists. For instance, a colleague (a non-engineer) always impresses engineers when he reminds them that their specifications of *individuals* are far looser than their specifications of dimensions. The latter will usually involve, first, the basic dimension, say 0·5 in., and then the tolerance allowed by the designer and required by the producer. The stated dimension thus becomes, say, 0·5 ± ·005 in.

When specifying an individual, whether in required characteristics or salary, the same basic dimensions and tolerances are required although the form in which they are stated is different.

Things would be easier if we could assume that all *technical* specialists understood one another, but we know that nearly every one of the many new specialisms is producing its own jargon and its own communication barriers. But, even so, there are strong movements towards a greater standardization of nomenclature and techniques, and the breaking down of specialist barriers. The modern computer, as an example of hardware, is encouraging many diverse specialists to agree upon a 'common language', and, even more important, a common understanding among uncommon specialists. A more intensive study of organization will help these integrating efforts, as it provides a meeting ground between 'things' and people, between theory and practice and between individuals and groups. But devising a common language is, as Esperanto enthusiasts have found, a slow business.

An interesting comment on the definition of organization is made in *Principles of the Self-Organizing System,* by W. Ross Ashby, who asks: 'What do we mean by it? As it is used in biology it is a somewhat complex concept, built up from several more primitive concepts. Because of this richness it is not readily defined, and it is interesting to notice that while March and Simon (1958)[1] use the word "organizations" as title for their book, they do not give a formal definition. Here I think they are right, for the word covers a multitude of meanings. I think that in future we shall hear the *word* less frequently, though the operations to which it corresponds, in the world of computers and brain-like mechanisms, will become of increasing daily importance.'

If I understand Ashby's rather abstruse paper properly his point is that a substantial part of the theory of organization will be concerned with 'properties that are not intrinsic to the thing, but are relational between observer and thing'. It follows, therefore, that 'organization is partly in the eye of the beholder', and being subjective is not apparently suitable for an objective definition. This is not, to me, adequate reason for an unwillingness to

---

[1] *Organizations.* J. G. March and J. A. Simon.

D

provide a definition, particularly in the person-to-person sense we are concerned with in this book. Ashby himself, by his constant reference to 'organization', surely emphasizes the importance of defining it.

Despite Ashby's comments, many definitions of organization do exist. Mooney and Reilly, in *Onward Industry*, define it as follows: 'Organization is the form of every human association for the attainment of a common purpose.' You will note their reference to the word 'form', which implies structure or shape, although they limit organization to 'human' activities. Note, finally, their use of the term 'common purpose', a phrase I have frequently used.

Sheldon in *The Philosophy of Management* defines organization as 'the process of so combining the work which individuals or groups have to perform with the faculties necessary for its execution, that the duties, so formed, provide the best channels for the efficient, systematic, positive and co-ordinated application of the available effort'. This is a bit of a mouthful, and in my view unnecessarily complicated. It is the sort of definition which frightens rather than attracts managers.

You will note that he refers to 'the faculties', which might be assumed to include *facilities*. If so, he includes within organization not only the human or personal requirements but other requirements too, such as planning, materials and finance.

This wider concept was accepted by Henri Fayol, in *General and Industrial Management*, who stated that 'to organize an undertaking is to provide it with everything useful for its function; materials, plant, capital, staff'. Fayol seemed to recognize two divisions of organization, the material and the human, and to some extent this broader concept of organization was embraced in *Industrial Organization and Management* by R. C. Davis, who stated that 'Organizing is the process of creating and maintaining the requisite conditions for the effective and economic execution of plans. These conditions are principally concerned with morale, organization, structure, procedure, and the various physical factors of performance.'

We might complete our list of definitions (there are many others) with three more recent ones. The first, in *A Methectic Theory of Social Organization* by Dr. T. T. Paterson, is rather involved. 'Organization in all groups, where a group is defined as an enterprise in being, can be expounded as the inter-play of the four subjective imperatives of obligation and expectation in terms of "rightness" and "goodness". The theory does not hold for abnormal behaviour, where there is impairment of moral judgement. Nevertheless this has its converse value. Abnormal behaviour, neurotic and psychotic, can be defined as incapacity to make moral judgement in terms of these subjective imperatives, which are necessary to social activity.'

One has the feeling that this quotation resembles modern art in the sense that one can't understand it, but finds it interesting.

E. F. L. Brech, in *Organization, the Framework of Management*, tells us that 'organization is an aspect of planning, concerned with the definition of

(a) the responsibilities of the executive, supervisory and specialist positions into which the management process has been subdivided, and
(b) the formal inter-relations established by virtue of such subdivided responsibilities'.

Brech seems to recognize, in this definition, only 'human' relationships. Should organization cover *all* relationships, between men and men, men and machines, and machines and machines, such as I discussed on page 42. Many managers talk of 'organizing an activity', which will often include non-human things like machines or facilities. Certainly the relationship of, say, one machine to another is important, just as is the relationship of one manager to another. But in industry we are likely to find the first being considered by a production engineer and the second by a top manager.

My final definition concerns itself more with the social rather than the business area. Wight Bakke[1] defines a social organization as 'a continuing system of differentiated and co-ordinated human activities utilizing, transforming, and welding together a specific set of human, material, capital, ideational, and natural resources into a unique problem-solving whole of whose function it is to satisfy particular human needs in interaction with other systems of human activities and resources in its particular environment'.

Readers may wish to read this again before absorbing its full scope and significance! It is a widely embracing definition and for the purpose of this book may be too ambitious. But, on reflection, is not a business or company a complete social organization, even if on a much smaller scale than the community? Are not the philosophies, attitudes and responsibilities of a manager similar in content if not in scope to the leader of a nation? Perhaps this infers that there is little difference between management 'science' and political 'science', although there are many people who would dispute this.

In *Principles of Social and Political Theory* Professor E. Barker, when discussing 'the social organism', reminds us that in its original Greek form 'organism' means 'that with which one works, a tool or instrument'. Barker notes in passing (on pages 127, 128) that the term has a special meaning to biologists: 'An organism is something animate which is a compound of parts serving one another, and serving thereby the whole which they collectively constitute, as instruments for the attainment of a "common purpose"; it is a composite living structure, in which the parts are "organs" or tools, mutually instrumental to the life purpose of the whole. We may accordingly say that the essence of the animate organism, in the reader of biology, is the instru-

[1] *Concept of the Social Organization.* E. Wight Bakke.

mentality of each part in relation to the life purpose of the whole.'

Do we not recognize in this 'definition' an analogy with organization as we are currently discussing it in this book? Barker himself felt that this biological notion could be carried over into the realms of social and political theory. I will discuss the essential differences more fully when dealing with the 'internal' organization of the individual and his place in the group. At this point I wish merely to stress that in Barker's view, and my own, the organism, or 'scheme of organization', as he prefers to call it, is centred on the individual and achieves its purpose through, *and for*, the benefit of the individual. This 'concerted effort, leading to a shared betterment, is an effort of individual persons, leading to a betterment of individual persons'.

This concept, Barker says, surely has its relevance in the economic field, as well as in the social and political. I too believe this, and in doing so am suggesting also that here is one concept, or definition, which stems from old philosophic roots, but is surely applicable to our modern community, and certainly to modern management.

What key points are likely to impress themselves upon a technically trained young manager after he has studied this varied group of definitions? What sort of thesis would he write which required him to develop common threads among such uncommon statements?

Let us isolate those terms which seem significant.

Puckey
(1) The organization structure or framework.
(2) The arrangement of people.
(3) People acting as one body.

Mooney and Reiley
(1) The form of every human association.
(2) The attainment of a common purpose.

Paterson
  (1) A group is an enterprise in being.

Brech
  (1) Organization is an aspect of planning.
  (2) It is concerned with the subdivision of executive, super-
      visory and specialist positions, *and*
  (3) The formal inter-relationships established through sub-
      division.

Bakke
  (1) A continuing system of human activities.
  (2) A welding together of various resources (human, natural,
      capital, etc.).
  (3) A problem-solving whole.
  (4) An integration with other systems to satisfy human
      needs.

Barker
  (1) A compound of individuals serving one another.
  (2) A compond of individuals attaining a 'common purpose'.
  (3) A composite living structure.
  (4) An effort of individuals, leading to a betterment of indi-
      viduals.
  Let us now carry out a further refining process:

Organization is concerned with
  (1) Individual persons.
  (2) Subdivision of personal responsibilities.
  (3) Inter-relationships between people.
  (4) Groups of people.
  (5) Achieving a common purpose.
  (6) A living structure.
  (7) Planning.

(8) Action.
(9) Utilizing all resources to satisfy individual human needs.

At the risk of oversimplification we might refine even more, and arrive at the following basic elements, which must be included in a definition of organization.

(1) The individuals.
(2) The relationships between individuals and groups.
(3) The groups of individuals.
(4) The common purpose.
(5) The living structure within which the individuals are grouped.
(6) The planning and achievement of the common purpose.
(7) The utilization of all resources.

A Restatement

In subsequent chapters I shall develop these basic elements in greater detail, with the exception of (7). Meanwhile, let me restate in a few sentences what this analysis tells us.

It surely reinforces our view that organization plays a key part in management, not only because of its own value but in the wider stimulation it gives to managers. The demands of organization are many. First, it requires managers to study people as persons, because the group is, basically, a collection of persons, and too often we are inclined to forget that every merger, take-over or group reorganization involves adjustments which may create serious personal problems. To the young manager a fuller study of personal problems within his group will soon convince him that we are only at the beginning of our scientific investigation into personal characteristics, emotions, responses and selection.

It is the duty of a scientifically inclined manager to keep abreast of this research, as a means of understanding people more fully and using them more effectively.

Second, the list of organizational elements reminds us that in our desire to understand and appreciate individuals we must study groups more intensively. We have all had experience of rational individuals who become, apparently, irrational when in a group. We all know, too, that a group's effectiveness may be (and usually is) far less effective than the sum of the individual values involved. For instance, many committee meetings detract from rather than add to individual effectiveness.

These possibilities should cause the scientifically minded manager to ask himself whether scientific research can be used more intensively to provide a better understanding of groups. He will review the vast amount of social research undertaken, and particularly those researches conducted under the title 'group dynamics', and he will realize, because of the *social* responsibilities of a manager, that research conducted in a wider social environment may also be applied to industrial organization (and vice versa).

Our young manager will be reminded, too, that organization is not an end in itself, but a means. He will realize that the 'end' should be identifiable and recognizable in a clearly stated and *widely understood common purpose*. No organizational effort can be adequate unless this common purpose is known to all the individuals.

The sixth 'element' in this list is of considerable philosophic and practical importance. Brech[1] alone of the various authorities selected limits his definition to the *'planning'* rather than the 'doing' concept of organization; in fact he is quite specific in saying that the dynamic concept of organization is outmoded, and that 'organization as a term relates to structure'. I do not think that the concept should be so limited.

The organizational relationship between planning and performance often raises difficulties, but clearly every manager must be responsible for both. A particular and important problem of

[1] *Organization, the Framework of Management.* E. F. L. Brech.

organization is to provide the best structure and relationships for ensuring a continuity of good planning *and* performance; we will discuss this more fully later.

Finally, the seventh 'element' suggests that organization is concerned with 'the utilization of all resources'. This, if taken literally, must directly involve the organizer with non-human resources also, and, as I said earlier, this may seem logical and acceptable to many people, particularly with the development of automation. I shall not, however, deal with it specifically in this book, which is devoted to human resources, and I would like to emphasize that I am concerned here with organization in relation to people although I realize fully that the management job includes a responsibility for all organization and all the resources of the group.

3

The Individuals

'THE GREATEST good for the greatest number' is, superficially, an ideal programme for a politician and a manager. But 'the greatest number' invariably leaves outside its ranks a minority (possibly only one individual) of people who do not conform to the larger group. This minority of people cannot be ignored, in fact they represent a vital element of company growth.

To the busy manager, minorities, whether in the form of groups or individuals, are usually considered a nuisance. They are the awkward squad who don't agree with the majority view or decision. Frequently they are led by one person, a nonconformist, a shop steward (often labelled a Communist, although ironically he would not last five minutes in Russia) or merely by an individual who feels more strongly than his fellows about a particular problem and may be quite right in doing so!

Managers must so order their affairs that sufficient time is made available to study and understand individuals, whether they are people with problems or perhaps seeking employment. It is frequently exasperating for a manager, but nearly always interesting, to find this time, but the manager who thinks deeply about what he has learnt from minority or personal cases will nearly always find that a lesson has been learnt which can be applied more widely.

How much should a manager consider individuals when he is planning a group exercise or designing an organization structure? I have stressed in a previous book, *Management Principles* (page 60), that in organizational affairs individuals are often considered at too early a stage, with the result that the organizational purpose is clouded too early by personal rather than by objective considerations. Too often Joe has been available and the exercise has been built around him rather than through the formulation of a plan which requires, to achieve it, a particular sort of chap who may be nothing like Joe.

Many an organization chart is filled with unsuitable individual names simply because certain persons were available or had to be fitted in because of family, service or take-over liabilities. Too often these appointments weaken the effectiveness of individuals and groups.

The views I have just discussed are, I find, often opposed by managers whose opinions I usually respect. Their view is that nothing is more sacred than one's obligation to and responsibility for an individual case, and, unfortunately for my argument, I am almost entirely with them in spirit. It is only in the timing where we differ. They consider the individual first when planning an organizational situation, while I consider him second. They first plan their basic objective around the individuals available, while I tend to plan first around the *objective*. After the objective has been clarified I try to match individuals to it.

In support of this approach I will refer again to the quotation with which I opened this chapter—'The greatest good for the greatest number'. The manager of any sizable group must assume that his decision (if reasonably planned and put over) will be acceptable to a *majority* of the group; he assumes rightly that he has a duty to legislate for the many, and that whatever the varying individual characteristics in the group, a majority will accept his proposals.

By this act he places the objective first and individual reactions second. Why, therefore, when he plans an organization should he not do the same thing?

Readers may at this stage be slightly confused. I commenced this chapter by stating that 'managers must so order their affairs that sufficient time is made available to study and understand [these] individuals'. This clearly requires me as a manager to have a high regard for individual attitudes, difficulties or points of view. But when I go on to say that in some circumstances organizational or group considerations should come first, I may be accused of disagreeing with myself.

Let readers be quite clear on this point. I have worked with (and occasionally against) so many exceptional individuals to have no doubt about their value. One man has often changed the fate of a company or country, which is another way of saying that £40,000 a year or more to the right manager may be well justified. But I have also seen exceptional men cut down in size, and the company with them, by wrong allocations of personal responsibilities and bad company organization.

I will repeat the statement made in my book *Management Principles*, page 11: 'A good organization structure should encourage the expansion of personal qualities; too often it inhibits them.'

I have tried so far to say two things. First, that a manager should organize his own time so that he allocates an adequate amount of it to personal or individual considerations. Second, that 'purpose' should precede 'people', and that having first agreed on purpose and structure a manager should then find the right individuals to achieve the objectives planned.

Let us reconsider the quotation 'the greatest good for the greatest number'. In 1825 Francis Hutcheson[1] propounded the philosophy of 'the greatest happiness for the greatest number'. It was, as Barker says, 'a shadow of the truth'. First, the term

[1] Professor of Moral Philosophy, University of Glasgow.

'happiness' is difficult to define, as it means different things to different people at different times. Second, this philosophy seemed to some people at that time, and seems to me today, to lay too much stress on the group and too little on the individuals within it. William James once said 'God does a wholesale not a retail business', and every manager, in his earthly sphere, faces the problem of deciding whether he is primarily concerned with the wholesale or retail aspects of people in managing his group. Most managers operate in the wholesale business.

I hesitate to discuss religious issues in this book, beyond stating my own conviction that there is, or should be, a personal relationship between God and each of us as individual persons. I believe, too, that in our earthly existence there should be the strongest possible link of understanding and respect between a manager and each of the individuals in his group. Perhaps this may be impossible to achieve, but it is not impossible to embrace as an attitude of mind.

There is no doubt that a 'wholesale' attitude towards people is all too easy to acquire when managers are pressed for time, where 'overall' discussions of policy become more frequent and complex, and where large numbers of individuals are involved. But many sociologists, with far less excuse, also take a wholesale view of social groups, and become so preoccupied with humanity that they have little appreciation of individual humans. Karl Marx was once described in such terms.

In dealing with the 'personal' aspects of his job a manager finds himself singularly short of scientific or analytical tools, and he usually has to fall back upon empirical methods. It is surprising, when we remember how long people have existed in the world, that we really know so little about ourselves as individuals. I suppose the answer is that in every civilization, and particularly since the Industrial Revolution, the individual has been studied largely in relation to his *external* environment, i.e. his group or society, and only through medicine has *the individual* been closely investigated in relation to his *internal* environment.

One of the most exciting developments of this century has been the greater interest displayed in man as a subjective person, and during my managerial life I have seen the growth of various activities which have focussed more attention on individuals. Medical research has greatly advanced on many frontiers, even if it is, according to many of its own members, still advancing too slowly, and in too disjointed a manner. The growth of industrial medical services has enabled far more doctors to understand the environment in which many of their patients worked, and from that knowledge to understand the individuals more fully. Parallel with this has developed a wide interest in individuals through psychological, psychiatrical and neurological techniques. A more recent development from the same stable is the investigation and treatment of 'executive stress', applied particularly to individual managers.

The twin development of bodily *and* mental health programmes has created greater interest in the relationship between the two. This is the field of psychosomatic medicine, and it provides the manager with one of his most fascinating fields of study. It shows him, in terms which he can sometimes understand, that there are relationships and reactions between physical and mental troubles which can often provide him with at least a marginal clue in dealing with individuals. It will open up new opportunities for closer collaboration between the manager and his medical adviser.

The social research worker has until recently displayed relatively little direct interest in the individual. Again, this is as expected, because social research has largely concerned itself with society, which is a group. Greater attempts must be made by social scientists to uncover the relationships which exist between groups and the characteristics of the *individuals* within the group. This will require a closer understanding between 'social' research workers and those concerned more particularly with research into individuals.

There is not at present enough pressure for this greater understanding to develop, although a few authoritative people are anxious to set up here something corresponding to the American Social Science Research Council. I believe that the many private social-science organizations already existing here could combine more effectively than they have already done, but it seems increasingly important for the government to provide a strong lead, possibly through the Ministry of Technology. Already it is, in various ways, working around the fringes of social science; with the development of cybernetics, ergonomics, psychosomatic medicine, to quote a few of the more important subjects, it will work inwards more deeply and will, I hope, meet the social scientists working towards it from another angle.

It is a truism that the group and the individual react upon each other, and each is now capable of being investigated more scientifically. Perhaps before long the manager will have placed in his hands some better analytical and decision-making tools for dealing with both.

In a discussion on individuals I must mention another important modern trend which appears, superficially, to denigrate rather than dignify the individual. This trend is towards what is usually called conformity and so far its discussion ground has been largely in U.S.A. It was W. H. Whyte, in *The Organization Man*, who stimulated international discussions on this problem through the use of the term 'organization man'. At a B.I.M. conference in London (March 1961.) Whyte rather indignantly refuted a suggestion that he had been responsible for the equation Organization Man = The Conformist = the Subjugation of the Individual. He inferred that other people had distorted his original term, which described an organizational trend, into one which was directly associated with loss of individual status.

One sympathizes with Whyte, as it has been the misfortune of many before him to suffer misunderstandings; semantics will always play an important part in understanding and misunderstanding. But Whyte must surely have realized that however right he was in drawing attention to an important organizational and social trend, most lay commentators would caricature his words beyond his intentions. In almost every social or organizational case-study the newsworthy reviews or discussions which follow are likely to concentrate upon the individuals who emerge in triumph or tragedy from the total situation. Perhaps this is as it should be.

Whyte's thesis, in simple terms, is that current organizational trends are producing too many men who conform to the trends, thus creating 'positive feed-back', and even more conformity. Managers would be more likely in future to be regarded and regard themselves as 'organization men' rather than 'individual men', and this would ultimately involve a serious loss of individual status and personal satisfactions.

If we consider again the phrase 'the greatest good for the greatest number' it is clear that in order to achieve this desirable state the majority of managers must conform to the company's organizational requirements. Up to this stage we are in favour of organization men. But in planning and legislating for the 'majority' a top manager may expect *all* to conform; the small area between 'majority' and 'all' contains many managerial and individual problems. It may well contain many strengths.

Later in this book I shall discuss the wider organizational problems posed by that problem child 'the organization man'. In this chapter devoted to the individual I can only restate what I have already said, that 'managers must so order their affairs that sufficient personal time is made available to study and understand individuals'. If every manager had this paragraph typed out and slipped periodically into his mail he would be unlikely to degenerate into the worst type of organization man, or to find himself saddled with more than the *desirable* number of 'misfits' or nonconformists.

How can we understand the individual?

A manager who decides to devote more time to the study of individuals finds himself, as I said earlier, 'short of scientific and analytic tools'. What information does, or can, he have available when faced by a personal problem? Let us list some possibilities.

(1) The 'problem' according to the individual (this is naturally subjective).
(2) The 'problem' according to the company or a colleague (this is *usually* subjective).
(3) Objective reports on (1) and (2). (This includes the use of scientific and analytical tools.)
(4) Managerial experience. (That is, an ability to weigh up the other three.)

(1) *'The Problem' according to the individual*

The individual who is in a minority always has a problem, however imaginary it might turn out to be. Many such problems arise from misunderstandings and often melt away when the true situation is explained in words of one syllable. It is remarkable how complicated we can make our explanations, and experience has taught me that a university don can as easily misunderstand or misinterpret a problem or decision as a less educated person, *particularly if the environment encourages him to do so*. A major managerial contribution to a greater amount of individual satisfaction is a constant attention to simplification in all its forms, and this is discussed more fully in Chapter 6.

But the minority individual may, even after adequate explanation, be left with his grievance, and every attempt must be made *to get him to agree on what his grievance is*. It is sometimes worth

E

while putting a man's grievance into writing, and getting his acceptance of the document, if by the time this document is ready for signature he still retains his grievance or minority view! I knew a Trade Union leader who insisted that when two individuals disagreed, before bringing their disagreement to him they should have *agreed* on the disagreement and put the precise nature of it into writing. It reduced individual disagreements enormously!

(2) *'The Problem' according to the Company, a colleague or supervisor*

Personal problems vary greatly. Generally the manager who is responsible for the solution of an individual case finds that there exists an equal and opposite point of view to that held by the individual, and the problem is to resolve the conflict without loss of essential principles or dignity on either side.

Frequently, problems are settled as a matter of expediency, that is, by giving way on principles in order to settle an 'individual' case. During the war we frequently faced such dilemmas; should you, for instance, side with the devil if he is currently opposed to your common enemy? Winston Churchill had no doubts on the answer after Russia entered the war when he declared that we would fight by the side of *any* country which fought Germany. This was the expedient solution, whatever the misgivings about the future. Perhaps there was no alternative to this and similar cases of expediency during a major war, but at the risk of being considered naive I must state my belief that the settlement of a problem by a concession of principle is bad. Too often the settlement is insecure and short-lasting, like, for instance, the Berlin 'settlement'. It seems to me that an 'end' is not worth while unless all the means of reaching it are worth while. But, having said this, let us be sure that our 'principles', 'means' and 'ends' are real. Too many of us stand on our 'principles' only to find, under examination, that we are on boggy ground.

We are reminded at this stage of the essential difference between 'compromise and integration'![1] The former often involves negative, short-term gain, while the latter involves a solution which is positive and satisfactory to all parties.

Many managers assume that the interests of the individual and company must be, and are, identical. Rodger and Cavanagh[2] said: 'We have spoken of people as being suitable or unsuitable for their work. Now we must recognize the need for yet another distinction, usefully enough expressed, perhaps, by the terms "satisfactoriness" and "satisfaction". A satisfactory worker is one who is satisfactory to his employer. A satisfied worker is one who is satisfied with his job. *Many satisfactory workers are dissatisfied, and many satisfied workers are unsatisfactory*' (my italics). Perhaps it is asking too much for the satisfaction to extend always to both, but the previous statement may be a clue to managers when they are dealing with 'dissatisfied' workers who previously had been thought to be 'satisfied'. I have seen many cases where an individual has, surprisingly and suddenly, wished to leave. His employer may feel aggrieved by this unexpected action, but he should certainly attempt to analyse more fully the reasons and the possibility of wider implications.

One difficulty I have frequently encountered when dealing with an individual's problem is the possibility that his colleague may be wrong. This colleague is often in a more senior category, and if he is proved wrong it is difficult to convince him of his error and yet preserve a good subordinate/superior relationship. These situations most frequently arise in worker/foreman relationships, and I am sure that one of the reasons behind the resentful attitude often taken by many foremen is their feeling that the dice is loaded against them at such times. If we consider a typical works situation we find that the joint consultation machinery, the Union pressures and agreements, and the

---

[1] Read *So You're Going to a Meeting* for a discussion on this subject.
[2] *Society*. Edited by Welford, Argyle Glass and Morris.

instinctive desire of most senior managers to be fair to the 'underdog', are too often likely to favour the worker rather than the foreman.

How can an integrated decision be achieved, instead of the compromise which often leaves a bad taste in many supervisory mouths? First, facts must be thoroughly uncovered and *agreed*. This is a major requirement and even if the contesting parties disagree on other things they should at least agree on the factual information. Unfortunately, reaching agreement on 'facts' is much more difficult than is often imagined. Facts, like religion, are sacred, but just as there are many interpretations of religion, so there are many variations of a particular fact.

Second, the decision should, as far as possible, be directly discussed and, one hopes, finally agreed between the contesting individuals. We must remember that the settlement of most cases of individual disagreement will still leave the two parties in the same supervisory relationship to each other; the solution must strengthen this relationship. One difficult lesson for most of us to learn is that a frank acknowledgement of our error often strengthens rather than weakens our status, and I value highly a comment once made to me by my chief at the time—that he 'respected greatly my willingness to admit error', having had it clearly demonstrated.

But admitting error to a superior is still not as difficult as admitting one to a subordinate. Perhaps the 'superior' in such a case can take comfort from my definition of a leader as 'someone who is more often right than wrong'.[1] This recognizes that a manager *can* be wrong and that other people, including his subordinates, know that he can be wrong (sometimes). But he will continue to earn respect as their leader if he is more often right.

Summing up, therefore, I believe in a frank admission of my own error (if proved) to a subordinate. In turn I hope that he

[1] See Chapter 7 for a more detailed discussion on leadership.

follows the same rule. I will leave him, and you, with the final thought that the *manner* of a settlement is sometimes more important than the substance of it.

(3) *Objective reports on* (1) *and* (2)

An objective report is generally assumed to be one prepared by someone who is independent of the particular problem being considered. Happy the company which can find these 'independent' individuals within itself, and I would rate my personnel manager very high if he enjoyed such a status among both managers and workers. The trouble with many companies is that too many 'organization men' abound who are unlikely to carry the respect of those who search for, or who are prepared to accept independent views. Every company would benefit by encouraging the creation and maintenance of a few such independent individuals. Outside or non-executive directors may (or should) possess these characteristics and even among the executives in most companies there will usually be found a few 'independent' characters who are more valuable than is sometimes admitted. We should, at least, hope to find them in the personnel and medical departments.

Before proceeding further let me emphasize that I am not, when I speak of independent assessors or advice, referring to arbitration, but rather to some form of additional advice or assistance in uncovering facts and in guiding discussion between disagreeing parties. Arbitration, in which two or more parties agree to hand over to an arbitrator their inability to come to a joint decision, is not, I believe, good practice. In many cases we have seen a refusal by one or other of the contesting parties to accept the arbitrator's decision, but even if both the parties accept it they have still failed to accept fully their own individual and joint responsibilities. A manager is selected, trained and paid to make decisions, which if right and rightly explained should be acceptable to those affected by the decisions. Any arrangement which encourages a manager to throw off part of this basic responsibility is bad. Any arrangement which, even indirectly, gives an impression to the 'minority' individual that the solution is imposed by someone other than his own chief tends to weaken the bond between them.

I referred earlier to the lack of analytical tools available to a manager when endeavouring 'objectively' to assess individuals. Psychological investigations into individuals have attempted to discover and uncover widely accepted traits and valid means of assessing them. Rodger and Cavanagh[1] said that 'traits of marked generality and persistence are, for selectors and advisers, characteristics of the utmost importance. They provide the main foundations for attempts to explain and forecast human behaviour.'

These 'foundations' provide the manager with better means of understanding and dealing with 'individual' difficulties; they are particularly useful in the earlier stages of selection, and if properly used at that time will reduce later on the number of individual misfits and problems. This basic selection is similar to the thorough inspection of raw material going into a factory. The better the initial inspection of all material, the less the number of individual rejects and service problems later on.

Psychologists will admit, in varying degrees, that they have much to learn in their quest to provide *managers* with better tools for assessing individuals. 'The ultimate problem we are seeking to solve is "How can we describe, predict and control human behaviour?" ' In these words a leading American psychiatrist stated the purpose of a joint meeting in New York City of the Academy of Medical Science of the U.S.S.R. and the New York Academy of Sciences.[2] Subsequent discussion at the conference showed how far they were from a solution.

Rodger and Cavanagh sum up current psychological thinking in this way: 'Let us return for a moment to our interviewer

[1] See page 67.
[2] 'Pavlovian Conference in Higher Nervous Activity'.

and his search for signs of general and persisting traits. We should now note that he is probably thinking of two kinds of trait. He is looking for some which will enable him to judge what his applicant is capable of doing; and for others which will lead him to conclusions about what he wants (or would at least be willing) to do. The first of these kinds we shall call capacities; the second, inclinations. This sort of classification of traits is, in one form of words or another, both old and widely used. Some have spoken of abilities and interests, some of aptitudes and preferences, some of talents and temperaments. A current way of thinking about the split is to be found in frequent references to skills and attitudes.

'In the notion of "intelligence" we have an important example of a general and persisting capacity. This label has been given to a trait which is held to play a large part in governing what we are intellectually capable of doing in tackling problems of many kinds (and is therefore general) and which seems to be only slightly modifiable by training and experience (and is therefore persisting). Burt (1935) defined intelligence as "inborn, general intellectual capacity"; and although some psychologists nowadays would shrink —a little to the left, perhaps—from the bold use of the adjective "inborn" and would prefer the less committal word "persisting", it is clear that the concept Burt here employs is still widely favoured.

'Some progress has been made in the identification of capacities less general and less persisting than intelligence, but broad and stable enough to warrant attention in some selection and guidance work. What is often called "verbal facility" is one of them, and "number facility" is another. Yet another is "mechanical aptitude", though this does not seem to be a very good name for it, because it is now plain that what it was meant to cover (that is, facility in grasping how mechanical things work) is an even broader capacity than used to be thought, and takes in appreciation of the structure and functioning of all kinds of contrivances, mechanical and non-mechanical.

'Less advanced is our knowledge about general and persisting inclinations. Burt (1935) has tried to show that, as a sort of opposite number to "general intelligence" (a better term than "intelligence") among our capacities, we can identify "general emotionality" among our inclinations; but few seem to have been convinced. More recently, Eysenck (1953), pursuing a similar line of attack and starting from similar presuppositions about the importance of what used to be called cognition, conation and effect, has sought to identify inclinations of high generality and persistence which he has labelled "neuroticism", "introversion" and "psychoticism". Burt and Eysenck have both made use of statistical techniques of factor analysis in reaching their conclusions. It is difficult to see how they could have reached them in any other way, but it is clear that this fact alone has been enough to make many psychologists look askance at them.

'In short, we in the occupational field have probably much to learn from our colleagues—in the educational and clinical fields particularly—in our thinking about traits, and in our ways of researching into them; but we must avoid the mistake of assuming that traits or factors or dimensions which will do for them will do for us. Ours should be derived not from contrasts between neurotics, psychotics and normals, but from contrasts between people who, in their work, prove suitable or unsuitable. Moreover, our traits should be given their proper status as "convenient fictions" and kept under constant review. Further, because suitability and unsuitability is partly dependent on the state of the labour market, and a person who is suitable at one time or in one place may not be suitable in other circumstances, it is clear that the traits we are after in the occupational field never stand still.'

It is probable, as the authors suggest, that we shall learn much, not only from psychology but from the educational and clinical fields, although we are warned that there are great differences between using a tool designed for one field in another; between, say, using it to measure educational success and also failure; to assess neurotics and psychotics, and also normals, and to decide between suitable and also unsuitable people at work.

The intelligence test has so far been the principal 'objective' tool available to managers who wish to measure an individual's capacity. I recall my own interests in Burt's[1] work many years ago, and my various attempts in succeeding years to measure my own and other people's intelligences in order to provide better managers. On the whole I am left today with a negative rather than a positive reaction, with a better understanding of what *not* to do rather than *what* to do. For instance, assuming the range of intelligence measurements to start with the 'A' level (highest group) and sink to 'E', I would not appoint anyone to any managerial position with a score lower than level 'B'. Below that level, however good a candidate's qualities might otherwise be, he just would not understand quickly enough what the subject under discussion was all about.

Two other aspects of intelligence add to my doubts about the value of existing intelligence tests taken in isolation. First, if intelligence is a measure of a person's ability to understand a problem, and presumably from it to visualize the right decision, why is it that many people of the highest intelligence are bad managers? It is obvious that, above a certain level, intelligence cannot be directly equated to managerial ability, at least not yet.[2]

Second, many tests have shown that at factory floor levels, working often on mundane jobs, there are many men and women of the highest intelligence. The cynic would probably say that 'they are too intelligent to take on all the worries of management', and occasionally, after a bad day, I would agree. I always have a feeling of regret, however, that such intelligent people are (apparently) wasting a scarce and precious asset, but whatever the

[1] *The Subnormal Mind.* C. Burt.
[2] For a discussion on the measurement of intelligence see P.E.P. booklet *Mental Subnormality.*

reason or solution it is clear that merely to uncover high intelligence in a person doesn't mean that one uncovers a manager or even begins to understand the whole person.

The principal of a well-known technological college said recently in my hearing; 'it is not lack of intelligence that holds chaps back, it's lack of motivation'. This remark was passed during a discussion on the desirable number of 'A' levels for entrants to degree courses and the general opinion was, subject to further experience, that above a certain level, additional 'A' achievements were unlikely to demonstrate a student's subsequent ability to achieve balanced stature.

No, I regret that the managerial tools available so far do not provide us with an adequate amount of objective help in understanding the 'subjective' problems of a particular individual. Let us hope that the increasing scope and volume of scientific enquiry, and the greater desire of managers for better tools, will one day correct this situation.

Some readers will wonder why I have not included the technique of interviewing in this brief survey of objective tools. It is certainly true that a skilled interviewer will have developed a considerable capacity for asking the right questions and at least encouraging the most productive responses. I will, therefore, deal with certain aspects of interviewing shortly under the more general heading of Managerial 'Experience', because, despite all that has been done, even the best interview can hardly be described, so far, as a tool which fulfils my 'scientific' specification.

(4) Managerial 'Experience'

One definition of 'experience' is 'a repetition of previous errors', and when I examine the many constantly repeated problems which arise in various spheres I am inclined to agree with the definition. Can we ensure, in the field of human or individual problems, that we learn adequately from experience? It has been said of politicians that they never look back—they daren't!

Perhaps the same applies to us. Some months ago I read through the many papers and lectures I have written over the years, and having first realized with a shock how many words I had spoken, I examined my earlier predictions in the light of today's scene. I suppose my forecasting accuracy was as good as average, but, as a psychologist once said to me, 'average is pretty low'!

Most of us conduct personal interviews unwilling or unprepared to use our experience to its fullest extent. We have probably not thought it appropriate to plan the interview too 'scientifically' as it might interfere with the warm friendly spirit we wish to create. We feel that we should 'play it by ear'. In this we are wrong, because the first duty of a manager or interviewer, when called upon to judge a man's application for a job, or to assess a personal problem, is to prepare adequately for it. Sir Winston Churchill once said that he spent many hours preparing an impromptu speech, and even I became convinced many years ago that to accept an invitation to speak meant accepting a responsibility to spend much time on preparation.

What preparations can be made? They may be divided into two groups—interview mechanics and personal considerations.

Interview Mechanics

It is no function of this book to instruct managers in the arts of interviewing, although as they do this many times a day it is obviously of great importance. Some excellent books exist which will instruct the reader in detail how best to conduct an interview. My purpose is served by stressing a few of the more important aspects of interviewing which experience has left with me. They are mechanics rather than 'principles', and they can be divided into two sections—the interview plan, and the facts of the situation. What do I mean by 'the interview plan'? Have you ever taken part in T.W.I.[1] exercises? If so you will remember that they required you to subdivide the task to be done, and to create

[1] Training Within Industry.

what were called 'key points', which had the same value as sign-posts on a complicated road pattern, that is, they helped you to keep on the right road.

In preparing an interview plan every manager must be guided by his experience and *his own* personal characteristics, and he must draw fully upon his experience of previous interviews. Have you, after conducting an interview, written up the key points and the interview 'pattern' as well as the purely factual information given or statements made? I said earlier that the manner of a settlement was sometimes more important than the substance, and it is this 'manner' or pattern which you should capture and build into your experience, and, possibly, your next interview plan.

I do not wish to imply that every interview should be conducted on the same plan, with the same key points, although I am sure that there are *some* common characteristics in every interview. What I am suggesting is that every personal situation varies because every person and his problems vary. In a previous book (*Management Principles*), I discussed this situation, and concluded that the infinite variability of human situations precluded a standardized solution to a personal problem. I went on to say, however, that *every* situation, whether it be a personal interview or a wider organizational problem, would respond to a 'scientific approach', using as far as possible the series of steps referred to on page 22 of that book.

For ease of discussion let me reproduce them here. A scientific approach involves the following steps:

(1) Define the object.
(2) Investigate the facts.
(3) Analyse the facts.
(4) Establish principles or laws.
(5) Validate (4) in controlled experiments.
(6) Apply widely.
(7) Validate widely.

Some readers may feel that this programme seems rather an elaborate one to use when considering an 'individual' problem. I can only repeat what I said earlier: that the problem of one individual is extremely important to that individual, to the other individuals in the group and to the manager himself. The latter will do well to realize that every individual solution may have a wider validity (step 5) which can be applied more widely (steps 6 and 7).

Let us turn to the second part of the interview plan, which is to collect the facts and to study and summarize them before an interview commences. It flatters the interviewee to realize that *you* have taken some trouble to find out the details, and it may leave him with the feeling that he had better not try anything on! Managerial 'homework' on a particular case often involves irritating detail, and may come at a time when you would really like to concentrate on that new merger. It is, however, essential homework, not only in order to brief yourself but to provide the right leadership of your colleagues and subordinates. You are appointed as a manager to set an example, and in no part of your total job can respect and trust be generated more firmly than in the care you take, and are seen to take, with individual cases.

Personal Considerations

Having dealt briefly with interview mechanics, let us turn to the personal problems and considerations which arise at most interviews. It is here that the pattern varies greatly, because individual problems, peculiarities and possibilities vary greatly. But there are some general considerations which can be isolated and adopted as key points in the interview plan. Let me mention a few of those I have found important.

The Personal Audit

I often find, when discussing a personal problem, that individuals refer to previous discussions, at which certain things were alleged to have been said (or, equally important, not said). The present interview is therefore likely to be one of a series, and may well repeat earlier errors of commission or omission.

Two possibilities emerge here: first, that previous interviews were probably not conducted with an adequate scientific approach, and, second, certain people (probably including yourself) failed to make themselves clear. Now there are two ways of being 'unclear'. You may not have cultivated the ability to express yourself in simple, understandable terms, or/and you have not found the courage to say what you really mean, or want, to say. A good manager should not fail on either count, but regrettably many do, a matter for serious consideration by those who aspire to teach management and select managers. I shall refer to this again.

It is understandable that two people (Britishers particularly) find it slightly distasteful to discuss *themselves* with each other; they would much prefer to discuss the weather, the order book or other people. But personal discussions should rank high in the managerial priority list, and their purpose should be to *avoid* potential problems, and not merely to discuss them when they arise. I was always amused at the title of the American 'grievance committees', which were set up under their various labour laws. The title implied that a grievance had to exist before it could be discussed, whereas wise managers know that more skill lies in anticipating a grievance. This can be done in two ways: first, by instituting regular discussions between a manager and his colleagues, where personal matters are frankly discussed, and, second, by creating an organizational pattern which encourages regular discussions on the shape of the future organization and the people within it.

I have for many years encouraged what I call the 'personal audit', where a two-way frank discussion takes place between (say) myself and one or the other of my immediate colleagues and subordinates. It is surprising how many incipient irritations or misunderstandings can be eased or eliminated by this procedure, and how many potential problems never become actual. The personal audit, conducted in this manner once or twice a year, can achieve as much as, and often more than, the annual medical check advocated by some authorities. Perhaps in co-operation they may achieve even more.

The Positive Question

There are questions and questions; some invite a negative response, while others encourage a positive reaction. In another book, *So You're Going to a Meeting!*, I said that the ability to ask positive questions is an important managerial quality, and I referred readers to the imposing questions asked of many people by Winston Churchill during the dark days of World War II. Several important points emerge from a study of these questions.[1] First, they usually *anticipated* trouble, and in this way they resembled the 'personal audit' mentioned earlier. The manager (or Minister) who can survey his wide field of responsibility and direct his (and other people's) attention to the right potential problems at the right time is valuable indeed.

Second, these questions were usually positive, that is, they asked for specific information to be provided to (the then) Mr. Churchill. Third, they ranged over a wide area of interest, which is an important 'managerial' requirement. Fourth, at least one of the selected questions (there are many others in this category) illustrated Mr. Churchill's desire to investigate personally any situation which was likely to have wider implications.

I cannot prove, except in a few cases, that the Prime Minister saw personally any but a small percentage of the replies, although organizational arrangements ensured an effective follow-up by his staff. I have found frequently that merely to ask a leading question is enough to stimulate action by a worthwhile subordinate, and it is very satisfying to check personally on selected

[1] *The Hinge of Fate*. Sir Winston Churchill.

subjects afterwards, and to find that the subordinate has seen the point and taken action without further pressure from you. Here are five questions, taken almost at random, which illustrate the points I have drawn to your attention.

'Prime Minister to General Ismay. 15 June '42.

'The attached should be considered by the Chiefs of Staff, and I should like to have their thoughts upon it as soon as possible. It may also be shown to the Planning Committee.

'The preparations for "Sledgehammer" and "Round-up" should be separated from Commander-in-Chief Home Forces. He has enough to do in other directions. Pray show me how this can be achieved.'

'Prime Minister to Chief of the Air Staff. 13 March '42.

'What is the position about dive-bombers for the Army? Surely it is more than a year ago that they were ordered by Lord Beaverbrook. Let me have the dates of the discussions on the Defence Committee. What is the forecast of deliveries for the next three months? What is thought of them from an air point of view?'

'Prime Minister to Secretary of State for War. 28 April '42.

'Let me see the strengths and composition of the Home Field Army before and after the reorganization under the following heads:

(1) Infantry battalions.
(2) Number of guns in the field artillery (including howitzers).
(3) Flak and anti-tank units.
(4) Machine-guns of all kinds.
(5) Armoured fighting vehicles of all types.
(6) Non-fighting vehicles of all types.
(7) Staffs of all kinds.

(8) Numbers of supply, transport and administrative services of all kinds.

(9) The total of officers and men of all ranks.

'In comparing these new tables with those of the German system it would be worth while to test our new organizations by comparing the percentage of staffs, divisional and brigade, with the numbers of men in the division. This might also be applied to signals, postal units, etc. It does not follow that the Germans are right, but I think it will be found that they serve more fighting men with fewer overheads.'

'Prime Minister to Secretary of State for War. 9 April '43.

'I should like to spend a morning or afternoon with a typical standard infantry battalion, in order to ascertain exactly the employment of every man in it. Let one be chosen within reasonable distance, and let it be placed at my disposal to check up with their establishment. I want to see for myself exactly how many men are employed on the machine-guns, mortars, anti-tank, signals, kitchens, clerical duties, etc. They must on no account be warned beforehand, nor must any changes be made in preparation. I am assuming an effective strength of, say, 770. I could do this one afternoon next week. I should be very glad if you could come with me.'

'Prime Minister to Minister of Agriculture and Minister of Food. 19 April '43.

'I understand you have discontinued the small sugar ration which was allowed to bees, and which in the spring months is most important to their work throughout the whole year. Pray let me know what was the amount previously allotted. What is the amount of sugar still issued to professional bee-keepers, and what is the saving in starving the bees of private owners?'

F

While on the subject of positive questions I must mention one that was recently asked, in my hearing, of a candidate for head-ship of an important college department. One of my colleagues asked each of the four candidates the question 'When did you last make a decision for which you were personally held respon-sible?' This proved to be an eye-opener in vacillation, and lack of clarity in the replies given by candidates. It certainly showed us that the problem of responsibility and authority is still little understood and practised.

I have occasionally been told that some of the questions I put to candidates are unfair. I wonder whether this is so, or whether my critics are confusing unfairness with directness. I can remem-ber no occasion in my career where a direct, positive question has caused more than a temporary difficulty. More often this form of question helps to create a more productive discussion, and, where job vacancies are concerned, a more satisfactory selection.

It might be appropriate to conclude by quoting the answer once given by a candidate for a job. 'I haven't,' he said, 'given you a satisfactory answer because you didn't ask me a satisfactory question!'

The Hidden Problem

Personal problems often resemble icebergs in the sense that there is more below than above the surface. In a long experience of labour difficulties (my own and others) I have rarely found that the obvious grouse was the true one; rather it was the last straw of several grouses, which had to be uncovered before the total problem was understood.

The interview therefore resembles an excavating exercise, which attempts to uncover *all* the so-called problems and to place them in some sort of priority. Frequently it will be found that solving one will solve the lot, a situation not unlike the shooting episode mentioned on page 34.

The Clinical History

Individuals and institutions are similar in the sense that it is not always so important to ascertain where they *are* but where they are *going*. For instance, are they moving upward, downward or are they static, which perhaps is the first stage of going downward? The interviewer should have prepared from the paper-work a tentative growth and decline pattern of the individual and, at the actual interview, should check his previous assumptions and modify this pattern accordingly.

It is extremely important, at the interview, to check previous assumptions, as one can be easily misled by apparently straightforward evidence. Having myself more than once deliberately gone backwards in my career in order (I hoped) later to go more rapidly forward, I realize that a constant rate of growth in an individual is not the only criterion of success. Neither is it necessarily a proof of incompetence that an individual finds himself out of a job, demoted or merely out of tune with his chief or colleagues. The principal fault *may* lie elsewhere.

It is important for the interviewer to assess the *long-term* pattern of the person confronting him, plotted against a time-scale, and the isolated problem, grouse, lapse or whatever it may be called, should not necessarily be regarded as serious, particularly if environmental causes appear to be present.

When discussing an individual with himself it is frequently difficult to find mutually agreeable 'frames of reference'. As I have said earlier, it is always essential to reach, as early as possible, agreement on the specific nature of the problem, or the reason for the discussion. There are, broadly, two approaches to this solution which must be faced by the interviewer. First, whether to assess the individual concerned in relation to 'absolute' standards, or, second, whether he should be assessed on 'relative' standards.

This is a problem of considerable importance to selectors and assessors of managerial capabilities, and much could be written on the subject. I shall refer to it again when I discuss the individual in relation to his group. At this stage I wish to observe that there is, usually, one safe, logical and, normally, mutually acceptable frame of reference or basis of discussion between interviewer and interviewee. This is: has the latter achieved what is expected of him, and, if not, why not? It recognizes the basic view that management, or a manager, cannot be considered apart from what is being managed.

One of the best methods of assessing the performance of a given manager is to measure what he has done against those responsibilities for which he is *accountable*. The term 'accountability' thus becomes important, not only in its basic definition but in our ability to measure an individual and make an objective comparison between what is expected of him and what he has actually achieved. This approach combines two important advantages. First, it encourages managers to create objective standards for assessing individuals, and, second, it relates individual performances to specific job performances, and not only to hypothetical criteria.

It is surprising and depressing how often a discussion based on an individual's performance (or lack of it) reveals that the individual can say, with truth, that 'he didn't know what was expected of him'. This conclusion helps managers to realize that for a subordinate to know something he has to be informed!

Discussion involving an individual's job performance may, however, leave the discussion on a level of group performance, schedules, targets and other *non-human* aspects of performance. The interviewer must at some early point firmly link *job* performance to *personal* characteristics, and to the relationships of the interviewee with his colleagues. The more clearly an individual's performance, or lack of it, is compared with what is expected of him, the easier it will be to discuss his personal characteristics, relationships, and rewards.

Management-by-Exception

It is appropriate, in this chapter, to discuss a phrase to which lip service has been given for many years, but which is neither understood nor practised widely. In this chapter we have been discussing the 'exception', that is, someone who, for one reason or another, stands out from the group. 'Exceptions' can, of course, be other than individuals, but because managerial responsibilities (and this book) are primarily concerned with human resources we will discuss management-by-exception as a technique which is applicable to human beings, and in particular to the *exceptional use* of human beings.

What is the popular (if such a term is permissible) definition of this term? It is usually meant to describe a technique which ensures that only exceptional or special problems, and *not* routine, go upwards for managerial consideration and decision. The higher the manager, the higher the category of decision, and the less the amount of routine he is expected to handle. We visualize management-by-exception, therefore, as a series of sieves which become progressively finer, so that each level of management, from bottom to top, is required to deal more and more with less and less.

What are the 'exceptional problems' in this context? I said earlier that *every* personal problem (indeed every person) is exceptional, and to find adequate time for dealing with them managers must obviously reduce the volume of routine which arrives at their desks. It seems, therefore, reasonable to conclude that the greater use of 'management-by-exception' will enable 'problem individuals' to be considered more fully.

But there are other individuals to consider. I once heard a foreman say, in response to a question: 'Of course I've got favourites; they are the people who work best for me.' Few of us would disagree with this definition of favouritism, but it raises, for our purpose here, another and wider aspect of 'exceptions'. Is not your *most satisfactory* worker an exception, as well as the one who is a problem in the group? It seems clear, therefore, that another most important category of 'exceptions' includes those who are exceptionally *good*, and that management-by-exception can be more comprehensively practised if a manager gives special attention to the 'good' as well as to the 'problem' individuals. Too often we take our good people for granted, and more 'exceptional' attention to them might well reduce some of the 'bad' exceptions. Perhaps we can go even further and say that the good manager should give exceptional attention to the complete spectrum of individuals, from infra-red to ultra-violet!

If management-by-exception is practised more comprehensively a manager must take particular care to ensure that his motives are clearly understood. Let us consider the first and the largest group, comprising all those normal individuals who make up the bulk of employees in most groups. Among such people the good manager performs a lubricating job, which he does by casual chats and contacts with as many employees as possible. He does this while walking around, awarding suggestion prizes, attending company functions and the like. But even the normal person is likely to feel some tension when a senior manager addresses him; he wonders 'why'. Argyris refers to this[1] when he quotes a worker as saying: 'Our boss hardly ever bothers us. In fact he tells us: "Don't worry if I don't talk to you. That means you are doing well. It's when I come looking for you that you should worry." '

Reactions like these may play havoc with the desire of a manager to make friendly gestures to random employees, and may cause unexpected difficulties, particularly if the exercise is spasmodically performed. In this type of 'exceptional' contact better results are likely if the contacts are made and are known to be regularly made as part of a manager's normal programme.

But if something becomes normal it is not exceptional any longer, and the use of the term 'management-by-exception' is inappropriate when applied to people in this way. Under no

[1] *Understanding Organizational Behavior*. C. Argyris.

circumstances should a manager regard the need to maintain a variety of personal contacts as exceptional, but rather as normal.

In dealing with administrative, organizational or technical matters management-by-exception has, I believe, considerable possibilities as an effective technique. Its significance will become greater as higher forms of control become better established, and a greater number of effective data-processing systems are installed. It is not particularly appropriate to discuss these in this chapter.

They will, however, encourage a situation where managers, as they ascend the hierarchy scale, live in increasingly rarefied air. Top managers may find (indeed are finding already for other reasons) that this upper atmosphere tends to put them out of touch with affairs and feelings at ground level. Management skill is best exercised by a judiciously planned combination of upper- and lower-level activities, of 'exceptional' high-level decisions, where most of the routine has been sieved-out on the way up, and also by frequent incursions and excursions into the personal problems and details which will bring a manager 'back to earth' and help him in a variety of ways to become a better top manager.[1]

To help them understand human relationships and personal problems more fully, managers must make certain that the 'sieves' they impose between their subordinates and themselves are designed not to stop but to allow special cases to get through to their desks. An ordinary manager helps to make himself an exceptional manager by ensuring that these human cases are dealt with by him as part of his *normal* job. It becomes normal to deal exceptionally with abnormals. (I use this word here to describe those who have a problem, rather than those who are mentally unstable.)

Management by Exceptional Managers

Let us go on to consider another aspect of management-by-exception. The conventional use of the term assumes the existence

[1] See the Churchill correspondence, particularly his letter to Secretary of State for War. 9th April 1943. Page 81.

of an organization which is designed to filter or sieve-out routine, and leave for managerial attention and decision only refined information or statistics. The success of this exercise depends almost completely on organizational skill, and on managerial conformity to a predetermined programme of administrative mechanics, where managers speak and decide only where and when they are told to, even if they previously designed their own programme and sieves.

But exceptional managers must never settle comfortably down at the top of a tidy organizational pile. Their task is not only to create a reasonable organizational structure but constantly to challenge the organization at its weaker points; they are builders who, having built, constantly prod and probe the structure to expose potential weaknesses. They are deliberately, in this manner, creating 'stress' conditions, and it is salutary for a manager, regularly, to say to himself that he is paid a high salary only because of his (presumed) ability to control his group effectively under stress, or in abnormal circumstances. It is the stress condition, the breakdown, the abnormal, perhaps the emergence of a bright new competitor, which calls for exceptional management and justifies exceptional salaries.

This concept of managerial responsibility fits well into the organization pattern we shall discuss later when we refer to the centrifugal and centripetal forces existing in a dynamic body, which in this context means a group of people. Managerial responsibility involves *three* things. First, creating centripetal conditions, or, if you wish, conformity; second, creating centrifugal conditions, non-conformity or, if you wish, stress, and, third, ensuring that a balance is struck between these two which maintains *reasonable* organizational fusion or cohesion.

It is not easy to be a 'three-in-one' manager, but we are, of course, talking about exceptional managers!

A Restatement

(1) Sufficient time must be made to study 'personal' problems. Managers are in the 'retail' as well as the 'wholesale' business.

(2) Personal problems often arise through organizational misfits. 'A good organizational structure should encourage the expansion of personal qualities; too often it inhibits them.'

(3) Managers are likely to learn much about the individual from physiological, psychological, neurological and psychosomatic research, which need to be interpreted more vigorously into managerial terms.

(4) Many 'personal' problems can be solved more completely by more skilful managerial attention to interview techniques. In particular, the following are important:

(a) Mutual agreement on the 'facts'.

(b) The undesirability of making concessions on 'principles' if we are sure that our principles are right.

(c) Recognition of the possibility that 'many satisfactory workers are dissatisfied, and many satisfied workers are unsatisfactory'.

(d) The need to obtain 'objective' advice from outside and inside the group. This does not necessarily, or desirably, mean arbitration.

(e) The need to use as many proven 'tools' as possible in assessing personal problems or capacities. The development of testing and assessment methods likely to emerge from (3) may help greatly.

(5) The interview plays an important part in 'personal' considerations, and can be made more effective by special attention to the following points:

(a) The step-by-step scientific approach method can often be used with advantage.

(b) The 'personal audit', if regularly and skilfully conducted, can reduce personal problems in number and seriousness.

(c) The ability to put 'positive' questions should be cultivated by managers.

(d) 'Personal' problems or difficulties should always be considered within the long-term record of the person involved. The person and his career should be looked at 'as a whole'.

(6) One of the most reliable and acceptable personal evaluations is to compare a person's performance in relation to what was expected of him. This assessment, in the absence of other reliable objective methods, or measuring tools, is most valuable. It recognizes that a manager 'cannot be considered apart from what is being managed'.

(7) The 'exceptional person' may be defined in various ways, and in particular these aspects of management-by-exception were considered:

(a) Every personal problem is an exception and requires special managerial consideration.

(b) Exceptional people can be one's most satisfactory, as well as one's problem, workers. This suggests that a manager should not take good performances for granted.

(c) If exceptional attention to individuals is given it should be regularly done, and known to be done. Suspicions and difficulties are easily aroused, when this is spasmodically performed, even if motives are good.

(d) The conventional management-by-exception sieves which are designed to prevent routine from appearing on top managers' desks must not isolate top managers from essential contact with, and consideration of, exceptional personal problems.

(e) Managers must be able and willing to dig into detail and attempt to expose weaknesses at all points of the structure. This can often be done by deliberately creating 'stress' conditions.

4

The Relationships between Individuals
and Groups

THIS IS the second of the basic elements tabulated on page 55, and readers may wonder how the subject matter of this title will differ from that in the previous chapter on individuals.

Many 'individual' or personal problems arise because of difficult 'group' relationships, where Johnnie has become out of step with his colleagues or they with him. There is a significant difference between an individual considered, primarily and subjectively, as an individual, and the same person considered as a member of a particular group; in this chapter we will begin to discuss individual relationships *within the group*.

Sir Julian Huxley in his Galton lecture on Eugenics in Evolutionary Perspective, 1962, reminded us that 'man's evolution occurs on two different levels and by two distinct methods, the genetic, based on the transmission of genes and gene-combustion, and the psychosocial or cultural, based on the transmission and variation of knowledge and ideas'. He points out that 'the tempo of cultural evolution is many thousands of times faster than of biological transformation', and this surely emphasizes the great and growing importance of group effectiveness in increasing the effectiveness of individual men.

Paradoxically, our first 'group' consideration starts *inside* the individual, because every human being is himself a group. It has long been known how one organ, or part of a human being, reacts upon other parts; it has long been surmised, but less well documented, that a close relationship exists between body and brain. It is still relatively little known how the brain and nervous system 'work' and how they control the complete group, i.e. the whole human being.

We now realize more fully that a better understanding of a complete human being may help us to understand *groups* of human beings. If we survey recent developments in 'human' fields we discover some extremely interesting trends, which, when synthesized and simplified, should help managers to understand individuals and groups more fully. Let us consider, first, the manner in which research has developed in the field of medicine. Sargant[1] says it is 'a modern paradox that rapid scientific progress often results when a field of experimental research is deliberately limited. For centuries, medicine was, in effect, controlled by those using a broad and comprehensive system of scholastic metaphysics to explain all forms of sickness; yet little progress resulted in the diagnosis of treatment of disease. Then from the moment when the medical profession decided to forget its metaphysical preoccupations—which had meant concentrating on the whole man in his environmental and religious setting— and simply set about examining the functional mechanisms of the lungs, the heart, the liver, and finally the brain itself, its present stupendous practical progress began. For hundreds of years before that, even the study of anatomy was thought unnecessary as an aid to medicine; scholastic philosophers claimed to explain satisfactorily the supposed workings of the body as well as those of the mind. The medical attitude of the Middle Ages, in fact, recalls some contemporary psychological views, such as that a satisfactory knowledge of metapsychology suffices to explain what may often be the varied results of normal and abnormal brain function. From time to time, the varied parts do have to be

[1] *The Battle for the Mind.* William Sargant.

reassembled into a new whole; but this is where the dangers of wrong generalization so often arise.

'Newton, being a philosopher at heart, and more interested in Biblical prophecy and alchemy than in the mechanical laws of gravitation, thought that his discoveries had contributed little to the stock of human knowledge. Towards the end of his life he reproached himself with having dallied on the shores of a wide ocean of knowledge, and there played with a few pebbles and shells. Yet, more than two centuries later, we still find ourselves without any philosophical understanding of gravitation, though its simple mechanical formulae, framed by Newton, have proved of inestimable practical benefit. And we are still faced with Newton's problem: where best to concentrate research on problems concerning the mind of man. Many thinkers bravely navigate too broad a philosophical ocean, only to find themselves caught in a Sargasso Sea of tangled weed or on unsuspected reefs of ineluctable physical fact.'

The so-called paradox mentioned by Sargant has its counterpart in other branches of learning. We have progressively, for many years, narrowed and subdivided our research activities, and generally have been much more inclined or encouraged to look at the detail rather than the whole. There has undoubtedly been great progress made on narrow fronts by subdivision and specialization, but we may have carried this too far—a point made by a distinguished doctor in my hearing recently when he said that *the* greatest need in medicine today was to 'get it out of the hands of the experts'. He called them 'white mouse doctors', and he presumably would have approved a trend noticed by another doctor recently during a visit to Russia. 'There was', he wrote, 'a perceptible tendency towards observing and treating the patient, as distinct from observing and treating the patient's symptoms.'

Readers who are interested in this subject may like to read *Man's Presumptuous Brain* by Dr. A. T. W. Simeons, which discusses psychosomatic illness in an illuminating way. Dr. Simeons is concerned, in particular, to bridge the gap between physician and psychologist, and in his own way emphasizes the problem stressed by Sargent in the recent quotation—that is, how to link together the specialists, and to consider more fully the whole problem, whether it be man or some larger entity such as a group.

The dilemma of all research workers is increasing rather than decreasing as new specialisms emerge and a greater number of 'discrete' areas are created. Those of us who are interested in applying all forms of research to management theory and practice will pay special attention to research into human beings, because we are likely to find an increasing number of analogies between the internal controls and communications required to make up a complete person, and the controls and communications necessary to make up a complete organization comprising many persons. But before we become too enthusiastic about the analogy between complete persons and complete organizational groups let us consider at least one essential difference.

The heart, for instance, exists with other organs in the body in order to sustain the whole, i.e. an individual person. But the whole individual person does not exist to sustain his group; in fact quite the opposite, i.e. the group exists to sustain the individuals within it.

What does this tell us? First, that the objectives of man's internal group (heart, brain, etc.) and his external group are identical; both are concerned with his betterment as a complete individual. They both exist, primarily, to help him, not he to help them. Second, that we must know at least four things if we are to provide this individual betterment. We must understand each of the 'organs' or parts making up a complete man, and each of the individuals making up a complete group. We must understand the relationships which exist between man's internal organs, and which enable them, collectively, to make him 'tick'. We must understand the external relationships between one individual and others, which collectively enables the group to function effectively as an aid to each of its individuals.

Let us consider the state of knowledge in these four areas. First, we have made great progress, as Sargent has said, in our understanding of man's internal organs, although the brain itself is perhaps the least well known.

Second, we know relatively little about the individuals who make up various groups. I said earlier that when we attempt to assess an individual in isolation we find ourselves short of analytical tools, and unless we develop a greater number of objective measuring-sticks which can be applied to individuals I do not see how we can fully understand the relationships *between* individuals.

The third area, which is the relationship between man's internal organs, is becoming more important as a field of study under the general term 'psychosomatic'. It is surely likely to provide us with many valuable clues to the way in which man's internal control and communication systems work.

The fourth area is concerned with man's *external* control and communication systems, that is, the group organization within which he and his colleagues function. The purpose of this book is to encourage a deeper understanding of group organization, and I am convinced that an increase in our knowledge of the third area, that is, man's own internal system, will help us greatly in our study of his external relationships, and through this to a greater appreciation of the whole man as a 'group'.

We will discuss these four areas in greater detail. The first area, that is, our understanding of man's internal organs, and the third area, that is, the internal relationship between these organs, will be considered together under the heading:

The Organization of the Whole Man

Some of the earlier writers on organization recognized fully the importance of studying the whole man as a basis for organizational understanding. Mary Parker Follett, whose great wisdom is less appreciated by modern managers than it should be, said in *The Psychology of Control*: 'I'm coming more and more to think that we cannot departmentalize our thinking in this way, that we cannot think of economic principles and ethical principles, but that underneath all our thinking there are certain fundamental principles to be applied to all our problems.' Here Miss Follett is referring to a very wide field indeed, and many would say that what she asks is unlikly ever to be realized. The canvas is just too large.

She goes on to discuss more fully what Dr. Mayo called 'the total situation'. If we have to undepartmentalize our thinking and get down to principles that are fundamental for all the social sciences, fundamental indeed for all the life processes, surely we have to do that especially for the subject of this paper. The aim of organization engineering is control through effective unity. If, therefore, we wish to understand control, we should begin by trying to understand the nature of unities. And as our thinking on this subject has of recent years been greatly enriched by the thinking in other fields, I want to speak briefly of what we are learning of unities from biologists, psychologists, and philosophers. Professor Henderson, a biological chemist tells us that we have to study a whole as a whole, not only through an analysis of its constituents. He says: 'The old physiologists described the circulation of the blood, the beating of the heart, or the properties of gastric juice, and could tell you separate facts, but could not connect these facts so as to make a satisfactory picture of the organism.' Again he says: 'Physiology is far from "seeing the organism as a whole yet, but we can put together the carriage of oxygen, or carbonic acid, the alkalinity of the blood, and see how these three are parts of one process. We can study how this bit of integration is itself an adaption." ' Professor Henderson is always looking on the functioning of a whole as the adapting and integrating of parts. (Is not that the chief job of the organizational engineer?) And he goes so far as to say—after stating the fact that doctors used to study separate diseases but now tend to study man as a whole—that 'this may be the beginning of a new science, the science of human biology'.

Again, Miss Follett[1] says: 'A very suggestive treatment of wholes has come from those who have been working at the integrative action of the nervous system. Sherrington has shown us convincingly that the simple reflex, which has been treated as an isolable and isolated mechanism, is an artificial abstraction, that the nervous system functions as a whole. Kempf, a psycho-biologist, deals with what he calls "whole personalities". He tells us of an integrative unity, of a functional whole. Many psychologists today are taking the idea of "organization", "integration", "total activities of the individual", as the pivotal point in their psychology. (Here again are words and phrases with which we are coming to be very familiar within business management.) The Gestalt school[2] gives us what is called explicitly the doctrine of wholes, which denies that physical, psychical or social situations are made up of elements in a plus-plus relation. The whole, they tell us, is determined not only by its constitutents but by their relation to one another. This is not new doctrine, but, being put forward as the cardinal feature of a whole school of psychology, it is having a large influence.'

Follett says later in the same paper: 'Why have I talked so long on the nature of unities? Because we cannot understand control without understanding unities. I said that the chief problem of the organization engineer was acknowledgedly co-ordination. That simply means he cannot get control without unity. Put this in the plainest language of your everyday job. In order to control a certain situation, you have to get the co-operation of those fellow executives who are also concerned in that situation. The degree of control will depend partly on how far you can successfully unite the ideas of these men and yourself.

[1] *The Psychology of Control.* Mary Parker Follett.
[2] For a discussion on this read *Theories of Personality.* Hall and Lindsey.

G

'I find this the law on every level I have studied. Those biologists, psychologists, and philosophers I have mentioned in this paper whose most fundamental thinking is concerned with integrative unities, tell us of the self-regulating, self-directing character of an organism as a whole. They mean that the organizing activity *is* the directing activity. The interacting *is* the control, it does not set up a control, that fatal expression of some writers on government, and also some writers on business administration. I cannot get up in the morning, I cannot walk to my work, without that co-ordination of muscles which is control. The athlete has more of that co-ordination and therefore more control than I have. On the personal level, I gain more and more control over myself as I co-ordinate my various tendencies. This is interesting to us from two points of view, not only as showing the operation of the same law on different levels, but because we are more and more using this knowledge in dealing with individuals in industry as well as to obtain effective group action.'

Readers interested in cybernetics will have noted Miss Follett's phrase 'the self-regulating, self-directing character of an organism as a whole'; I shall return later to her emphasis on co-ordination, which to her is not an aspect of control but control itself.

Another earlier writer on organization, Henry Dennison,[1] put this question of man's 'wholeness' in another and more picturesque way. 'There is a sort of New England town meeting going on inside our heads all the time. The animal, the savage, and the child are sitting on the benches, eager members of the assembly. They debate every question that arises. Each wants every question settled his way. All sorts of odd opinions, dead doctrines, ancient hatreds, wily superstitions, unworth loyalties and foolish fears are also there.

'But the educated man is the chairman of this meeting in his brain. The effectiveness of every man's life depends upon his being a good chairman.

[1] *Organization Engineering.* Henry Dennison.

'He must see to it that the animal, the savage and the child do not run away with the meeting. He must see to it that the real "order of business" for the day is not upset or set aside by the hatreds, the superstitions, the fears and the outworn opinions that are in the meeting.'

When a manager takes the chair he always faces this situation. It is perhaps difficult for him to realize that he himself is subject, internally, to these varying forces, but it reminds him that co-ordination internally is a desirable preliminary to co-ordination externally with other people.

Which comes first: dissecting a person or an organization, or putting him or it together? I am convinced that a consideration of the whole is a necessary prelude to dissection. In any case, when we dissect a person in the manner described by Sargant we must put him together again; having dissected an organization and isolated one or more individuals within it we must put it together again. The 'scientific approach' is a dissecting operation, with each 'part' or step requiring its own research and practice ground. But a number of good individual steps do not automatically make a staircase; a variety of good individual 'parts' do not automatically constitute a complete person or organization.

Perhaps at this point I may introduce a term which has been the subject of philosophic discussion for many centuries, and yet paradoxically has never been more in need of earnest consideration than today. That term is 'holism', which our dictionary defines as 'a tendency in nature to form wholes that are more than the sum of the parts. . . .' How wonderful if we could become more skilled in achieving this in individuals and organizations!

Whatever the field, one sees many examples where vision has stopped short of its wider possibilities. The specialism has hidden the possibilities of holism. Within industry we find examples in design, where the technical and aesthetic specialists pursue their separate ways, often ignorant of, and occasionally antagonistic to, each other. How much one sighs for the 'complete design'. In accounting one finds all too much evidence of narrow specialization. Today's manager requires his accountant to be in at the birth of ideas, projects, budgets and the like, as exemplified by the modern phrase 'management accounting'. Most accountants, however, act the role of coroner, presiding at the inquest on figures dead and gone.

I find also, today, an increasing tendency for individuals to speak from a narrow platform. Someone will say, 'now, speaking as a Christian I would do so and so', or, 'speaking as a teacher I think that this should be done'. One wishes that more of us would 'speak as a complete person'.

In many fields of activity I find people preoccupied with narrow projects and studies, and with little desire to examine their place or possibilities as part of a 'whole'. In management circles much the same outlook prevails. It is, for instance, much easier to get a full house at a managerial conference where specialist subjects are discussed. It is obvious that either the delegate or his chief, or both, want immediate value for money, and subjects which cover a broader canvas and which are likely to be discussed in philosophic mood are not in that category. Organization itself suffers as much as any other activity from narrow vision, and I constantly see organizational changes which are narrowly conceived and narrowly executed. A specialist, rather than a generalist, view prevails, and it is no wonder that some organizations end up like a patchwork quilt, full of little unrelated bits of change.

The narrow attitude often discourages a search for the real truth, and this is particularly so in the case of strikes, most of which are ostensibly sparked off by one grievance; most managers know that there are probably other causes, covering a wide area, and the publicized reason may be only the last straw.

There are signs that wholeness, or holism, are once again becoming more attractive, and, one hopes, more valuable as scientific and managerial preoccupations, when more of us are encouraged, as Professor Brinser said recently,[1] 'to develop the power of mental cross-reference'. A colleague put it another way when he stressed the need for three-dimensional managers. Dealing particularly with those activities bearing upon organization, we see the emergence of new terms, which, even if the fundamental ideas are old, give then a new look by clothing the older ideas in new scientific and technological apparel. Cybernetics is a case in point, where its definition, including, as it does, such terms as 'control' and 'communications', 'men' and 'machines', assumes that the 'whole' is being studied. This concept of the whole is encouraged by the manner in which *some* (but not all!) exponents of cybernetics are organizing themselves. It is true that in cybernetics yet another specialism is emerging which adds to the great number of 'isms' existing. But if in so doing it brings together, or integrates, many different scientists, the net result may show gain. It seems inevitable that medical specialists, in co-operation with mathematicians, physicists, engineers and philosophers, will produce a more complete picture of man and machine, which can be used more effectively by managers.

In a similar, and perhaps equally important, way, ergonomics, another old/new term, is encouraging a greater appreciation of man in relation to his rapidly changing environment. I have already referred to the effects of the environment upon individuals, and I make no apology for repeating that all persons, individually and in groups, can be helped by studying their physical environment more fully. A man may be conditioned by a chair as well as a colleague. An informative booklet[2] was once issued by D.S.I.R. which, under the challenging caption 'Man designed for machine', said that a lathe in current use had its controls so designed as to require, ideally, an operator 4½ feet

---

[1] Brinser Professor of Resource Economics, University of Michigan.
[2] *The Industrial Use of Ergonomics.*

tall, 2 feet across the shoulders, with an 8 feet arm span! Few such men exist, but many such badly designed machines do.

Such examples exist more often than we imagine and they point to the need for a more complete understanding of the term 'design'. Too often the latter is applied in a narrow engineering sense with little realization of the human aspects required. At a conference on ergonomics[1] Dr. O. G. Edhoem referred to the new opportunity it presents for specialists like biologists, engineers, psychologists, physiologists to unite into composite teams. He told us that in future we should require scientists to be trained in more than one discipline, which is another way of saying that we may have gone as far as we should go in division, and must now encourage the wider outlook. One small but significant contribution to this development is the sponsorship, by Granada, of a series of public lectures, usually at the Guildhall, London, where many aspects of 'communication' are ably dealt with by prominent speakers.

Modern computing and data processing systems are encouraging us to think more deeply about the whole situation. This form of development is particularly important because it is a product of modern science and technology, and its further development will encourage other specialists, including those in the 'social' fields, to collaborate more effectively. This point was brought out by Dr. Maarschalk when he reported[2] on an Integrated Data Processing Conference in Holland. 'The second issue at the conference', he said, 'is the confusion caused by the fact that different sciences and arts, which our educational system, so far, has kept separated, have been thrown together because they use the same information processing machine. This means that delegates had a variety of education, background, sphere of work and objectives. A balanced integration of these specialists around the

[1] D.S.I.R. 1960.
[2] *B.C.A.C. News*, July 1962.

gravity centre of information processing still has to be reached, for which purpose a suitable vehicle has to be made.'

Perhaps a computer may seem an odd gravity centre for the encouragement of 'holism', but we cannot neglect any such influence, whether it is a piece of equipment, a college, a conference, a new specialism, or an attitude of mind.

A reference to colleges reminds me of yet another argument for 'holism' which was made by Oscar Handlin in an article entitled 'Are the Colleges Killing Education?'[1] He says: 'No other system of higher education subjects its students to the endlessly badgering tests of the American college. The examinations of French and English universities are difficult, but they come where they belong, at the terminus of a stage of education. And they probe not fragments of courses, but the mastery of a whole field of knowledge, however and whenever acquired. These methods cannot be simply transferred to our own situation. But they indicate that we can safely do without the recurrent, meaningless hurdles we now set in the way of our students. We can aim at a mode of valuation that will judge the whole man as he leaves the campus, not the bits and pieces of him we glimpse as he passes through it.'

Continuing with our discussion of the four 'areas' referred to on page 95 let us consider briefly some possibilities in the third area, which is:

The Comparative Assessment of Individuals

What can research tell us in this field? Like most managers I claim only a superficial knowledge of biological, neurological and psychological developments, but I do bring a deep interest and a lively imagination to bear on the many developments which are currently in hand. Few specialists in these fields have themselves the willingness to cultivate holism, and this reluctance makes it imperative to promote better means of co-ordinating the

[1] Oscar Handlin, Professor of History, Harvard. *The Atlantic Monthly*, 1962.

separate researches, and to ensure that a greater amount of synthesized knowledge emerges which can be understood and used by other specialists, particularly managers.

Let us consider the problem of fitting an individual into a group, which is a problem all managers face frequently. Management-selection specialists have in recent years made an intensive study of this problem, and even if, so far, they have not accumulated a neat set of selection principles, they have at least amassed an experience which is far greater than that possessed by most managers, whose selection experience is usually small and spasmodically used. I referred earlier to the lack of effective testing or selecting tools available to us when an individual is being selected for engagement and promotion in, or even firing from, a company. Few tools are also available for those who wish to assess an individual's suitability for membership of a particular group within the company. Experience has taught us that very few people can adapt themselves to almost any group, and we now realize more fully that to fit an individual effectively into a particular group we require to know three things: the characteristics of the *particular group* into which an individual is to be fitted, what the group requires from the individual, and the characteristics and requirements of the individual.

What tools or techniques are required in order to select and fit an individual into a particular group? Let us leave until the following chapters some of the basic characteristics of groups and at this stage concentrate upon the individual to be fitted in. To some extent, for some purposes, individuals can be placed in fairly precise categories. For instance, you and I have, or should have, a blood category which is vital when our blood has to be grouped or transfused with others. We have been, or could be, measured and placed into other categories, some medical and others which show our intelligence and manual dexterity.

Andrew Cooper, writing in *The Director*, August 1962 issue, related his experiences while investigating some psychosomatic techniques developed by a Dr. Viard in the French company of Telemechanique Electrique. An attempt was made to show that a viable correlation exists between the endocrinal organs, certain physiological and psychological tendencies and the desired social role of an individual. As make-weight a geometric test is thrown in which relates to the 'golden' ratio of 1·00/0·618. Many golden ratios should apparently exist in an elegant human body, and significant departures in any individual indicate departures from the desirable norm in the character and emotional traits of the individual.

I am afraid that the 'typical report' which Mr. Cooper extracted from this company's files seemed disappointingly conventional and made no reference to the interesting measurements discussed in the article. One is therefore tempted to give a verdict of 'Not proven', although any new study in this field by someone of repute is surely worth investigating. There may be something in it!

There may, too, be something in another measurement which was mentioned in the *Electrical Times* in June 1962. Recorded voice-prints can give as reliable an identification as fingerprints, according to the Bell Telephone Laboratories. 'Effective disguise is impossible.' Not even 'such drastic measures as removal of teeth, tonsils, adenoids or fitting the mouth with marbles seriously modify the pattern'. I have not yet discovered how to use this information in aid of better management, but one day . . . you never know! You never know whether tests such as those recently described in *The Financial Times*[1] may prove more valid than the subsequent correspondence showed them to be. It was, for instance, suggested that 'the right-hand side of your face is what you are born with, and the left-hand side is what you have become'. Many years ago the right side of my face was slightly distorted by a hockey ball, and I fear, therefore, that I would carry little weight if evaluated on that particular test, or indeed on the

[1] 'One Way to Choose Top Executives'. 10th November, 1962.

others described which required managerial candidates to select psychopaths and play trains with pegs as proof (or disproof) of their abilities.

It is unwise to be wholly sceptical about a new test just because it seems slightly absurd. But in the field of management selection the validity of tests is even more important than in many other spheres, because the penalty of wrong selection is severe and far-reaching.

I said earlier that the intelligence test is, so far, the only one which is measurable in a reasonably consistent manner, and (apart from medical checks) is available for managerial selection purposes. It has, however, considerable limitations when we attempt to use it for fitting an individual *into a particular group*. We have not yet, for instance, done much research into the reaction of various intelligence levels upon one another in a group situation. An interesting possibility was suggested by Grey Walter, in *The Living Brain*, who said that 'the tentative classification of simple brain records has indicated a wide prospect of diverse and fluctuating personalities. Intelligence as estimated by arbitrary and already obsolescent tests, finds no parallel in our tracings, but versatility, ductility and certain special imaginative aptitudes, are beginning to be recognized as dynamic interrelations and transformations within the framework of normal variation.'

The tracings to which he referred are those recorded by electroencephalograph (EEG) tests, which produce measurable rhythms, even if, as yet, these measurements are not precisely understandable or applicable. But Grey Walter goes on to suggest some applications in and adjacent to the field of management. For instance, he says: '. . . in these days of protracted international wrangling how many negotiations may be frustrated simply by the fact that one of the negotiators is an extreme P type and the other an extreme M type! Like Peggy and Michael they want to agree and eventually may come to agreement, but meanwhile the peace of the world is in jeopardy through mischance of alpha grouping, just as a man's life may be imperilled by a mistake in blood-groups. Academic examinations are designed to discover character as well as capacity, but these basic mechanisms of mental behaviour, the characteristic operations of a person's way of thinking, are masked by all manner of social and intellectual tricks. Competitive examination does not reveal them; it is not a question of one type being superior to another. Even the most extreme types are undesirable only, like matter, in the wrong place, in the wrong company. It might be well to index all politicians, and his alpha designation should certainly be on the passport of every diplomat.'

It is surely a short step from this to a classification of members of a board of directors or a management group, where the relative alpha designations offer new opportunities to fit people 'more scientifically' into a group.

Perhaps we should pause here while some managers express their horror that any such technique should ever be applied to human associations or groupings. But is it really such a revolutionary idea? Surely, as I suggested on page 42, we have already committed ourselves to 'the machine' in many forms, ostensibly to help ourselves and society in one way or another. We have committed ourselves physiologically to many tests and measurements, which presumably help us to become and remain effective members of a group and society. We have not yet committed ourselves psychologically or neurologically in the same way, but only, surely, because we do not yet know how to do it. Let us remember that research into mental orders and disorders is still pitifully small, and, according to Mr. I. Henderson,[1] only '0·67 per cent of the total money spent on the national health service went on research. A smaller proportion of this was spent on investigating mental disorder although sufferers from these conditions filled nearly one half of the total hospital beds available.'

[1] Chairman, Mental Health Research Fund. 20th November, 1961.

If only this small sum is spent on mental *ill health* how much is, or should be, spent on the more positive programme of mental *health*, which is very closely associated with satisfactory personal relationships. It reminds me of the grievance committees I mentioned earlier in the sense that the best way is surely to *anticipate* trouble rather than to cure afterwards. A striking example of the positive approach in the physiological area was the tubercular Mass X-ray project, in which I was privileged to play a small pioneering part. As much as any other method it helped to anticipate and finally to reduce greatly the incidence of TB. I see nothing wrong in considering a similar programme in the mental area.

When we talk of measurements we must be careful to avoid making too precise a comparison with normal measuring concepts and standards. Engineers measure fairly precisely, physicists very precisely, doctors less precisely, and managers, on the whole, roughly. As Grey Walter says: 'E.E.G. signs correlate better with "how" than "how-much". The superficial E.E.G. differences are linked more closely with personality than with intelligence.' But managers *want* new types of measurement, such as one which measures *how* someone is likely to act or react. I would certainly like to know 'how much' of various characteristics a manager has, but I would also very much like to know 'how' he is likely to approach a situation or work with others.

Perhaps, however, the possibilities such as those I have been discussing are still too far off for us to become immediately excited about their advantages or doubtful of their dangers. At present it is probable that, as Grey Walter says, subjects like this also have their Gresham's Law—half-truths drive out full understanding! But surely this is a half-truth, because few would (less should) claim today to know the whole truth. One purpose of this book is to encourage young managers to search more widely for more organizational truth, and if, along the way, they pause, contemplate and possibly try out a half-truth it may be better than trying nothing new at all. 'It's better to have . . .'

The Individual's external relationships with his group

This is the fourth and last of the 'areas' referred to on page 95, and it is, of course, the aim of this particular chapter which attempts to show that a greater understanding of man's 'internal' relationships and his characteristics should help us to improve his group relationships.

Much interesting work has been done by various researchers into the relationships of an individual with his group, and several such projects are analysed by Mason Haire in *Modern Organization Theory*. Under the subheading 'The Conflict between personality and organization' he reminds us that 'Whenever we join a group we give up some individual freedom' and therefore 'the calculus of the balance between the two (the individual and the group) is a problem'. It is, to me, the core of the problem.

Argyris[1] makes the basic assumption 'that human beings are need-fulfilling, goal-achieving unities', and one of the various strategies they create is to *organize* themselves. This to a manager seems to imply that he has an individual's full and natural support in his managerial desire to merge that individual into a group. The individual wants to join the club and this surely is an important basic consideration. It seems to follow that if the individual and the organization go sour on each other the principal fault is likely to be organizational rather than personal.

Despite some particular cases to the contrary I largely support this theory, and it has long conditioned my attitude to personal problems which, when they arise, are first approached by me as organizational, rather than personal, failures.

Argyris refers to the possibility of help from biologists, who, 'because of their long experience in studying organizational phenomena', have much to offer us. In amplifying this statement he says the following: '. . . some students of social organization believe that it is possible to understand organizations by breaking

---

[1] *Understanding Human Behavior in Organization.* Chris Argyris.

down the complexity into smaller and more manageable units (through the traditional independent-dependent-variable design). The organization, they reason, will be understood when the results of the separate experiments are finally synthethesized.' This strategy has much in its favour, and the author uses it in some of his research. It tends to be more vigorous and the variables more easily quantified. However, it has limitations, some of which were highlighted at a recent symposium on biological theory. Paul A Weiss, for example, in criticizing such procedures states quite clearly that organization is not something one can understand by synthesizing the result of several carefully controlled experiments (that focus on parts of an organization). Organization may be something which has *stability only if the components are present all at the same time*.

Here we find another aspect of 'holism' where it becomes not a synthesis of various activities but the total purpose of the complete individual, or the whole organization, without which, as I suggested in *Management Principles*, no 'detail' can be understood fully.

Argyris developed a model,[1] which should be studied more fully by those interested. Briefly, he outlined the development of the human personality from infancy to adult existence, and said that when that person becomes a member of a group he is likely in most cases to suffer a variety of frustrations, which themselves are exhibited in a variety of ways, such as regression, aggression or tension. An individual will often adapt himself to these conditions by a variety of *informal activities*, which are, so to speak, his personal reactions to the formal organizational chains which attempt to bind him.

These thoughts prompted Argyris to form his own 'tentative conceptual definition' of organization, which is:

'(1) A plurality of parts,
(2) Each achieving specific objective(s), and

[1] *Understanding Organizational Behavior*, page 63.

(3) Maintaining themselves through their interrelatedness and,

(4) Simultaneously adapting to the external environment, thereby

(5) Maintaining the interrelated state of the parts.'

Readers may like to compare this definition with those on pages 50 to 55.

In this and, more particularly, in a later study Argyris refers specifically to the attitudes of foremen and the conflicting attitudes and loyalties which are present among individuals in groups. Any research into the place of the foreman in a group is extremely important, as in my industrial experience I have never really been satisfied that we have understood fully, and organized effectively, these relationships, either with 'top' management or with the workpeople.

Argyris makes an important point which should be fully appreciated by managers; this is that there may be 'an increase in *individual* disturbance while there isn't, as yet, any inferrible *organization disturbance*'. He rightly says that 'It would give us much needed insight into the tolerance of the system for stability and change. Such knowledge might lead to understanding why, when and how some organizations explode, and why some do not.'

But surely the wise manager *has* means available to measure the increasing 'temperature' and pressure of a group. He can examine regularly the individuals within it, such as by the personal audit discussed earlier. He can carry out an occasional social audit[1] of the group; he can check other personal and 'group' performances, too, such as quality and quantity of work produced, absentee or lateness records, and other indications of exceptional or unusual activities. As I referred earlier and specifically to *foremen* it is certainly important to 'measure' as accurately as possible what

[1] 'Social Audit of the Enterprise'. F. H. Blum. *Harvard Business Review.*

foremen and junior managers are thinking about the group, because they really are in a key position between 'top' and bottom. Too often they feel themselves to be between the upper and nether grindstones, and even Argyris separates them from the 'men' by referring to their attitudes towards 'the management'. Many years ago I lectured widely on 'the foreman as a manager', but even today we really do not accept him as part of the management team, and generally he knows it.

In this chapter I am dealing specifically with the relationship between *an individual* and his group; later I shall discuss foremen again when I examine the problem of *groups* within a group, which is a wider aspect of the individual problem. There are some essential differences to consider.

One vital group requirement is the need for the group to express itself through an individual, or the individual to represent himself, or others, to or through a group. An obvious example is the relationship between a managing director and his Board, and vice versa. This relationship requires a continuous understanding between the individual and his group, and many company failures or misfortunes are directly connected with the inability of an individual, usually the chairman or managing director, to maintain adequate relationships. Sometimes this failure is due to the individual; more often it is due to group deficiencies. Whatever the reason, this problem emphasizes the importance of individual group relationships at the top level, which, if achieved, will encourage similar satisfactory conditions lower down.

An interesting contribution to managerial group relationships and responsibilities is made by Bakke[1] when he discusses the need to 'preserve the unique and dynamic wholeness of the organization'. He says that at least three 'synergic processes' can function in a social organization to fulfil this need. They are

[1] *Concept of the Social Organization.* E. Wight Bakke.

(a) The Fusion Process.
(b) The Problem-Solving Process.
(c) The Leadership Process.

I shall discuss these more fully in later chapters, but here I wish to discuss only (a). The Fusion Process 'attempts first of all to reconcile or *fuse* these expectancies and bring them into closer harmony with each other, and in the process the organization, the groups, and the individuals are changed, and their behavior is changed.

'The second need for the Fusion Process arises from the fact that the organization as such is related to more comprehensive organizations, and to other autonomous organizations, integration with some of which is essential to its existence. The same dual or multiple directional-process of mutual attempts of one organization to make an agency out of other organizations results in the need for a fusion process as between an organization and others external to or comprehending it.

'In other words, the function of the Fusion Process is to maintain the integrity of the organization in the face of divergent interests of individuals, groups, other organizations, and the organization itself, which each hopes to realize through its contact with the other. Its aim is to establish and maintain for the organization an internal and external integration which will at least leave its capacity to perform its function unimpaired, and at best will improve that capacity.

'The major symptom of ineffectiveness in the carrying out of this process is the persistence (not necessarily the occurrence) of tensions, friction, and factionalism in the organization, rebellious acts of individuals and groups against activity or standards of activity required of them by the organization, indifference and apathy of participants towards the needs of the organization, lack of interest of participants in defending the organization.'

Bakke's comments remind us of Argyris (page 109), who referred

H

to the basic need of human beings to organize themselves. Once created, the organizational group defends itself against attack, which may come from inside and outside, and almost certainly from *individuals* within it. Every manager must face the conflict of interests which are present within most groups, although I hope he realizes that *if no such conflict existed there would probably be inadequate 'dynamic wholeness'*. Every worthwhile group must have its tensions, its individual problem-raisers, its Johnnies-out-of-step, its critics. These must be overcome by constant attention to the 'Fusion Process', which becomes a continuous operation as long as any *diffusion* possibilities exist; that is, as long as any dynamic constituents remain in the group. The ideal group is one where fusion only marginally wins!

Mason Haire, in *Growth of Organizations*, refers to the relationship of an individual and his organizational group in 'mechanical' terms. He says that 'As the organization grows, the force that seems likely to destroy it is the centrifugal force arising from the fact that the members are individuals and tend to fly off on tangents towards their own goals.' He makes the interesting point that, in his observations, 'most management time and effort is spent in holding the thing together as a single working unit'. Surely this must be so, because unless the centripetal force is stronger than the centrifugal, disintegration of a structure would occur.

Haire uses the word 'cohesion' instead of 'fusion' and both words seem appropriate although I prefer the former. Weiss and Jacobson[1] said that in their studies of a company they were able to isolate 'liaison men' whose principal job was to provide the cohesion for holding the groups together. Out of 200 in the company 18 per cent were identified as having this function.

Summing up, we are constantly faced with the centrifugal tendency of individuals to fly off at a tangent, to break away from

[1] *A method for the analysis of the structure in complex organizations.* R. Weiss and E. Jacobson.

the group in one manner or another. This is a continuous possibility as long as dynamic movement of the group exists. Centripetal or contra-action can be taken in several ways; first, by providing enough structural strength in the organizational mass to resist reasonable tangential or centrifugal stresses; second, by ensuring good relationships between the individuals in the group, so that those who are thinking of flying off are restrained by the greater force of cohesive argument and treatment; third, by the appointment of 'liaison' individuals, who have a deliberate and specialist responsibility for maintaining reasonable group stability. Perhaps the obvious example of such a liaison man is a good personnel officer.

Robert Dubin, in *Stability of Human Organizations*, has some interesting things to say on the relationship of the individual to his group. He discusses the case of an individual who is considering the desirability of making a career, a condition particularly important in management circles today, where there is a greater willingness of senior executives to move around in order to find one. Dubin refers to the conflict which may exist between 'professional' status and functional specialization. I know of many such cases, where an individual has achieved high professional respect as, say, a scientist, but remains firmly stuck in a relatively narrow specialist groove. His chance of achieving a high post is in inverse ratio to his present success.

This problem is likely to increase as more specialisms arise, and more specialists are appointed who, as in a number of cases known to me, tend to become frustrated individuals and awkward group members through their failure to leap out of specialist into managerial rank. It is an individual/organizational problem of growing importance and Dubin's studies are worth more careful thought than I can give here.

Finally, Rapoport[1] deals with yet another aspect of the individual in relation to his group. He questions the value of an

[1] *An Experimental Paradigm.* Anatol Rapoport.

'individual' as compared with a 'group' task, a problem of particular interest to all managers who constantly face the necessity of considering how best to solve a given problem. 'Shall I appoint an individual, or organize a group, to solve this problem?' This is frequently met at Board level, and often, perhaps too often, 'solved' by appointing a sub-committee to report back. I say 'too often' because in many cases the best Board 'solution' would be to allocate the task to the most appropriate *individual* and let *him* report back. I shall refer again to this situation in the next chapter.

Rapoport also discusses this problem as it affects the relationship of the chief executive with his group. He says, for instance, that 'the executive (in a group of, say, three) may, if he wishes, ignore the other two completely, since the information from the apparatus is directly available to him. The frequency and the extent to which this is observed will tell us something about the value of this role division, for example, whether it is felt to be an unnecessary burden or an advantage. It may happen that many an executive, impatient with the complex group-process, will decide to by-pass the others but will show only a pedestrian performance compared with team performance.' He goes on to say that 'The entire question of individual *versus* group efficiency in the solution of problems is a difficult one to answer meaningfully. . . . For instance, if in the group approach there is an opportunity for one individual to take leadership, it may happen that the most competent individual will most frequently take leadership, with the result that the average of an n person group performance will really be the average of the best of n randomly selected individuals, which will always be higher than the average taken over single arbitrarily selected individuals. Contrariwise if the conditions of solution are such that *every one* must understand the solution, it may be that the least competent in the group becomes the pace-setter. These statistical efforts obscure the question originally asked: 'How do co-operative groups and individuals compare in the solution of certain problems?'

The varying leadership possibilities posed by Rapoport seem to suggest at least two desirable requirements. First, that the most competent individual must take leadership (and keep it), and, second, that he must make special attempts to see that the weak links are strengthened by an adequate understanding of their weaknesses, and by constant attempts to raise their understanding and performance to nearer that of the leader. Groups, like chains, have weak links, which cannot always be completely eliminated, but their weaknesses can, by careful design and good management, be reduced.

I am very conscious of the importance of the subject matter of this chapter. In an earlier chapter I stressed the importance of the individual, and the not always obvious fact that 'importance' is a relative term and therefore individuals can only be fully assessed in relation to other individuals, or to the groups within which the individual exists. This surely implies that the relationship of an individual to his group is a most important problem for an organizer or manager; a full understanding of this relationship requires not only a knowledge of the individual as a complete person, but also an understanding of groups and their characteristics.

In this chapter I discussed first the individual as a complete person. Internally, man has so far been studied more fully in 'bits' rather than as a whole, and, as Sargant says, 'remarkable progress has been made in biological understanding'. But we must admit that no such progress has yet been made in mental or psychological understanding. We have only to realize the amount of mental *ill health* which exists to realize that we are far from understanding how to maintain a high degree of mental *health*.

Much of the work in this field is still conducted in specialist grooves, and there is, I believe, an increasing need to bring them together and particularly to translate new knowledge into management opportunities. Managers do not know much, indeed cannot be expected to, about the highly specialized pieces of research now being conducted in the physiological, biological, psychological and psychosomatic fields. There is a great need for new tools which will enable managers more 'scientifically' to measure those human characteristics which can be used to classify, select and in other ways assist individuals to work more effectively. Managers will, I hope, pay particular attention to the developments in psychosomatic medicine, where body and brain are being 'put together', or at least where the association between the two is being more closely examined. This is a firm step towards a greater understanding of the relationship between one 'part' and the whole, and what the 'whole' really is, in both the individual and group sense.

In addition to his need to understand 'man' more fully as a person, a manager needs more help in fitting that person into the group. So far, outside the medical field, intelligence tests are the only ones available which can measure appropriate human characteristics in a reasonably consistent manner, and even these tests have severe limitations when used to assess an individual's suitability for a particular group. Interesting work is proceeding in the neurological field, and it may well be that eventually better tools will become available for assessing the ability of a particular individual to fit into a group, and indeed to assess the group performance of a particular combination of individuals. This possibility, while some way off, is not, I suggested, as revolutionary as it might appear, and it seems a logical, even if difficult, step forward from those 'personal' measurements and specifications most of us accept as desirable today.

I drew attention to the researches of various workers in this field. Argyris and others refer to the conflicts within groups, which are often stimulated by a variety of *informal* activities by individuals. It is suggested that a most important managerial task is constantly to assess and measure these individual disturbances, and to ensure that the group's internal temperature and pressure do not rise to exploding point. This is even more important in the foreman, or middle management, group, where upper and nether strains and stresses are likely to be concentrated.

Bakke uses the 'fusion process' and Haire the word 'cohesion' to describe the force necessary to maintain reasonable internal stability. Haire does in fact use the 'mechanical' analogy of centrifugal force which is likely, in a dynamic group, to send some individuals flying off at a tangent. To counter this, centripetal action must be taken, which can be done in a variety of ways: by certain informal activities, by constant study of the individuals, by group measurements, such as lateness, output, etc., and by the appointment of certain liaison people whose specific responsibility it is, on behalf of the top managers, to help in maintaining stability.

I referred also to a special aspect of individual activity within the group, that is, the increasing desire to see a career pattern ahead, which is a personal requirement of growing importance in these days of greater managerial mobility. This requirement emphasizes not only the need to give more attention to individuals, but the increasing importance of organizational skill in providing the best growth climate for these individuals within a group.

This was emphasized also in my final research reference, where Rapoport refers to the possibility of comparing individual and group performances in the achievement of a particular task. Unfortunately, present evidence is not conclusive, but it does at least point to conclusions already reached through other researches that, in every group, leadership is important, and that one of the leader's most important jobs is to increase the strength of the weaker individual members of the group.

Perhaps a final word from Haire's *Modern Organization Theory* is appropriate: 'Conflict between individual and organizational demands is omnipresent. Often, in current writings about organizational theory, there seems to be an implicit assumption that it is inevitably deleterious. Certainly some conflicts—between personalities and between individuals and the framework—are harmful and expensive, but others seem to be fruitful, stimulating, and productive of growth. If they were absolutely eliminated, the organization, relaxing in a bovine acceptance of its pattern on the part of the members, would have no protection from its own mistakes and no hope from a "divine spark of discontent".'

And so say I!

A Restatement:

(1) Most personal problems arise from group relationships, and an individual cannot be completely understood without reference to his group.

(2) Before considering 'outward' relationships between the individual and his group it is desirable to look inwards at the individual, who is himself a group of elements making up a complete human being.

(3) Man's bodily development has probably made more progress through 'internal specialization' than through 'holism'. To a lesser and more modern extent similar progress is now being made through specialized research into mental areas.

(4) The development of psychosomatic understanding is beginning to give us a wider understanding of the whole man, and the relationships which exist between various internal functions and organs. This may well provide managers with new and valuable means of assessing individual persons and their group relationships.

(5) A greater understanding of 'the whole man' is essential if managers are to ensure that the whole man is greater than the sum of his internal parts.

(6) Greater interest in 'holism', that is, in the 'complete man', is essential to good management. There are signs that some scientific, technological and organizational trends will encourage quicker progress towards this goal.

(7) One of the most important requirements of a manager is to assess an individual's suitability for a particular group, and vice-versa. This involves an ability to measure more accurately both the individual's and his group characteristics and requirements. To measure an individual more accurately, managers must ensure that progress is made in the many areas of research discussed in this and the previous chapter. In assessing an individual's group suitability the following considerations are important:

(a) It is necessary to resolve the inevitable 'conflict between personality and organization'.

(b) 'Human beings are needfulfilling, goal-achieving unities', which means that they *desire* to organize themselves. If, as this suggests, they 'want to join the club', subsequent failures point to 'club' or organizational, rather than personal, deficiencies.

(c) These 'formal' difficulties often encourage individuals to take counter-measures by 'informal activities' which become 'personal reactions to the formal organizational chains which attempt to bind them'. Unless carefully controlled, these informal activities create positive feed-back, which can wreck the group.

(d) It is particularly important to control the informal disturbances mentioned in (c), as they may not immediately show up as *organizational* disturbances. Many managerial techniques are available which can measure personal and group temperatures and performances so that early action can be taken to correct bad trends. Foremen or junior managers play a key part in this activity, both in creating and controlling difficulties.

(8) An important aspect of the individual/group relationship is the need for most groups to express themselves through an individual. Important examples are the managing director and a shop steward. This need underlines the

necessity of maintaining a complete understanding within the group, and with its leader.

(9) In preserving 'the unique and dynamic wholeness of the organization' several processes are at work, of which particular mention is made in this chapter of fusion or cohesion. Every manager must face the inevitable 'conflict of interests' which is present in every group, and realize too that 'if no such conflict existed there would probably be inadequate "dynamic wholeness" '. The ideal group is one where fusion, or cohesion, only marginally wins.

(10) Specialist appointments create special difficulties between individuals and their group. This requires managers to give special attention to the relationships between 'functional' and 'professional' responsibilities and to promotion possibilities between one and the other.

(11) Finally, reference is made to the inevitable problem of individual versus group tasks. This is important in at least two ways:

(a) Its effect on the training of individuals and the achievement of objectives. There is a tendency to 'refer' problems to sub-groups when it would be better to assign them to individuals.

(b) The effect of individual action by a manager on those colleagues he may by-pass, either accidentally or by design. Whatever the justification for this, the leader must ensure that the weak links are strengthened in order to maintain dynamic wholeness.

5

The Structure of Groups: I
Size, Shape and Internal Structure

As GROUPS have existed since Eve it is remarkable how little we know about their structural characteristics, and the interpersonal relationships within them. Looking back over my own working life I recall much discussion with fellow managers about the theory and practice of group organization, and many managers are interested in this subject. But what contributions have been made to a better understanding of group organization? I find disturbingly few which have become widely accepted by industrial managers as theories or principles, and we must go back forty years to the Hawthorn experiments to find a really significant contribution to the subject; this gap compares very unfavourably with almost any other 'scientific gap' known to managers.

I believe that a fairly close reciprocal relationship exists between the size of this gap and the progress of management. The fewer the guide posts along our path, the more unsure our progress, and it is probable that the slow progress in scientific management deplored by Urwick[1] will not quicken until more direction posts of the Hawthorn quality are designed and erected for the use of practising managers.

In previous chapters we have worked our way through two

[1] Page 19.

'components' of the group; first, the individual, and, second, the individual in relation to his group. Now we arrive at the group as a composite whole, which is a most complex structure, in purpose, shape, size, internal arrangement and external relationships. Every group exists in a constantly changing relationship to other groups, and needs constant attention to its own particular characteristics, and to other groups, in order to remain viable. Together, all groups exist, act, react and provide purposeful life to the master group called Society. Society exists to provide purposeful life to individual people, and so we attempt to provide an ecological chain of stability.

The industrial manager rarely finds time to consider his own group in such a wide setting, but he will do well always to remember that no group, just like no island, is complete unto itself, but is joined, as Donne[1] said, to a continent, or at least to a wider group. The relationships and responsibilities are multidimensional.

Before we consider what are the more important group dimensions let us return again to the scientific approach, and consider Stage 1—'Define the Objective'. What objective have we in mind when we decide to analyse the structure of groups? Surely it is to design the best *organization structure* for the 'purpose' we have in mind.

Perhaps I may remind you once again of the preparatory work embodied in a previous book, *Management Principles*, page 29, where I attempted to define these terms:

(1) The organizational structure.
(2) The organization.

I used various analogies to convince you that the structure was 'the framework, the plan, the basic organization chart which the managerial architect draws up to help in achieving the objective'.

[1] John Donne. 1571-1631.

I then said that the 'organization' is produced when individual names and titles are added and the 'dynamic' life of the group starts. The dynamic feature of an organization is provided by a combination of personal, internal group and external environmental forces. 'Only when these three are maximized is "the ability to act as one body" at its strongest.'

Our 'objective' is therefore to maximize these three forces. The first two have already been considered in previous chapters and in this particular chapter we shall consider their relationships with good structural design. What do we require in order to design the best organizational structure? Desirably, we should have this information:

(1) The company purpose or objective.
(2) A number of 'growth factors' which show company growth from past to present.
(3) An extrapolation of these past patterns into a future growth pattern.
(4) A limited number of specific requirements, some of which inevitably involve 'personal' considerations.

Let us briefly consider each in turn.

(1) The Company Purpose or Objective

I have already discussed, in *Management Principles*, page 53, what this is, and why it should exist. It is the 'common purpose' of the company group, expressed in terms which will answer reasonably such leading questions as 'Why are we in business?' or 'Is the proposed merger desirable in the light of the company's declared objectives?' Whenever a major reorganization or appointment is being considered the company purpose should be in the foreground of the discussions. The 'purpose' may be modified by agreement, but it should always be available in its latest agreed form, and is of great value to the organization engineer, who must provide structural shape within the framework of the accepted purpose.

(2) *A number of 'growth factors' which show company growth from past to present*

With companies, as with individuals, it is not so much where you are as where you are going that matters. A stroboscopic picture of a company in motion shows the 'static' view of a dynamic situation; but the company may be speeding up or slowing down, gaining or losing energy, and to assess a company's future we must know and assess its rate of growth, which means plotting growth curves.

The number of specific curves selected is a matter for individual choice, but, as 'people' are vital components, we must ensure that they are adequately included in one category or another. Certainly *total* numbers of people are important, as a group structure, like a building structure, depends greatly on the number of people likely to live within it. We should not be too concerned at this stage with subdivision of individual skills, specialisms or types, as these refinements will arise later. In any case, the finally agreed structure must provide for the utmost internal flexibility to accommodate changing personal, technical and other trends.

(3) *An extrapolation of these past patterns into a future growth pattern*

Here we attempt to place our third 'dot' on the growth charts. We have already plotted the past up to the present, and now these curves must be carried forward into whatever future period of time we consider desirable.

What is a desirable future? In designing a building we plan for at least twenty-five years of life, and most last far longer. In designing an organization structure what is the basic consideration? Some might say 'No time at all', because, they say, we can modify, or even demolish, an organization structure at a single meeting of the Board. But this is an oversimplified aspect of most company structural situations, and rarely is it possible (or desirable) to make drastic organizational changes without full consideration of the individuals already in the organization, those who may be required to join it, the shareholders, and, in a public company, the Stock Exchange. It is a good thing that company organizational changes are now attracting wider attention than before, and I for one hope that this interest continues on the part of shareholders, of the City and the Press. Organizational importance will then more surely come into its own as a contribution to company prosperity.

Let us return to the problem of structural life. I said earlier that structural considerations should be relatively independent of personal considerations. But when a structure exists, as is the case with the majority of organizational changes, people are already inhabiting it and therefore structural changes are intimately bound up with personal changes. Consequently we might consider what is a desirable time-span for an existing managerial team, and use this period of time as a basis for projecting organizational growth patterns into the future.

How long should, say, the managing director of a company remain in that capacity? The answer varies with every individual and his environment, but one short answer is, 'a shorter rather than a longer time'. I say this because, on the whole, a quickening rate of change is desirable in British industry, and this is stimulated by personal changes, particularly at the top. It is not difficult to prepare a personal growth chart which projects individuals into the future, so that reasoned and reasonable managerial succession is assured. It will probably show that a maximum of, say, ten years as managing director is desirable, as otherwise the promotion pipeline tends to get clogged.

Weighing up the various aspects of structural change it seems reasonable to project growth patterns at least ten years ahead, perhaps divided into two five-year plans.

Most Board chairmen would say that it is difficult enough to see one year ahead, let alone ten, but this argument dodges the real point. Organization planning must always *anticipate* actual growth, and if a company already has a reasonable past it must attempt to anticipate a reasonable future. It already possesses a group of managers, most of whom are probably committed to the company until retirement; certainly the company is committed to them through service and pension agreements. Its inescapable commitments make it necessary for every company to project into a reasonable future those significant curves which will provide growth patterns.

An interesting contribution to the possibilities of long-term forecasting was made by Lovewell and Bruce.[1] They describe the work started three years ago at Stanford on technological forecasting, and although it is obviously impossible as yet to prove its long-term value, the authors believe that it will not only provide better long-term (say, fifteen years) guide lines to product development, but will help to predict 'the future of the "soft" sciences—economics, sociology, psychology and the like—as well as management methods'. They make the interesting point that in the present state of the subject, mathematical skill is likely to play less part than the availability of 'knowledgeable people who are capable of keen analysis and creative interpretation. Logical sequential thinking is the best alternative in view of the inapplicability of mathematical techniques.' I suppose we could say that 'logical sequential thinking' is another way of describing the scientific approach!

What will this extrapolation tell the organizer? He will, at the least, have 'guesstimates' which will tell him what the top managers have in mind about the number of people likely to be employed, and, approximately, the main divisions of the company's product range and scope. He will be able to analyse this basic information so that not only can he recommend a structural form and

---

[1] 'How we predict technological change'. P. J. Lovewell and R. D. Bruce, Stanford Research Institute, California. *New Scientist*, Vol. 13.

growth in broad outline, but also, perhaps, certain personal changes. In short he will be better able to provide the Board with the design of a future company 'building' and some suggestions on internal 'shape'.

(4) *A limited number of specific requirements, some of which inevitably involve 'personal' considerations*

Before completing his suggested design the organizer will have born in mind certain specific requirements which were probably laid down by the Board when he was given his assignment. Most new houses provide for certain personal or special features which are required by the immediate occupiers. The organizer should be restricted by as few of these 'requirements' as possible, but it would be asking too much to ignore the idiosyncrasies, convictions or even whims of existing top managers; these individuals should, however, when planning for the future bear constantly in mind that the future structure may not contain them but their successors. It is therefore desirable to consider the views of these successors who, if an adequate management succession plan exists in the company, will be available for consultation.

Few top managers are prepared to go this far in planning for the future, but there are sound reasons why they should place more confidence in their successors. A little consideration might convince the existing top men that the more they become linked to the company, in terms of shareholding, options, pensions, consulting fees, etc., the more they must rely, after retirement, on the success of their successors. It seems good sense to let those successors have a hand in the design of the future organization structure.

An Analysis of Structure

In this chapter we have so far prepared the way for a more detailed structural design. The Board has furnished its best estimates of growth, certain basic information has become

I

available and the organizer is now ready for a more intensive analysis. Let us use a simple mechanical analogy to clarify what we are trying to do at this stage. I have already described a typical group as a composite unit possessing its own special combination of internal 'parts' and its own special size and shape. It is a multi-dimensional dynamic entity. It has a constantly changing relationship with surrounding groups, which gives it positive and relative motion as a *complete* group. In its motion it keeps a constant eye on other groups which are also in motion.

Isn't this something like an automobile, which is a unique collection of specially designed 'parts', all fitting together into a complete entity and providing, internally, co-ordinated and controlled power which allows it to proceed under effective 'management' in a variety of directions. The objective will be realized best if the automobile is designed well, with the best arrangement of internal parts, with efficient fuel and lubrication, and a driver who steers it towards the objective, bearing constantly in mind the other automobiles in motion, often indeed in competition, with him!

The sub-structure of a group

What are the principal 'parts' or assemblies within the composite group structure? Bearing in mind recent chapters, we can say, with some truth, that there are as many parts as individuals within it, because every individual is different from another, and requires, as we have stressed, individual treatment. But I am concerned at present with *structural* or relatively non-human considerations, and, continuing with our previous analogy, am more anxious to prepare a sales specification of our automobile than a spares parts list.

Let us consider the following structural factors, and discuss each in turn:

(1) Size.
(2) Shape.

(3) Internal structure.
(4) Communications.
(5) Fusion (cohesion).
(6) Group direction.
(7) Leadership within the Group (Decision Making).

(1) SIZE

Josephine Klein had some interesting things to say on this and
other aspects of groups, and I find her book, *The Study of Groups*,
most readable and likely to be reasonably understood by practising and practical managers. She refers, when discussing group
size, to an analogous situation in economics—the marginal
contribution. 'One does not arrive at the total strength of the
group by adding the individual "strengths" of members. Each
man's contribution is a marginal one. Thus, the effect of co-
operation in the performance of a task is interactive, that is to
say, the group product is the result not only of the strength of
each member but also a result of the effect that each member's
effort has on the efforts of other members.'

This conclusion followed a discussion which started by asking
a question many managers have frequently asked—'Why form
a group, and, if so, what size shall it be?' Klein says: 'Our problems in the present chapter are such as these: when is it worth while
to form a group in order to solve a problem? When does a group
perform a task more efficiently than an individual? When is a
larger group more efficient than a smaller one? Let us therefore
consider what we imply when we use the word "efficient".

'Generally efficiency is measured in terms of speed of solution,
or accuracy of solution, or both. But when we refer to the speed
with which a solution is reached by individual or group, we may
find ourselves thinking of time in two senses. If one person
performs a task in five hours and three persons perform the task
in three hours' co-operation, how justified are we in saying that
the second method "took less time"? For in terms of man-hours,

the first solution took five, and the second three times three, or nine, hours. Husband (1940) has shown that while for certain tasks like decoding and jigsaw puzzles individual workers take more time than do pairs of workers co-operating, the pairs never worked for less than two-thirds of the period required by solitary subjects. Only if they had taken half the time would the total expenditure of time have been equivalent in the two cases. Was co-operation an "efficient" way of performing this task?'

What relationship, if any, exists between the size and efficiency of a group? Moede[1] studied the increased strength of a group as more members added their weight to a rope-pulling exercise. It was found that 'with each addition in group membership, the effect of each man's effort was lessened'. Managers are generally more concerned with wire-pulling than rope-pulling, but I do not find it difficult to visualize similar management group situations to the one described here. It and other researches show that as group size increases, only marginal increases in efficiency occur.

It is interesting to equate these findings with the statement that 'the whole is greater than the sum of the parts'. Applied to a group or company this statement means that *something* can be added to the sum of individual people; presumably this 'something' is the company spirit, or the group or organization value. Paterson[2] refers to it as moral authority, with its ability to *enhance* 'the structural right to command'. It is the 'additive', the upper-cylinder lubricant, which provides that little bit more (often a great deal more) than the standard fuels and oils. But the rope-pulling and other such experiments show us that the whole under certain conditions may become *less* than the sum of the parts, and if we wish to increase group size we obviously must ensure that the group value or, if you wish, the value of 'the organization' becomes positive if the whole really is to become more than the sum of the parts. Put in another way, the manager's

---

[1] *Die Richtlinien der Leistungspsychologie.* W. Moede.
[2] *A Methectic Theory of Social Organization.* Dr. T. Paterson.

job is to see that the marginal losses usually involved in adding more individuals to the group are made good by better organization of group effort.

Another experiment[1] provided a rather different, but connected, result. It was shown that more interaction between members may have an *adverse* effect upon the total output of a number of persons and it seemed to follow that the greater the number of people involved, the more the interaction, and the less the output per person.

It is easy to draw false conclusions from these and similar experiments, but one feels that in their varied ways they help to stress the organizational advantages of smaller rather than larger management groups for performing certain tasks. It is certainly worth bearing in mind that additions to any group may have a marginal value, involving the law of diminishing returns.

The larger the group, however, the greater the possibility of various and separate 'experts' within the group, and 'the higher the probability of a speedy solution'. How do we reconcile the apparently diminishing value of the larger group with the greater possibility and advantage of finding an expert and therefore a solution within it? How would we balance these possibilities when appointing a Board of Directors, or forming a managerial group? How difficult it is to be dogmatic about the application of specific research findings to other conditions; Klein, in *The Study of Groups*, stresses this when she suggests that in almost every group situation one must start with certain assumptions. Solutions are likely to be valid only if the assumed conditions are present.

Klein's assumption 3, 'Let the correct solution be unverifiable', is frequently applicable to Board meetings, where all too often the discussions are based on many opinions and few facts. 'Here', as Miss Klein says, 'there was no truth which became self-evident once it had been demonstrated.' Each member of the group had

[1] *Do groups think more efficiently than individuals?* G. B. Watson.

to be convinced by argument. The more members there are the longer this is likely to take.

To improve this situation Maier[1] advocates 'that the expert should have skill to minimize the tendency to persevere on an unfruitful or narrow approach'. The expert, or leader, facilitates good discussion along the following lines:

'Do not present the group with the problem but instead determine from the group whether they have a problem. Recognize all suggestions but influence direction in thinking by asking for further suggesions. Protect individuals from criticism of other group members by interpreting all remarks in a favourable light.

'Make a list of all suggestions so that all types of considerations are included. When the list is fairly complete, probing questions may be asked, i.e. "how would that work out?", etc. Do not hasten the solution by capitalizing on the first good lead or in any way reflect your preferences.

'Always work toward the ideal of removing undesirable features from the job. Make your objective one of resolving differences in the group.'

On the assumption that most top management meetings contain experts, but that, equally, most solutions are not immediately self-evident or verifiable, we seem to arrive at the conclusion that (a) a group should contain fewer rather than more members, and (b) that all experts, particularly the leader, should receive more training in personal relations and communications. This second point will arise again.

When I study the many scientifically conducted psychometrical experiments I realize, humbly, how many variables exist in every human group situation. How difficult it is to draw viable conclusions unless every important assumption is clearly stated, and clear limitations set beyond which the conclusions are not likely to be valid. Unfortunately most managers have neither time,

[1] *The quality of Group discussion as influenced by a discussion leader.* N. R. F. Maier.

money nor inclination to conduct experiments of this magnitude, and they must constantly be seeking short cuts, or at least broader generalizations on which to base managerial decisions. The present problem, that is, the relationship between individual and group, is one of the more important in which social scientists should endeavour to provide better and broader managerial 'guide-lines'.

Let us look at the problem of size in quite a different way by considering the analogy between organizational and biological structures. Two recent writers have contributed their views on this and I will refer briefly to their salient points. Haire, in *Growth of Organizations*, believes that the biological model seems analogous in many ways to our present subject.

This model, he says, provided us with 'the problem of integrating the parts into a single functioning unit, of maintaining communication among them, and of developing and co-ordinating specialized functions'. Thompson[1] told the story of Jack the Giant Killer who had nothing to fear from the Giant if the latter was built as he was pictured. His (the giant's) mass would be 10^3 or a thousand times a man's, because he was ten times as big in every dimension. Unfortunately for the giant the cross-section of his leg bones would have increased only in two dimensions and they would be only 10^2, or a hundred times as big as a man's. The bones would not support the giant's weight, and he would break his legs. He was, as Haire says, 'trapped by a simple principle called the square-cube law which points out that in normal spatial geometry, as volume increases by a cubic fraction, the surface enclosing it increases only by a square'.

It seems clear, therefore, that 'A man cannot grow as big as a giant, and still have the shape of a man. A deer cannot grow as big as an elephant and still look like a deer. The size cannot vary completely independently of the shape.'

During the writing of this chapter the proposed take-over of

[1] *On growth and form.* Sir D'Arcy Thompson.

Courtaulds by I.C.I. was being discussed, and *The Economist*, 23 December, 1961, had this to say—'The question is not merely one of principle; it is also one of capability. Has the top management of I.C.I., plus whatever it recruits from the younger group within Courtaulds, the capacity to handle anything so big? Foreign comparisons here are less telling than they might seem. Together, I.C.I. and Courtaulds would have assets and turnover comparable to those of Du Pont; but they would have twice as many employees. Their labour force comes to about 175,000; Du Pont has 88,000, and the largest European chemical-fibres group, Montecantini, has 67,000. And the ultimate strain upon management is number of people, not tonnage or money. The performance of the British chemical industry since the war has been impressive compared with some other British industries, when compared with other chemical industries in the world, not quite so impressive as all that. I.C.I. may feel, as it seemed to feel earlier this year, that it has supermen to spare. Courtaulds is clearly short of talent even for running it at its present size. Does adding the two together ensure competence to manage something one and a half times the size of I.C.I.?'

This question is partially answered by Haire in *The Growth of Organizations*, when he says 'it is customary to see the specialized function of the chief executive as the limiting factor leading to diminishing returns with increase in size. . . . It seems likely, however, and empirical evidence seems to suggest, that the limitations also come from other implications of the size-shape-function relationship. As the organization grows, its internal shape must change. Additional functions of co-ordination, control, and communication must be provided and supported by the same kind of force that previously supported an organization without these things. If the relationship were linear, there would be no problem. If each increment in size produced one increment (or one plus) in productive capacity and needed one increment of additional supportive function, there would be no limit. However, in the organism, the proportion of skeleton needed to support the mass grows faster than the mass itself and puts a limit on size as a function of the environmental forces playing on it. Similarly, it is suggested that, as the size of a firm increases, the skeletal structure (needed to support it against the forces tending to destroy it) grows faster than the size itself, and hence comes to consume a disproportionate amount of the productive capacity of the organization. If this is so, it becomes important to identify the skeletal support of the firm, the forces it resists, and the rates at which the support must grow.'

A speaker[1] at a Management Conference in Australia said: 'As one whose interests were zoological before they became managerial, may I interpose at this point the obvious fact that the cult of size has never been, biologically or historically, a pursuit that has led to sustained success? The initial triumphs of apparent success lead inevitably to failures in co-ordination and ultimate collapse. The same has been true of empires as of animals. The realms of Alexander the Great, Caesar Augustus, Charlemagne, Philip II of Spain, Napoleon I, and even perhaps Adolf Hitler, collapsed either because the giant had feet of clay, or because there was no successor to take his place when he had gone.

'The great and luxuriant Age of the Reptiles, of vast dinosaur and clumsy pterodactyl, creatures which for millions of years were apparently successful, collapsed before the onslaught of the tiny mammal and the feathered bird. . . . Both mammal and bird were organisms whose body temperatures were thermostatically controlled, and therefore who could flourish in any climate. Both had the improved internal communications that go with small size, the mammals had brains far larger in relation to their total bulk than any saurian. Both developed methods of nursing their young which provided for a qualified succession. The parallels with human organization can be extended almost

<hr>

[1] *Organization Decision-making.* Lord Verulam. International Congress of Scientific Management, 1961.

indefinitely. Those who doubt the validity of the simile can go hence to study the fascinating marsupial fauna of this Australian continent; they have survived only because Australia was cut off from Eurasia before the evolution of the true mammals; the Australian marsupials are at this moment perishing, unhappily, because the rat and the dog, the sheep, the cow and man himself, are more efficient than they are.

'In the industrial world of today, where the cult of organization is more important than many of the finer points of engineering or process techniques (which are in substantial degree available to all who want them), it is not difficult to claim that the larger concerns are those that can claim to be the most successful. This may be true for the moment, because of the paramount ability of one or two men at the top of whatever pyramidal hierarchy may exist in the undertaking in question; it is not true permanently. It is very seldom that the man who builds a large and successful organization succeeds in appointment, and giving full authority and experience to, an equally competent successor, before he himself succumbs to (or is made partially ineffective by) old age or fatigue or arteriosclerosis. Even if the difficulty of succession can be surmounted, in any one case, it is most unlikely (and probably undesirable) that any human society will evolve which can produce a sufficiency of capable men competent to manage a very large number of very large concerns.'

Other organizational situations of interest to us are discussed in this thoughtful paper, written by a man whose early death so many of us mourned. They will emerge later. Perhaps I have said enough at this stage about the factor of size as such. It will arise again in our consideration of the other factors listed on pages 130–1.

A Restatement

(1) The 'total strength' of a group must be defined. It may involve numbers of persons, ability to solve problems, or even the geographic area it covers.

(2) Size and strength are intimately related. 'One does not arrive at the total strength of the group by adding the individual "strengths" of members.'

(3) 'Total strength', or size of a group should always be greater than the sum of the 'parts'. Additions to size show only a marginal increase in strength, and may, at a certain point, involve a weakening rather than a strengthening of the group.

(4) Total strength involves a total contribution, and the group leader must ensure, through good personal relations and communication, that all members of the group contribute to total group effectiveness.

(5) There is a close analogy between organizational and biological structural size. Neither animals, man, nor groups can grow indiscriminately and maintain linear strength. As an organization grows, its shape must change, because a disproportionate amount of effort is taken up in maintaining its own strength, leaving proportionately less to achieve its purpose.

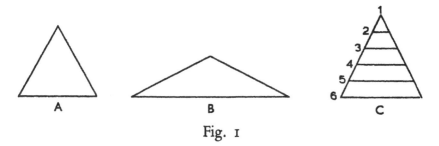

Fig. 1

(2) SHAPE

The conventional shape of an organization structure is pyramidic, as shown in Fig. 1A. It assumes a single authoritative individual at the summit and a varying and widening number of horizontal managerial layers below. But even the conventional pyramid has many variations of shape, ranging from, say, Fig. 1B to Fig. 1C.

The former may have only two 'layers' of responsibility, and the latter (say) six. Between these extremes are many alternatives, and it is not easy to be dogmatic on the best shape or the optimum number of 'layers'. It was once stated that the ideal organic shape was provided by the Catholic Church which comprised two layers, with the Pope at the apex and the parish priest at the next level. When one considers the duties of a parish priest one might concede that in him is vested in miniature every responsibility vested in the Pope himself. But this fascinating conclusion fails when we consider, for instance, the election of a new Pope, where another layer, in this case the Cardinals, must inevitably be present.

The problem of layers, and therefore shape, is intimately bound up with the form of group concerned. For instance, a conventional de-centralized manufacturing group can support a larger number of layers than a centralized professional group, all members of which must maintain a personal relationship with the man at the top. In the latter case, a wider span of control can be faced with more confidence.

No consideration of shape (or indeed of other factors) is complete without an investigation into the way it is likely to be influenced by new developments and particularly by new technological systems of control and communications. Let us consider the organizational aspects of automation, where the emphasis is on 'flow', which can be applied to materials, components, assemblies, control and communications. Consider, for instance, an automated line which starts, or at least appears to start, in the raw material stores, continues on through a variety of production or processing units into a finished part stores, producing on the way anything from bottled or canned beer to a capsulated spare assembly. Authorizing this physical movement of components, and accompanying it in one form or another, is the control information which is available to the controllers at all stages of progress through the plant. It is important to note in passing that much more of this control network will in future become automatic in its working, and will depend less and less on intermediate supervisory or administrative activities. I foresee great developments in this field, and although relatively few *comprehensive* examples are as yet available, much theoretical and practical experience is being gained in departmental applications.

Let us consider the organizational aspects of automation and automatic data processing, and in particular their effect on structural shape. The conventional pyramid Fig. 1A (page 139) includes, usually, a mixture of 'line' and 'staff' functions performed by various *production* and *service* departmental heads. The opportunities given by an automated line may enable us to eliminate a number of intermediate management functions, and to establish more controls and communications directly between top and bottom, or between the centre and circumference. It is not difficult, in a growing number of cases, to visualize a structural shape something like Fig. 2, where we preserve for the time being the apex of top-level managerial responsibility (level A). Reporting

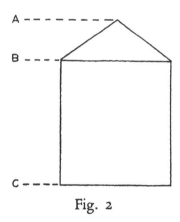

Fig. 2

to the top manager are various specialists (horizontal level B), whose authority goes down to level C, which is the actual 'production' level.

It must be admitted that this form of structure relates more to an advanced technological situation than to current normal practice. It is, however, important for younger managers to reflect upon the growing impact of technology on organization structure and two writers are worth quoting on this. Jasinsky's book *Adapting Organization to New Technology*, was, in my earlier book quoted as saying:

'Traditional business organizations run on a vertical line, relying almost solely on superior-subordinate relationships. Orders and instructions go down the line; reports and requests go up the line. But technology, including both integrated data-processing and integrated machine production, has developed on what might be called a horizontal plane; that is, the machine cuts across superior-subordinate relationships, affecting the jobs of people in different areas, departments, and work groups. Typical of the kinds of relationships required by modern technology is the progressive fabricating and assembly line. Here the need to make the right decision or take the necessary action at the right time at the right place is immediate. Managers, in order to solve an immediate problem, have to deal horizontally with their peers and diagonally with people at different levels who are neither superiors nor subordinates. To follow established, formal routes would be too time-consuming, too costly, and too disruptive.'

Joan Woodward refers to this relationship when she says[1] 'Organization also appeared to change as technology advanced', and emphasizes her point by stating that 'The span of control of the chief executive widened considerably with technical advance'. This statement supports the structural shape of Fig. 2, where these conditions apply.

Another modern trend which influences structural *shape* is the merger or take-over. Consider two companies with similar if unequally sized structures—Fig 3, A and B.

---

[1] 'Management and Technology'. D.S.I.R. Report No. 3, 1958.

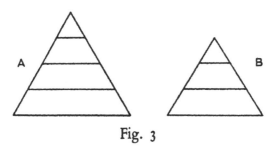

Fig. 3

A has five 'layers' of managers, and B has four. Company B is taken over by A, and the resultant *combined* structure may well be shaped like Fig. 4.

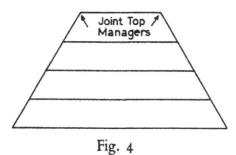

Fig. 4

At the top, 'joint' management may be the only compromise acceptable to the top men in the two companies. At the bottom of the pile there will be a 'wider' group of employees to control and therefore a greater number of junior managers, although the number of horizontal layers of management in the combined group may not increase from those formerly existing in Company A. The effect of the merger or take-over is therefore to create a structure which is flatter, and in which career opportunities may be more attractive to a specialist adviser than a potential top manager, who sees in the new structure a reduced opportunity for promotion.

I shall discuss other aspects of shape when Structural Division is being considered. In the meantime, it is worth commenting on a research paper which attempted to show whether there was a correlation between, among other things, shape and personal satisfactions. Meltzer and Salter attempted to evaluate[1] an earlier study by James Worthy.

Their conclusion was that 'the advantages inherent in large organizations can be enjoyed without . . . detrimental consequences if a "flat" or broad type of structure is employed. When few levels of administration *intervene* [my italics] between the top management and rank and file employees, the span of control of every supervisor is increased, making it necessary for each to delegate authority and responsibility to his subordinates. Thus employees work in an atmosphere of relative freedom from oppressive supervision, and have a sense of individual importance and personal responsibility which other types of structure often deny.'

It is significant that Worthy's theory was 'not proven' and the commentators remarked that much more research is needed in this field. In endeavouring to equate his conclusions with my own experiences, I have doubts on at least two of them. First, I do not think that 'intervention' between leaders and subordinates is the right word to use, and later I shall make a special reference to the need for active, rather than passive, leadership. Second, a wide span of control does not automatically lead to greater delegation, but possibly to reduced face-to-face understanding and more frustration.[2] I shall discuss the span of control in more detail later (pages 158 and 269).

A Structural Analogy

Let us look at shape in quite a different way, and consider whether the organization engineer has anything to learn from the structural engineer, to whom shape plays a vital part in strength, flexibility and aesthetics.

[1] *Organizational Structure and the Performance and Job Satisfaction of Physiologists.* Leo Meltzer and James Salter.
[2] See *Management Principles*, pages 78–81.

It may require considerable imagination to visualize a managing director receiving as much satisfaction from a contemplation of his group's organizational shape as from the aesthetic beauty of, say, Waterloo Bridge! But there will be a great step forward in organizational understanding and appreciation if the care given by a structural designer to shape is given also in the organizational field. Perhaps we can learn something from the manner in which shape is approached in other technical fields.

It is obvious to most engineers that shape and strength are intimately connected, and equally obvious that greater strength is required at those points where greater strains are likely to arise. Let us consider, for instance, a wider appreciation of the term 'span of control'. In a bridge span the 'control' of strain may well be taken care of by a shape such as Fig. 5a or Fig. 5b.

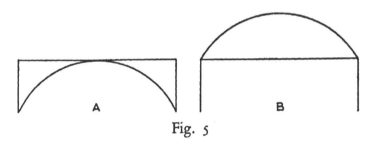

Fig. 5

Whether one or the other is chosen depends on a variety of conditions, but in both cases greater strength is provided where greater strains arise, even if the shapes appear, superficially, to vary greatly. Let us consider again the words of Haire, who was quoted earlier. He says in *Growth of Organizations*: 'In general, as physical objects get bigger but retain the same proportions, they get weaker, and a larger and larger proportion must go toward supporting their own mass. Consequently, with increase in size their forms are modified to resist the force associated with size. The appropriate modification is a clue to the force. The appropriate support for a physical structure is a perfect diagram of the forces tending to destroy it. Similarly, in the industrial

K

organization, special attention to the modification of form as size increases may give us at least a clue to the strength of the force tending to destroy it, and to its point of application.'

But even if we give this special attention to an organizational 'form', we find it is more difficult than in engineering to analyse and calculate the forces tending to destroy the structure. How then can we design the best shape in the absence of this information? Let us consider again the analysis on pages 125 to 129, which I said should be made to determine the growth pattern of the company. This, if done thoroughly, will enable us to plot the relationships between past growths and the strains they produced. This will help us to anticipate new growths, and new strains, and provide at least some guesstimated data for reshaping or strengthening the existing structure.

Haire shows us the growth slopes of four firms of varying sizes, and attempts to establish equations which if more widely applicable will increase the fund of data required in organizational structural engineering. I will not reproduce them here, because I assume that those interested will study his work in more detail. Sufficient to say that the implications are considerable, not only in their effect on *overall* shape, but on internal arrangements and responsibilities, such as the changing relationships between line and staff. I shall discuss these again in a later section.

I will end this section on shape with a comment on *balance*. This is a word which is widely applied, and the musician may seek to provide a balanced composition just as the engineer seeks a balance structure. It is important to the organizational engineer, who also wishes to obtain balance in *his* structure.

If, as I said earlier, we design a structure so that its strengths match the strains likely to be put upon it, we do of course achieve balance. But there is an overall concept of balance which top managers must always have in mind, and balance, therefore, becomes not only a structural design problem but a company 'purpose', which puts it on a higher plane of importance.

How often have we all heard someone say of a situation, department or group that it is 'out of balance'. This condition can be achieved in many ways, such as by the unwise purchase of other companies whose product range is out of step, or by the internal growth of too much fat in certain places, just like some of the unbalanced bodily shapes one sees around.

One aspect of balance arises when one considers Newton's 1st Law of Motion. 'Every body continues in its state of . . . uniform motion in a straight line, except in so far as it may be compelled by force to change that state.'

In business terms this means that a company is likely to go on doing what it has done before unless force is applied to change direction. This analogy has, of course, a connection with 'positive feed-back', which, once a body has gone out of balance, creates an even greater out-of-balance.

Many old-established companies go on doing what they have done for years and have probably gone out of balance in the process. This is not usually a deliberate action, but comes about largely because most people cling to things known. Given clear reasons for change, and a climate which encourages it, most of us are willing to change direction and restore balance to the company. But a strong managerial effort is always needed —we must be 'compelled by force to change'.

In Chapter 8 I shall refer to the Principle of Balance, and I suggest that this principle and its implications should be borne in mind by the organizer when he is considering the problems of structural size and shape. It will certainly help him when he moves on to consider the next section, Internal Structure.

A Restatement

(1) A wide variety of structural shapes is possible, depending greatly on the purpose and activities of the group. The number of 'layers' of authority in a 'professional' body, where each person is vested with a greater 'self-contained'

authority, can be much less than a group which contains a large number of semi-skilled workers.

(2) New technological developments, particularly in automation, are likely to influence shape greatly. Central control and communication systems will rely less upon conventional chains of command, with their vertical/horizontal bands, and more upon diagonal co-operation between various levels. The span of control is likely to increase.

(3) Mergers will also influence shape and may, in passing, create more personal problems as the ratio of subordinate to senior posts increases.

(4) Organic structural shape, like size, has an analogous relationship to other fields. In particular, these engineering aspects of shape are of special interest to the organizer:

(a) With an increase in 'size', shape must be modified to support the increased mass.

(b) Modifications must be applied at the points of increased strain. 'The appropriate support is a perfect diagram of the forces tending to destroy the structure.'

(c) It is difficult to calculate the forces tending to destroy an organization structure. Attempts have been made to prepare growth slopes which may, if developed more fully, allow us to establish equations and calculate shape more accurately in the light of changing requirements and environment.

(5) Overall balance must be maintained. This will be achieved by a periodic consideration of company purpose and structural shape.

(3) INTERNAL STRUCTURE

This factor is, I warn readers, likely to be rather complicated in its ramifications and somewhat inconclusive in its conclusions. In discussing it we must examine the internal divisional arrangements within the total structural shape; we must attempt to show why divisions are necessary, how they should be arranged for optimal effect, how they link to or communicate with each other, and how a reasonable balance should be achieved between fusion and diffusion, or between centrifugal and centripetal forces. In discussing these matters I must again refer readers back to the factors and considerations already discussed, and, as before, say that those structural factors yet to be considered, namely 4, 5, 6 and 7, play *their* part in designing the internal, and therefore the total, structure.

Why divide the total structure?

Even in a 'one-man' company there must be an agreed subdivision of duties, with the individual entrepreneur having a choice of several hats; as soon as he engages an assistant, a *sharing* must (or should) be agreed. The more employees a company engages, the more complex will become the division of duties and structure, and the more difficult, and therefore the more important, it is to organize the many so that they achieve a 'common purpose'.

It is as important to approach 'division' scientifically as to consider in this manner the structure as a whole. Let us turn back to the growth curves mentioned on pages 126 to 129, where I said that, *at the initial stage*, the organizer should not be concerned with too much subdivision. Now, however, he must give it more attention, and he will wish to investigate the growth curves in detail. He will wish also to give deep consideration to the alternative and widely varying ways in which he can divide the total structure into viable pieces. He is presented, on a grand scale, with the problem confronting many people when a carving knife is thrust into their hand and they are asked to dissect the Christmas turkey. 'Where does one start, and where is one likely to finish?'

In an earlier book *Management Principles* I briefly discussed the problem of division when I referred to centralization and de-centralization. I suggested that at least three principal groupings existed:

(1) Product specialization.
(2) Functional specialization.
(3) Geographic specialization.

Each of these could be achieved by a variety of organizational forms:

(a) Divisions or departments.
(b) Wholly owned subsidiaries.
(c) Partly owned subsidiaries.
(d) Consortiums.

The organizer, now facing fundamental decisions on the divisions of the internal structure, must carefully consider each of these possibilities and, to add further complication, must realize that in most cases two other complications exist. The first is personal, that is, the existence of senior executives around whom he may be required to erect structures. We hope that the organizer is not unduly restricted or inhibited in this manner, but just as long as senior people exist so will this problem confront him.

The second complication is TIME, which is present in every managerial consideration. Later in this book (pages 197 and 284) I shall refer to the time factor in reorganization, and it will suffice to say here that most long-term reorganizations desirably require interim groupings of a different nature from the final form. The time scale of change is important.

Our organizer, therefore, finds himself confronted by the need to consider at least five different groupings or factors:

(1) Product specialization.
(2) Functional specialization.
(3) Geographic specialization.
(4) Personal factors.
(5) Time factors.

Later, on page 157, I shall introduce another factor.

With these in mind let us consider the long-term purpose of the Board, and the evidence that has been collected and embodied in the growth curves (page 126). We will, in the light of the stated purpose, now consider in more detail two growth curves which play key parts in divisional specialization. First, the subdivision of the product range, and, second, a classification of the total numbers of people likely to be employed. Let us discuss each in more detail.

The subdivision of the product range

A feature of modern science and technology is that it forces managers to give increasingly early consideration to the development of products. An aeroplane is not, today, the only product which is 'ordered off the drawing board', and is considered obsolescent almost as soon as it is produced. Companies who are in the market for computers, automation equipment and nuclear plant, for instance, find great difficulty in deciding at what stage of development they should freeze their doubts and unfreeze their order forms. The makers of these products are in even greater difficulty than the customers, as they must *anticipate* customers' requirements by a margin large enough to retain competitive strength. Neither they nor their customers are too sure of the technological future, although both know that development costs and failure ratios are likely to be extremely high.

Yet, more than ever before, a company should endeavour to retain control of its product design policy, and not lose the initiative to competitors who can forecast or design better. It may not be possible to forecast a precise range of future products by a projection of product development curves, but experience convinces me that at least a pattern of development can be produced which enables a company to be more prepared for swift action. For instance, it will be found that earlier attention to technological trends will enable a company to appoint a new specialist, or organize a new group, to anticipate new developments. Any such action which can reduce 'lead time' is most valuable. It leaves a company better 'poised' for swift action. (See page 128 for another discussion on forecasting.)

The breakdown of total numbers of people

Two considerations are important here. First, the effect that future total numbers have on 'size' considerations, such as floor space, division of plant or office areas, decentralization and product specialization. Second, the effect that numbers of people have on managerial, supervisory and specialist requirements.

In dealing with total numbers managers should always remember the square-cube law discussed on page 135, not necessarily because of any restriction this law might place on the growth of people in a group, but because of its reminder to managers and organizers that as total numbers increase, both the overall structural shape *and* the internal divisions must be modified and strengthened, not necessarily in linear fashion.

The relationship between the number of internal divisions and total strength

A building structure may present, externally, a satisfying, clean exterior. This is likely to have been achieved not only by aesthetic considerations but by many calculations, involving many alternative structural patterns. Consider, for instance, the simple external 'shape' Fig. 6. The 'roof' section can be designed in a variety of ways, such as in the illustration. The internal area can be divided into a number of horizontal and vertical divisions, making up an internal matrix.

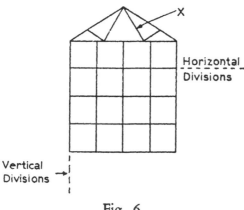

Fig. 6

Much the same can happen to an organization structure, although the matrix may vary much more and the treatment is usually very empirical. To some extent this will always, relatively, be so because of the wide *variety* of organizational variables existing, ranging from changing group purposes to variable product ranges. But *some* theoretical considerations are possible, and some attempts have been made to encourage a scientific approach to the problem of providing an internal divisional matrix which, in a given set of conditions, provides a structure within which the individuals may specialize, co-operate, communicate, work effectively, and be led towards achieving a common purpose with desirably a 'clean' exterior to the structure. Let us consider first the 'top' of the structure. I showed in earlier diagrams that the 'slopes' could vary between, say, Fig. 1b and 1c (page 139), and that there are strong trends towards the shape, Fig. 4 (page 143). The wider the base of a structure, the more intermediate members are required to support the superstructure. Stating this in near-managerial terms, the wider the span of control the more effort must be made to prevent the 'span', *and the apex*, from sagging. A simple structural example of intermediate supports is shown in Fig. 6, where the span is supported by a variety of members.

A building structure contains, mostly, vertical and horizontal 'divisions' in a variety of types. They may be walls, external and internal, floors, columns, struts. Often the 'roof' section is supported by diagonals like those at X in Fig. 6. Together, they make up an interlocking, intersupporting, whole.

Surely this is what we seek in an organization structure? Here the 'divisions' are, in most cases, created at the borders, or boundary lines, of departmental responsibilities, such as at the division line C in Fig. 7, which is the boundary line between executives controlling departments A and B.

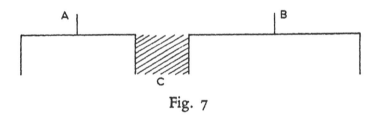

Fig. 7

Let us consider this organizational boundary division between individual spans of control. Ideally, we might assume that when two departmental responsibilities *coincide* at their mutural boundary lines, the two separate lines at C. Fig. 8 merge into one, as with a butt welding operation. In order to link effectively with each other, however, the two executives A and B must plan for a certain amount of *overlap* in structural form, and in management responsibilities. Whether this is described as 'overlap' or 'butting into other people's territory' is a matter of choice, but it is an important organizational requirement and its managerial implications must be fully understood.

Division lines between two or more bodies (material *or* human) are potential weaknesses unless special efforts are made to overcome this tendency. If we consider a mechanical structure, whether it is a building or a motor car, we usually find that excessive friction, or a failure of the bolts, screws, rivets, etc., which should hold them together, creates weaknesses and possible disintegration of the total structure.

To some extent, also, a division line may be considered as a crack in a structure, where, if abnormal strains occur, we would expect the cracks to worsen and disintegration to be hastened.

These possibilities surely infer that structural forms should be designed with as few division lines as possible. In material structures this is easier to achieve than in human organizational structures. Every designer is constantly faced by the problem of achieving the best design for a given purpose, and if this can be done with the *fewest possible* number of component parts so much the better. I recollect, for instance, a recent case where, in a counting unit, about fifteen separate components in various metals were replaced by one nylon component, which was cheaper, had a very 'clean' exterior, and was functionally quite as satisfactory as its predecessor. Its 'internal divisions' had been completely eliminated.

In designing an organization structure, a manager does not have this wide scope, because he faces one inescapable fact, *that every individual person in the group will always remain a separate component*, and however the individuals are *grouped* for convenience of purposeful organization, they still exist as individuals. There will always exist in every group approximately as many 'divisions' as individuals within it.

There is another important factor which must increasingly be born in mind when division of any structure is being considered. I said earlier that a divisional line between two or more separate components is potentially a weakness. But it may become a strength if two possibilities are borne in mind. First, that each 'component part' is specially designed for its own special purpose, and, second, that the 'parts' are linked together effectively. Let us consider a mechanical analogy. In a typical electro-mechanical assembly, each component part is likely to be specially designed for its particular purpose. The electrical components are made from materials which have certain *electrical* characteristics. Other components may require greater strength or appearance characteristics. Each component performs a *specialist* role, and is designed accordingly. Together, all the components are assembled with skill and represent 'a complete design'.

Just as, for instance, a wider range of materials is now available for specialist use by mechanical designers, so there is a wider range of specialist skills available to the manager or organizer. In place of the 'general practitioner' is the group of specialists, with each individual an expert at his own special job and linked with the other specialists by a skilled organizational and managerial effort. Under the right conditions this specialist use of specialist skills will achieve much more than the alternative use of 'generalists'.

For many years managers have made use of specialists, and the 'staff' concept of organization recognizes that specialists can be of value in assisting 'line' executives. Many companies have worked out a satisfactory relationship between staff and line functions and individuals, which enables the special skills of the former to improve the output of the latter. But in recent years a great increase in specialist activities has taken place, and unfortunately more skill has been used in separating out and developing these specialisms than in improving their integration with each other, and their contribution to the purpose of the overall group.

In organizational affairs it is a constant and constantly varying problem to resolve in optimum terms the relationship between 'special' and 'general' skills. Elsewhere in this book[1] I discuss, for instance, the subdivision of labour, which is another aspect of this

[1] Page 170.

problem, shown at its most advanced or least progressive state (depending on the point of view) on an automobile assembly line. Under the subheading 'Communications' I shall refer to the greater misunderstandings likely to arise when more 'divisions' are created. Under these circumstances 'division lines' become not only cracks but chasms over which essential communications find it more difficult to jump.

On page 151 I said that five factors confront the organizer when he begins to consider internal division of the structure. I am now saying that he is confronted by yet another factor which, in some ways, is interwoven into at least the first four of them. If, for instance, we consider (2), Functional specialization, how many 'special' functions should the company provide in order to achieve its purpose? An engineering company might provide itself with four principal functions—Research and Development, Production, Sales and Finance/Administration. But at the next 'layer' down a case might be made for many subfunctions, each of which would give special attention to an important phase of company activity, present or future.

Are there any guide-lines available to the organizer when he is faced, as he often is, by this dilemma of 'division'? In a period of great technological change it is important that special and specialist attention should be given to new possibilities. In organizational terms this can be done *ad hoc*, or permanently; that is, either by creating a temporary commando force which looks into a new possibility, reports back, and dissolves, or by creating a new specialist group. Generally, permanent changes in structure should not be made too lightly, and every group should be designed and encouraged to adapt itself to new possibilities without changing its 'permanent' structure too often.

The following points should be considered by the organizer when confronted by the necessity to decide how and how many more specialist functions, and how many 'division lines', are required to satisfy the factors on page 151.

(1) Every specialist, individual, group or function should exist only if it can thoroughly justify his or its separate existence.

(2) Every principal division or group should pay continuous attention to new developments, and should provide *ad hoc* specialist attention to their investigation and development.

(3) If any specialist development is likely to show continuous and significant growth, consideration should be given to a permanent recognition of this in the form of reorganization.

(4) Every 'division line' creates a potential weakness, which tends to reduce the 'specialist' *advantages*. Special attention must therefore be given to the linking arrangements (cohesion, communication, etc.) so that the advantages are maintained.

The final result will depend greatly on how we design the divisional links. If the divisional patterns are designed to use specialist skills fully; if the divisional links overlap rather than underlap; if the *inter*-communication aspects are borne in mind, then we shall develop greater strength by the greater use of specialists, and the greater subdivision of the structure. The cynic may well say that there are many 'ifs' in this programme, and I must agree that the present trend towards greater specialization is a weakening rather than a strengthening force. Perhaps a fuller realization of this will encourage us to examine organizational divisions more carefully.

The Span of Control

The span of control is one of the most popular 'principles' of organization. At least it is popular in the sense that, like the classics, everybody talks about it and few study it. The span of control plays an important part in 'divisions', so let us discuss what the term means, what are its implications and its validity.

Many writers have written extensively on this subject, which has been elevated to 'principle' status, and I can do no better than quote Urwick's words[1] in supporting its usefulness: 'We all know that the number of individuals who should report directly to a Chief is limited. There has been much disputation about the principle and organization known as "the Span of Control" but all experience, and indeed, ordinary commonsense, support its validity.'

It was Graicunas who formulated the number of relationships with and between subordinates. The formula used is:

$$\gamma = N \left(\frac{2N}{2} + N - 1 \right)$$

where γ = number of relationships
N = number of subordinates.

If a manager at the apex has four subordinates who are directly linked to him, he would have forty-four possible relationships with them (direct and across). If the four are increased to six the relationships would increase to 222. The impact of this considerable increase in relationships is supposed to convince a top manager that a modest increase in direct reportability creates a relatively much greater load on his control and co-ordinating ability. I am interested in mathematics and much in favour of greater mathematical precision in organizational affairs. It is one of the tools of a scientific approach. But this particular formula encourages too elaborate a view of managerial relationships, and it is of greater value in considering the problem of communications, which we shall discuss shortly. It has limitations when we consider only the question of personal reportability.

The most important value the principle of the span of control has is its reminder to managers that direct reportability is a basic consideration when 'dividing up' the structure. Some readers

[1] *Leadership in the Twentieth Century.* L. F. Urwick.

will already have read in *Management Principles* why I believe this is so, and although I appreciate Urwick's reference to 'total relationships', I agree entirely with him 'that leaders, *however busy*, should *make time* for close, easy and intimate relations with those directly responsible to themselves'. This involves, in my terms, face-to-face relationships.

There is, however, a strongly held view which says that there is better opportunity for personal development of subordinates if the span of control is 'wider', and gives *less* rather than more opportunity for face-to-face discussions with the chief. Under these circumstances it is thought that the subordinates are forced to make their own decisions, and to develop proportionately faster. Like all points of view this has something in it, but I have often seen it carried to excess with results which are not at all as suggested above. The subordinates become frustrated, isolated and often lacking in common purpose. Today's relationships must rely much more on interdependence than independence.

What are the *facts* of control spans? I have already quoted Miss Woodward, who reported widely varying spans of control among those companies investigated. A more recent American report[1] covering a survey of over 1000 companies showed the following spans of control among various groups of companies.

Number of employees	Number of Individuals reporting direct to the Chief Executive	Median Concentration
Under 100	2– 7	4
100– 199	2–12	5
200– 299	2–23	5
300– 499	3–11	5
500– 999	3–17	5
1000–2000	3–11	5
Over 2000	3–45	6

[1] Research Institute of America. Management Report, 30 August, 1962.

One, no doubt exasperated, chief executive, on being asked how many reported to him, replied, 'Dozens,' but the results above show that on the whole there is a remarkable median conformation to the 'ideal' suggested by organizational theorists.

Prys Williams[1] discusses the span of control and suggests that the major reason why direct reportability should be kept to a low number is the possibility of two or more subordinates wishing to drink 'at the fount at any one time'. In other words, it becomes unduly difficult for any one subordinate easily to see his chief. He goes on to say that 'the frequency of reference can often be reduced by the prescription of action appropriate to the more normal and routine situations'. This means that the chief would say to his subordinates: 'Come to me whenever you want or need to do anything not clearly prescribed in the regulations.'

We can visualize some companies better able than others to create *and maintain* comprehensive regulations within which subordinates can make decisions without worrying their chief too much. But, in my experience, managing by regulation has severe limitations in the more vital areas of management, and however much we may strive to 'programme' decisions we must allow more rather than less time for the unprogrammable decisions, which in a dynamic group must involve easy and frequent face-to-face discussion.

A recent case came to my attention which is worth quoting. The managing editor of a publishing company faced three alternatives when deciding to reorganize the relatively small group of twelve 'professionals' involved. The first alternative is illustrated in Fig. 8.

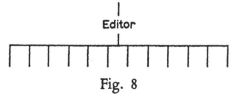

Fig. 8

[1] *The Limits of Business Administration and Responsibility*. G. Prys Williams.

L

Here he accepts the wide span of control, and a direct reportability to himself by each of the twelve subordinates.

Fig. 8A illustrates a refinement which reduces his span and creates three sub-editors, who report direct to him.

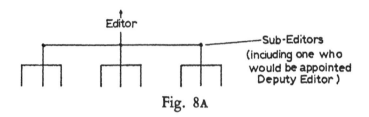

Fig. 8A

He finally adopted Fig. 8B, which, under an executive editor, grouped the subordinates into three 'loose' groups, each having a reasonably cohesive functional objective.

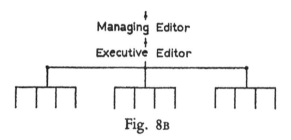

Fig. 8B

He felt that this alternative would reduce the number of individuals reporting direct to himself, and yet encourage a greater amount of delegated discussion and decision *within* the three groups, which would be encouraged by the cohesive properties of each group.

However much this appears to 'pass the buck' to the executive editor, this is a legitimate *first* organizational step. It is, however, inevitable that leadership problems will arise in each of the three groups and may involve, later, a change towards the shape of Fig. 8A. If the editor wished, in Fig. 8B, to maintain reasonable contact with *each* and all of the subordinates, and even if he ultimately adopted Fig. 8A, he could build in the double-link control which I shall discuss later on page 190.

I refer later (page 169) to the experience of Sears Roebuck in experiments with the span of control, and readers may well conclude that their experience, which favours *wider* spans of control, may be a special case and not one to be applied generally without deep thought.

Line and Staff Divisions

Another largely vertical divisional consideration involves line and staff relationships. More words have been written on this subject than on almost any other organizational matter, and I hesitate to add to them. Many of the so-called differences between 'line' and 'staff' are artificial, and have done much to perpetuate one of the worst features of administrative and financial practice, i.e. the division of men and money into 'direct' activities and costs, and into 'indirect' or 'overhead' categories and so-called 'on-costs'.

Every person in a group has *direct* responsibility and authority for something; everyone is *directly* concerned with the prosperity of the group or company. It is undesirable to complicate structural divisions any more than is absolutely necessary, and more complications exist today than are 'scientifically' necessary. Let us consider a few simple cases. In an engineering works a production operator is classed as 'direct' and has a 'line' relationship upwards. An inspector is usually 'indirect' and has a 'staff' relationship. But many companies are endeavouring to eliminate the separate inspection operation, either by making the *production* people responsible for the quality of their own work, or by production techniques which automatically check quality. In effect, this allows a production man or machine to decide whether a component is in a fit state to go forward. Much the same service is provided by a computer which provides checks within its own programme.

This example illustrates many changing relationships, where the line takes over duties formerly performed by the 'staff'. An opposite example is provided where, in a growing number of automated groups, the *direct*, or line, activities are being taken over by 'staff'. Consider, for instance, an arrangement where the maintenance workers in an automated line now combine the dual function of maintenance *and* production supervision, and therefore perform both staff and line, or 'indirect' and 'direct', duties.

How would you classify these men? It seems organizationally desirable to simplify classifications, although to eliminate the terms 'line' and 'staff' may be asking too much, particularly from accountants, who are still largely steeped in tradition. I am probably, also, asking too much from other 'staff' workers, who often feel a 'head-office superiority' in being so classified. But the loss of this doubtful advantage may be outweighed by the creation of a deeper feeling among 'indirects' or 'overhead' types that they really are of *direct* value to the group.

Horizontal divisions

We have, up to this point, been discussing, largely, vertical divisions, such as that shown in Fig. 9 where a chief executive A has four managers, B_1, C_1, D_1 and E_1, reporting to him. We will assume that B_1 and C_1 are so-called 'line' executives, responsible for two divisional production groups, while D_1 and E_1 are so-called 'staff' specialists, advising on their specialisms. We have many inter-relationships between executives B_1, C_1, D_1 and E_1, which should be maintained *across* the vertical division lines which 'separate' the fields of activity for which these executives are responsible. But if these cross or horizontal relationships are desirable at this level, they are also desirable lower down between the junior executives controlled by executives B_1, C_1, D_1, and E_1; that is between B_2, C_2, D_2 and E_2, etc.

We might liken these lower cross connections to rungs in a ladder which has four 'upright' members, B, C, D, E; it is desirable

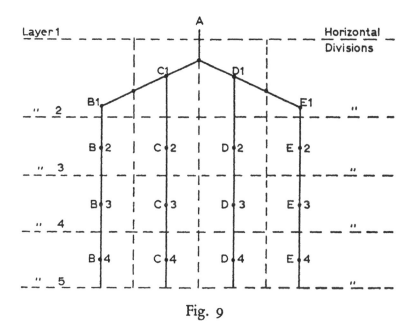

Fig. 9

that those working on the lower rungs should be able to move freely sideways, and if necessary diagonally, in the execution of their agreed jobs. This pattern of movement and communication is difficult to describe in a diagram such as Fig. 8, which is two-dimensional, and we really require in organizational studies a new form of presentation to show adequately the many relationship patterns which exist, even in a simple structure such as Fig. 10.

Let us consider the plan diagram Fig. 10 which shows just a few of the forty-four possible person-to-person relationships which exist between executive A and his four subordinates, B1, C1, D1, E1. This plan illustrates only two 'layers' of relationships: layer 1 at the level of chief executive A, and layer 2 at the next level below, which is occupied by the four executives B1, C1, D1, E1, who report to A. Each layer of supervision below these becomes progressively more difficult to illustrate diagrammatically, not only in the relationships at the same

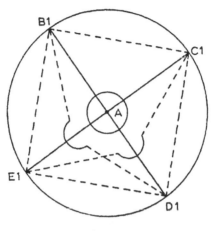

Fig. 10

layer, but those which exist between individuals or groups on one layer and those on others, that is, the diagonal relationships.

It is possible for a communication engineer to design a multi-channel network which enables a variety of individuals to communicate in a variety of patterns. It is much more difficult to control the personal complications which are likely to arise when communications take place across divisional or boundary lines, and which cause trouble in most organizations.

Modern technological trends encourage multi-directional movement of paperwork, controls and communications and it is, for instance, easy to envisage the need for a direct communication between executives B1 and E4 on Fig. 9. But it is even easier to envisage the resentments that may be caused when the vertical and horizontal barriers are crossed without the full agreement of those whose territory is crossed. Many senior executives know that even a direct line communication between (say) executives B1 and B4 (Fig. 9) can lead to resentment by the intermediate executives B2 and B3, and horizontal barriers are no easier to cross than vertical ones, in fact they are often more difficult.

I shall discuss communications more fully in the next section but at this point we must realize that communications and internal divisions are intimately associated, and we cannot consider the former without careful attention to the latter.

Before attempting to bring together the various aspects of 'division' let us consider more fully the problem of horizontal 'layers'. If we refer back to Fig. 9 we see a five-layer supervisory structure, where between the chief executive A and the factory floor workers are five divisional lines, each of which represents a barrier, a link, a gap, or a limit of direct reportability, whichever you may prefer to call it. Each represents a potential strength or weakness. Each may provide more personal problems in the organization than almost any other factor.

What conditions govern the number of supervisory 'layers' in a structure? If we study some of the nine considerations on page 171, particularly 4, 7, 8 and 9, we might easily conclude that the greater the number of 'layers' of management the less well designed is the structure. Is this true—or false? In organizational as in other subjects 'the best' is usually found only when the circumstances of a particular case are fully known.

But there may be some *general* considerations which we should have in mind when considering how best to carve up the structure horizontally. First, we must realize the close relationship between the number of layers and the span of control. The wider the latter, the less normally the number of layers required. On balance, I believe that it is better to provide smaller spans of control even if this increases the number of 'layers'. Let us remember that a greater number of layers *may* create a stronger feeling among subordinates that the ladder of promotion is less restricted. I am sure that the restricted upward vision and the 'flattened' structure created by some mergers is a serious bar to managerial satisfactions, just as a hill is less inspiring to look at than a mountain.

Perhaps, however, there is a flaw in this reasoning, particularly when we consider very large groups such as the N.C.B., British Railways, or even I.C.I. In these cases, the number of horizontal layers from bottom to top is necessarily large, and may create in a junior manager a feeling that the downward pressure of the superstructure is likely to defeat the upward pressure of his ambition. This is an interesting subject for further research, as I find little conclusive evidence so far to show preference trends among young executives for attaching themselves to various sizes or shapes of companies. They will certainly find a greater demand for their services within the larger firms because more of the latter are coming into existence. One review (*Company Assets Income and Finance in 1960*. H.M.S.O.) showed that the number of companies with assets of £5 million and over grew from 361 in 1957 to 423 in 1960. Mergers and take-overs will continue to influence this trend, and will, if my experience is typical, tend to increase the numbers of layers.

The report quoted on page 160 gives also some information on the number of layers existing in over 1000 American companies.

LAYERS OF SUPERVISION

(Counting Chief Executive as one)

Number of Employees	Range	Median Concentration
Under 100	2– 5	3
100– 199	2– 8	3
200– 299	2– 7	4
300– 499	2–12	4
500– 999	2– 8	5
1000–2000	2– 8	5
Over 2000	2–15	6

My only comment is that, despite some of the *advantages* I have said are present in a multi-layer structure, I see little future among those supervisors in the 'over 2000 group' who are the low men on a company totem pole which supports fourteen others above them.

One last comment on 'levels' comes from C. Millard who wrote an article 'How many levels of Management?' in *The Australian Manager* (October 1962), and who cites the experience of Sears Roebuck. This company organized two groups of stores, one with a 'tall' structure with short spans of control and multi levels, and the other with a 'flat' structure having wide spans of control and fewer levels. Experience showed that the latter was superior.

This, and other evidence, supports at least the conclusion that the span of control is a flexible principle, and can vary greatly numerically. The important thing, as in many other managerial matters, is to study its implications fully in the light of the particular circumstances before deciding the *best* structure. It is important to consider the comments made on page 161, and the possibility that in this particular case 'management by regulation' might be more easily achieved than in other cases.

It must be realized that promotion does not always involve a vertical movement from one layer to another. Within each supervisory layer is a band of opportunity, which allows someone to be promoted vertically, horizontally or diagonally in the same layer, possibly with salary increases within the limits that may be set for each layer. It is, in a way, analogous to the building shown on Fig. 6 where the greater the number of floors and the more rooms on each floor, the greater, presumably, is the opportunity for satisfying individual preferences and opportunities.

Are these arguments valid? They appear to support an organizational concept which provides a greater rather than a smaller number of 'divisions', layers, or whatever we like to call them. I said earlier (page 156) that in technical fields it is increasingly possible to divide the total assembly structure into a greater number of separate components in order to achieve the best design. I appear now to be advocating the same sort of division in the organization structure, so that we make the fullest use of a variety of specialists, and the greatest opportunity for personal movement and promotion. But I also said earlier that the greater the number of divisions in the structure, the greater its structural weakness unless we provide more strength along the division lines. The best solution seems, on balance, to be found by strengthening the multi-divided structure rather than reducing the number of divisions.

But this conclusion is too facile when we consider certain other trends which are noticeable today. Friedmann[1] wrote in a most interesting manner on the subdivision of jobs. He suggested, with much supporting evidence, that we have exceeded common sense and good management in our efforts to divide labour into ever smaller specialist packages, a condition brought to its ultimate absurdity by Charlie Chaplin in *Modern Times*. In my own life I have seen and taken part in production engineering trends which for many years subdivided individual tasks into smaller ones in the interests of specialization and presumed efficiency. But I have seen more recently a noticeable change in philosophy and practice and one type of production organization described in *Management Principles* (page 121) is an example of the new trend.

Perhaps the main reason for this new trend is the growing realization among technologists that an increase in job content is likely to lead to a proportionately greater personal satisfaction and overall efficiency among the workers. I believe this is a valid and important reason, but as with other trends it is difficult to know how far the pendulum should be allowed to swing in the new direction. It is difficult also to decide whether this particular trend has a specific application to organizational design and whether it will affect *managerial* job content, the number of specialist appointments, the number of 'layers' of management, spans of control, and the simplification of the organizational structure.

[1] *The Anatomy of Work*. Georges Friedmann.

Summing up, I must admit to a rather confused concept of structural division in the light of present evidence. There is much to be said for a structure which, to provide the fullest use of specialized skills and (apparently) better promotion opportunities, has more rather than less divisions in the total structure. But if groups are becoming larger it may become more important to challenge this trend. It is natural for a group as it grows larger to become more complex, managerially, organizationally and technically; perhaps one of a top manager's most important tasks is to build in a *simplifying* counter-force so that every tendency towards greater division is challenged, and made to justify itself fully before becoming embodied into the structure.

However, despite all such counter-action, we are and will continue to be faced with the problem of structural 'divisions'. It seems, therefore, that we must face this problem squarely and decide to make the best of its advantages. In doing so we must endeavour to minimize its disadvantages by ensuring the best cohesion, communications and control in the interests of overall strength.

How can we maximize cohesion?

We have already seen that structural weaknesses are more likely to show up along division lines, just as we would expect mechanical failure to occur where two pieces of metal are joined together. Good design in both cases must ensure good connections between separate 'parts', and the provision of certain other design features which add to the total cohesive strength.

Therefore, in considering total cohesion we must study the total pattern and particularly the following:

(1) A group has a natural tendency towards cohesion among its members.

(2) Personal divisions and difficulties are, however, potentially present, and tend to reduce cohesion; they act as 'flaws' which may suddenly become apparent.

(3) Lack of understanding of group purpose tends to reduce group cohesion.

(4) Cohesion is basically a condition involving people, and structural divisions and weaknesses are therefore basically between people.

(5) Greater cohesive strength should be provided at points, or divisions, of maximum stress and strain.

(6) Cohesion is increased by better co-operation, which is multi-directional.

(7) A basic element of cohesion and co-operation is communication. The communication matrix plays an important part in maintaining cohesive strength.

(8) Communication is, basically, between people, and its effectiveness is directly related to the opportunity for personal discussion and reportability. This makes the span of control an important element in cohesion.

(9) Communication, being basically a condition of mutual understanding, should encourage simplicity, rather than complexity, of structural shapes. The formal means of expressing internal divisions, i.e. the group organization chart, should be as simple and understandable as it is possible to make it.

I am tempted to go further and to apply these nine considerations to specific cases. I shall, however, leave you, my reader, with this opportunity to consider how, for instance, your own group's structure measures up. I hope the result will not create too much 'division' between you and your colleagues!

Let us return, finally, to the present situation where, in so many cases, I find a greater tendency to create divisions than to strengthen cohesion. If we consider more fully the nine points above we shall improve the cohesive force, but there will always be a tendency among individuals and groups to build 'Berlin walls', or to ignore, or fail to recognize, flaws which are potential sources of weakness and may, under stress conditions, crack the total structure. Many divisions are logically designed, and encourage reasonable co-ordination and communication across the lines. In some cases, however, we set up 'artificial' divisions which become barriers to mutual confidence. There is, for instance, the Head Office barrier, which is often artificially created and weakens rather than increases total strength.[1] I referred also to line, staff, direct and indirect categories, which are often needlessly maintained, and tend to create unnecessary barriers. If we must have divisions let us make quite certain that each is really necessary.

A Restatement

(1) When a sharing of duties takes place, the internal structure becomes divided; the greater the development of specialist allocation of duties the more complex the structural division becomes, and the more important it becomes to ensure that the structure has adequate cohesive strength.

(2) Division of a group's product range becomes a major reason for dividing its organization structure. For this reason a long-term product policy is required around which to plan organizational changes and maintain strength.

(3) Division of a group's total personnel is another important consideration in producing structural divisions. In particular the square-cube law affects greatly the size, shape and internal divisional pattern of a group.

(4) Overall shape also affects the divisional pattern, and therefore the 'shape' considerations discussed earlier should be remembered when divisions are being considered.

(5) The potential weaknesses present at division lines can be improved if we plan for overlapping of responsibilities, which must be understood to mean 'taking the strain' rather than butting into someone else's territory.

[1] There is something in the 'law' which states that 'morale rises with the square of the distance from Head Office'.

(6) A division is potentially a weakness *and* a strength. It can be a crack which can cause disintegration of the structure, or a potential strength if it allows each separate divisional area to be designed for the fullest use of specialist strengths. The latter must, however, be accompanied by stronger *inter*-communication and co-operating links.

(7) Spans of control create divisional lines and problems.

(8) Line and staff relationships also create divisional lines and problems. It is desirable to avoid as many 'artificial' divisions as possible, and line and staff relationships can often be simplified with a consequent strengthening of the divisional pattern.

(9) Horizontal divisions are likely to increase with the development of new systems of control, and this tendency, in conjunction with (1), may create a complex and weakened divisional pattern, which will increase the difficulty of communication and weaken the total strength.

(10) Another important divisional consideration is the tendency to subdivide the job-content of many varieties of workers. Reactions against this are now becoming evident which, if followed through, will simplify the divisional pattern.

(11) It is difficult to strike a balance between those forces which are currently increasing and decreasing the number of divisions in an organization structure. On balance, there is possibly a tendency to weaken the structure by an inadequate consideration of divisional weaknesses. For this reason a simplifying counterforce should be provided, which challenges every 'complicating' tendency which attempts to embody itself in the structure.

(12) Finally, an attempt is made to show how cohesion can help to strengthen divisional areas and provide greater total strength.

6

The Structure of Groups: II
Communications and Cohesion

(4) COMMUNICATIONS

As ASHBY reminds us, we can define 'parts' as being organized when communication exists between them, although this makes the two words 'organization' and 'communication' relational, and not interchangeable. The reminder has value in emphasizing the importance of communication in organization.

It is interesting to reflect upon the increased use of the word 'communication' in recent years. It has moved out of the sphere of transport systems into the realm of people; it is moving into the sphere of global electronic systems and networks and becoming, in the process, a more sophisticated word and, paradoxically, less easily communicable in the process! It is now being treated by The Institute of Directors as a serious enough business problem to merit the provision of special courses at top management level.

It is too easily assumed that if individuals freely communicate with each other all is well. This may not be so, and in an earlier book, *So You're Going to a Meeting*, I referred to the possibility of communication as a destructive rather than a cohesive or co-operative medium. It is frequently better to say nothing, or to avoid a meeting, on the basis that 'the less said the soonest mended'.

It is also too easily assumed that when something has gone

wrong in a group there has been a 'failure to communicate'. Frequently, the 'communication' has been understood but rejected, because there was a failure of top managers to ensure that the communication was 'complete'. This will only be achieved if the communication is mutually understandable *and acceptable*.

There is an old Chinese proverb which suggests that the reason why we have two ears and only one mouth is that it is more important to listen. Perhaps another way of looking at this is to assume that it requires twice as much effort to understand something as to say it. This is not a bad reminder to managers. But the importance of two ears takes on a modern look when we read of some useful experiments which were reported[1] under the heading 'Listening with Both Ears'. Rapoport, in a government-sponsored project, increased the capacity of voice communication systems by discovering that those messages having a greater significance to an individual became focussed within his brain by the stereo effect of listening with *both* ears, in comparison with irrelevant messages which went through only one ear. In a test of the system devised to exploit this, it was found that messages sent to a particular listener, if sent simultaneously by a different channel to each ear, were much more clearly understood even in the presence of increasing background 'noise'. This system has many technical possibilities, and its implications are important to the manager interested in better communications.

The spread of integrated data processing systems is causing us to enquire more deeply into the desirability or otherwise of better communication. Consider the company which set up a so-called 'drudgery factory',[2] where inter-company statistics were processed, and made available to all in the company who required them. It was soon found by the staff of the drudgery factory that

---

[1] *Research for Industry*, Vol. 14, No. 5. Stanford Research Institute.
[2] So called because it was presumed to reduce statistical drudgery among managers.

such was the speed of modern computing and printing equipment that more copies of many statistical forms could easily be printed. 'Why not', therefore, they said, 'send copies to everybody?' Sub-managers soon found that statistics previously sent only to them were now sent also to their bosses, and, worse still, arrived earlier than their own (mail boys started deliveries in the front office). Where formerly subordinates analysed the statistics and passed the *conclusions* upwards in good 'exception' style, now the top manager was asking questions before the subordinates had, sometimes, even seen the statistics. This was clearly a case of too much communication too quickly, and it emphasizes the significant point that 'channels' are also very important. They can cause difficulties when they are opened up as well as when they are clogged.

I know a manager who always seems in too much of a hurry to 'pass on' information. Cases often arise where a Board decision involves passing on decisions, by, say, the managing director to his subordinates. Now, it is one thing to decide, another thing to decide how to carry out the decision, and the wise manager should take enough time out to plan his communication campaign so that he creates the right effect. Hurried communications can often spoil the desired effect.

What do we want from 'communications'? Shorn of much of its mystique it is surely a means to an end, and not an end in itself, which some people seem to think it is today. In this book I have frequently said that the purpose of organization is ultimately to ensure a greater number of individual satisfactions, and presumably, therefore, better communications will help us achieve this condition.

Let us, at an early stage, consider how communication networks can be built up, so that whatever is sent along the channels is sent in the most efficient manner. Earlier in this book, on page 159, I reproduced a mathematical expression of the relationships possible in any given span of control, and it should be remembered

M

in passing that a 'relationship' involves a two-way communication channel.

By calculation we find that:

A four-member group, that is, a manager and three subordinates, involves eighteen possible relationships.

A five-member group involves forty-four possible relationships.

A six-member group involves 100 possible relationships.

Let us now show in Fig. 11 a graphical representation of communication links between members of similar-sized groups.

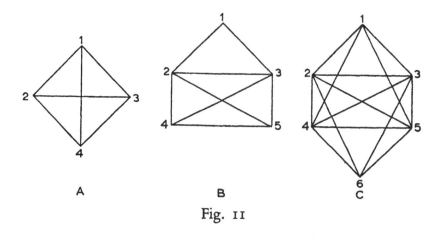

Fig. 11

For a four-member group the number of links are six.
For a five-member group the number of links are ten.
For a six-member group the number of links are fifteen.

The reader is immediately struck by the considerable difference in the number of 'relationships' and the number of 'links', in a group comprising a given number of individuals. For instance, in a group containing an executive and three subordinates there are (using the Graicunas formula) eighteen possible 'relationships', but only six 'links' (Fig. 11). Let us tabulate the relationships in a group containing four individuals, 1, 2, 3, 4.

There are

Relationships between	Links between
1–2	1–2
1–3	1–3
1–4	1–4
2–1	2–3
2–3	2–4
3–1	3–4
3–2	
3–4	
1–2/3	
1–2/4	
1–3/4	
2–1/3	
2–1/4	
2–3/4	
3–1/2	
3–1/4	
3–2/4	
Total 17	Total 6

What does this tell us? First, that 'relationships' include the possibility of two or more individuals 'ganging together' to form relationships with others in the group, and it is interesting to note, in passing, that the Graicunas formula on page 159 is not complete if we take this sub-group possibility fully into account. We can increase still further the number of relationships calculated by that formula by assuming that a *sub-group* can have a relationship with another sub-group, and that any one individual can have a relationship with a sub-group comprising *all* other members of the group. In the particular case under discussion we therefore add six more relationships, making twenty-three in total.

$$1/2–3/4$$
$$1/3–2/4$$
$$1 \quad –2/4/3$$
$$2 \quad –1/3/4$$
$$3 \quad –1/2/4$$
$$4 \quad –1/2/3$$

It all looks very complex, and indeed it is, when we realize that each of these relationships must rely upon channels of communication.

The second point to note from this tabulation of possible relationships is that it recognizes the existence of 'two-way' communications. For instance, at the top of the list (page 179) we see a relationship between individuals 1 and 2, and lower down a relationship between 2 and 1. It is important, as I said earlier, to remember that if individual No. 1 communicates with No. 2 it does not automatically follow that No. 2 communicates with No. 1. It is a feature of the Graicunas formula that it reminds us of the need for providing both channels.

There is considerable opportunity for a scientifically inclined manager to develop linkage diagrams which enable him more clearly to understand and improve his group's communication channels. Linkage diagrams are similar in purpose to organization charts, and it is probable that those who value the latter also value the former. There are some managers who try, usually without success, to combine the two by drawing a variety of wandering dotted 'communication' lines between various executives on the organization chart. They attempt too much on one chart.

Technological trends are tending to make linkage diagrams more complex. Older organizational terms like the 'chain of command' will lose some of their former validity and value through the greater need for interdepartmental co-operation *across* the chains of command, which in turn may bring about more widely a situation envisaged many years ago by Mary Parker Follett when she said that 'control', which is an integrated aspect of the chain of command, will be more effectively exercised through 'co-ordination', which thus *becomes* control.

In designing a linkage system we must remember its 'purpose', which will be achieved if channels are made available in number, direction, and strength to bear the desired traffic. We must remember particularly a statement made earlier when discussing shape (see page 145), which was that 'greater strength is required at those points where greater strains are likely to arise'. This applies as much to communication linkages as to structural designs and road systems.

In this book I use several linkage diagrams to illustrate various conditions, and I can only suggest that you study them thoroughly, and endeavour to design your own for a given situation. I hope you will bear in mind the engineer's creed, which is that in a surprisingly high number of cases, something which doesn't look right isn't right. Perhaps it is asking too much of managers and organizers to look at a communication network with such skilled eyes, but when I remember some of the complicated-*looking* diagrams I have seen, which purport to show relationships between people, I cannot help repeating what I said earlier about the need for greater simplicity.

Finally, I wish to return again to the rapidly growing theory of communications and, particularly, to its graphical expression. (For a more complete discussion see *The Potential Contribution of Graph Theory to Organization Theory*. Dorwin Cartwright.) Just as a well-designed organization chart enables a trained manager to 'see' the total group organization, so a well-designed graphic representation can help him to 'see' more vividly its communication pattern.

Graph theory has advanced in step with mathematics, and

together they will provide more valuable tools for managerial use. An interesting and growing use of a graphical expression in the development of P.E.R.T. (Programme Evaluation Review Technique) was seen in *The Financial Times* where it was applied to the building of a house, an area of activity where planning has often seemed to the layman to be conspicuous by its absence. Since then P.E.R.T. and its variations have been widely applied in conjunction with computers.

People vary in their appreciation of visual forms, and Grey Walter in *The Living Brain* has some interesting things to say on this subject which are particularly important in the teacher/ learner field. Some of us, myself included, prefer a graphical or analogue form of expression, and can visualize a particular situation better if it is expressed in this form. Others prefer the tabular, statistical, or digital form of expression, which in some applications has been proved to be more valuable. The Medical Research Council has conducted some research in this field, but its application has been slow.

Organization is likely to be more thoroughly understood if we use whichever form of expression is appropriate to a better understanding of the various elements of communication.

The Elements of Communication

In what logical manner can we discuss the principal elements or factors of communication? I find it difficult to decide how and how much to subdivide a subject which is in many ways indivisible. The very nature of communications encourages a comprehensive treatment, and yet one feels that an understanding of the 'whole' is more likely through an examination of its most logical areas of division.

Four such areas come to mind. These are:

Communication for information or instruction.
Communication for collaboration or co-ordination.

Communication for control.
The time and cost of communication.

Immediately we visualize the possibility (and the desirability) of any one of these impinging upon the others; a number of communication situations must satisfy all four requirements.

Before we examine each of these four areas let us consider whether the 'act' of communication is fundamentally different in various circumstances. The most significant difference I have found in practice is, whether there is a direct communication between one person and another (or others), or whether it is 'indirect', that is whether it passes in series from person to person before full communication is achieved.

I will discuss these differences as they arise in each of the four areas. I would, however, particularly draw attention to the error-possibilities inherent in series-communication, and the opportunities which now exist for these to be reduced by automation.

Let us proceed with an examination of the four areas mentioned above, which, I believe, provide a logical division for consideration.

Communication for Information or Instruction

This is, I suppose, the most important single objective of communications. Each of us is born with certain instinctive and potential abilities, but from the moment of birth we are informed and instructed in countless ways during the rest of our lives. The 'purpose' presumably is to enable us to attain knowledge, health, wealth and happiness, and for us in turn to communicate these virtues to others, so that dynamic purposeful growth is assured among as many individuals as possible.

When the term 'communications' is used today by managers it is usually assumed to mean 'informing others', which is one, but not a complete, aspect of instruction. One of my early lessons in management was a realization of the value of feed-back, or, putting it in more simple terms, the effect that the 'managed' should have on the managers. The term 'joint consultation' has too often degenerated into one-way information-*giving*, or communication downwards, where a body of junior managers or worker-representatives are told something, but are not encouraged to feed back to top managers ther own interpretation of company affairs.

Few managers realize that information-giving or instruction is a two-way process, and that communication channels must be designed for giving and receiving; for sending information and instruction down and up. It is even more important to ensure closed-loop feed-back conditions in personal communications than in automation.

The art of information-giving or instruction is one which is undergoing considerable change, and in particular the impact of 'learning machines' may have a profound effect, and not necessarily all good, upon the relationships between givers and receivers. Efficiency of instruction is affected by a variety of elements, of which the clarity of the original instruction, the design of communication channels and the 'receptiveness' of the recipients are important.

Leavitt[1] gave each of five members a card on which appeared five (out of six possible) symbols. In any set of five cards there was only one common symbol, and the problem was for every member to find the common symbol. The members were asked to do so by means of written communications. I will not quote all the details, but briefly report the conclusions, which comment on the different reactions experienced by the various groups under observation. Incidentally, there were four such groups, each with a communication pattern fixed in accordance with Fig. 12.

---

[1] *Some effects of certain communication patterns on Group Performance.* H. J. Leavitt.

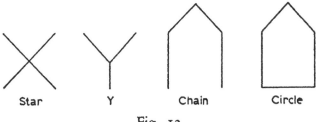

| Star | Y | Chain | Circle |

Fig. 12

(1) The Star was the most efficient in terms of speed and lack of error.
(2) The Circle was the least efficient.
(3) The Star was the least enjoyed.
(4) The Circle was thoroughly enjoyed.

These results seem, on the face of it, to be obvious. Action and interaction, as in the circle, is fun, while the star, by giving one key man information which he may or may not pass on to the others, gives satisfaction to him, but not necessarily to the others.

We seem to arrive at a consideration of the relative attractions of efficiency, speed and enjoyment. Ideally, we want all, and we can envisage situations where, if solutions are speedy, enjoyment comes too. But in some situations, particularly where there is already a low morale, the results may, in the star organization, make for even lower morale.

'People like to exercise their skills. If the communication pattern is such that they cannot, they dislike the situation. Where using one's wits is the real end of the group, the formation of restricted communication-paths, either by the experimenter or because of other social influences, reduces the pleasure taken in the group. This is confirmed by Back[1] (1948) in his study of inter-personal relations in a discussion group. The barriers to communication in his case were created by the members themselves. Some of them just talked so much that others could not get a word in

[1] *Interpersonal Relationships in a Discussion Group.* K. Back.

edgeways. Here, also, a marked lack of enjoyment was shown by members deprived of the opportunity to talk when they felt like it.'[1]

It has been shown that under some circumstannce as individual does a better job than a group, and one reason may be that information is clear and unambiguous. More time may be spent trying to understand other members than solving the problem. Heise and Miller[2] constructed some three-person networks, which produced interesting results. The networks are shown in Fig. 13, and the order of good performance was, in descending order of quality—1, 2, 3, 4, 5. This result, according to the

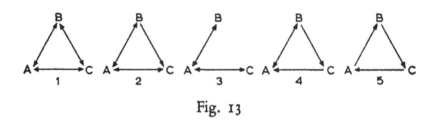

Fig. 13

researchers, is entirely accounted for, and I will extract some significant comments. The first is that 'when two members cannot communicate mutually, the communication of the one to the other is likely to act as a disturbance and not as a help. Because in this way all messages may be delayed, both the performance of the task and the efficient organization of the group will be more difficult in networks of this kind.'

The second is that 'Mutuality of communication obviously helps the group to perform efficiently. One reason we have shown is that if two members do communicate simultaneously to a third, one of them can be asked to wait. No intermediary is necessary to transmit that (organizational) message. Second, if A has sent information to B which contradicts B's store of knowledge, it

¹ *The Study of Groups.* Josephine Klein.
² *Problem Solving by small groups using various Communication Networks.* G. A. Heise and G. A. Miller.

can be cleared up very much more easily if the two can inform each other directly of the existence of the discrepancy than if this correction has to be mediated by a third. Learning depends directly on the possibility of correcting errors. The greater the possibilities of error, the more important such feedbacks become. This is true both for learning information which is available through others, and also for learning which channels of communication one must use in order to arrive speedily at a solution.

'Third, in a network in which there is a mutual link between some members and not between others, members differ in centrality. The more central members have more information sent to them or through them than other members. They are therefore in a better position for spotting discrepancies in information sent from two different sources, and they can co-ordinate the efforts of others. We shall see from the next experiment that co-ordination may be very important. Lastly, we know that the central members may reach a solution before other members do so. If they then transmit the solution through the network the group as a whole possesses the solution; they need not each wait for all messages to reach them—a valuable saving of time.'

Much of the evidence in Klein's Chapter 5 implies that 'a group with mutuality of communication and a clearly recognizable central member or co-ordinator' (in other words, a typical top management group) 'are best suited to solve problems in which each member possesses information useful to others, and which are so complex that a co-ordinator is required'. Routines of communication are in a way desirable, as people know with whom they should communicate, and so go speedily on with the actual job. But top management groups should avoid letting routine become ossification, and one experiment (*Communication and Learning in Task-oriented Groups*. Christie, Macy and Luce) introduced ambiguity into the task of decision. Their results 'show some interesting consequences of rigid structuring or wrong learning. If very similar tasks are performed a number of times and then the nature of the task changes, what results can we predict? All that we know seems to point firmly to the hypothesis that the circle will do better than the chain, and the chain better than the star. Let us examine the evidence. First, the better a routine has been learned, the more reward its rigid keeping has brought in the past, the less willing will members be to abandon it now that they are uncertain and in stress. They will not be able or willing to recognise that the change in the nature of the task involves a change in the structure of the group. (See also Homans, *The Human Group*, 1950.)

'Second, the members in the circle have been enjoying themselves. They have been participating actively. In the star, on the other hand, there are four members, and in the chain two, who have had nothing to do but to send out information at their disposal and then wait for the correct answer to come back to them. The members in the circle are therefore more strongly motivated to perform their task with zest. In the other two networks, members have learned to sit back and to leave the thinking to the central members. It is nothing to them that they now leave the central member in a mess. Third, let us look at the networks again.

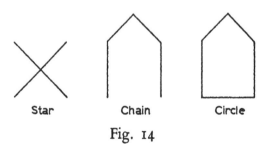

Star   Chain   Circle

Fig. 14

'In the star (Fig. 14) the central member now gets ambiguous or even contradictory information, and no one else gets any information. Therefore, even if the central member asks "What do you mean by 'yellowish?'" there is nothing in the experience of the peripheral member that will enable him either to interpret the reason for this question or to place it within a range of yellowishness, and its shadings into browns, reds or greens. In the circle there are sufficient inter-connections for everyone to realize that something odd is going on. Since everyone transmits every-one else's messages, there is sufficient information at the disposal of members for them to sort things out if necessary, each for him-self. Moreover, the circle members tend in any case to send more organizational messages than do other networks (Leavitt, 1951),[1] and to arrive at all kinds of short cuts. If they have learned any-thing at all, it is how to cope with uncertainty. (Bavelas, 1952.)[2]

'Similarly with the correction of errors. In normal conditions, without noise or ambiguity, errors in the star are corrected by the central member or not at all. Other members cannot get a chance to learn to do this. In the same conditions everyone in the circle has practice in checking items of information against one another. Leavitt has shown that the members of the circle learned to correct many of the great number of errors they made. They did not correct many to begin with, but they learned to do so as the trials proceeded. This learning also is carried over to the new situation. The star and the chain are less adept at the reduction of error, having had less practice in doing so on their previous task.'

The leader is always a teacher, and my own experience of group leadership has confirmed the importance of the teaching role and the necessity to make face-to-face contact at regular intervals with more than one level of managers. In a previous book *What is this Management?* I referred to 'double-link control', an 'overlapping' device which ensures that not only does a manager maintain contact with his *immediate* subordinates, but also with those immediately *beyond* his span of control. Those interested might care to consider the diagram I used, which is reproduced here.

[1] *Some effects of certain communication patterns on Group Performance.* H. J. Leavitt.
[2] *Communication Patterns in Problem Solving groups.* A. Bavelas.

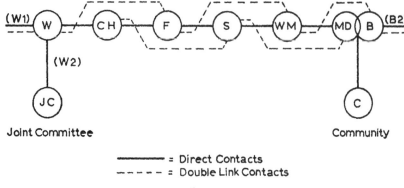

Joint Committee   Community

——————— = Direct Contacts
— — — — = Double Link Contacts

Fig. 15

This device can be applied to a variety of occasions and levels, and I personally found its use most effective when organizing regular management sessions, at which certain important decisions required to be communicated widely. The 'double-link' series of meetings gave regular opportunities for overlapping layers of management to meet, and more thoroughly to understand each other and the subjects discussed. In passing I must admit that top managers did not generally find it easy to convince middle managers that *they too* should practise double-link communication further down. Foremen, for instance, are nearly always more loquacious on the need for *receiving* information from above than on *giving* it below! This is an important teaching problem, bound up intimately with the many interesting things Argyris has to say in *Understanding Organizational Behavior* about the attitude of foremen towards top managers and workers.

Other similar means of ensuring close-knit communication structures are available which develop common purpose, teacher/learner possibilities, and therefore group effectiveness. Lickert in *Motivational Approach to Organization* describes a team with overlapping group memberships, and refers to it in these terms: 'In most organizations it will also be desirable to have various committees, staff activities, etc., which involve effective groups and which help further to tie many parts of the organization together. These links are in addition to the linking provided by the overlapping members in the line organization, and strengthen further the interaction-influence system. Throughout the organization the supervisory processes should develop and strengthen team spirit and group functioning. This theoretically ideal organizational structure, when properly used, provides the interaction-influence system called for by the modified theory. It will result in an organization characterized by high capacity for efficient, full communication in all directions, high loyalty and trust, and high motivation to achieve its goals.'

Communication for Collaboration or Co-ordination

Is there a significant difference between the two words 'collaboration' and 'co-ordination'? Of the two, the latter is the one most used today by managers, and it has a veneer of modernity which makes it popular. I prefer the word collaboration, which implies a mutual relationship *and responsibility* between two or more people who are concerned with a particular task. The word co-ordination implies that the collaborators require to have collaboration imposed on them by a third party, usually a senior. Collaboration[1] implies a *delegated* responsibility from seniors to juniors, which seems a desirable attitude to encourage.

Let us, in this section, assume that the two words are interchangeable, and are covered by the word collaboration. In what way can it be improved by better communications? It is at this stage that we might consider more fully the added problems introduced by the need to bring several people into the picture. This is, of course, present in almost every group task, including that of teaching, because most communications require to be 'passed on' in one form or another to other people.

Here I wish particularly to emphasize the *added* difficulties

[1] I have frequently used collaboration in preference to co-ordination in previous chapters.

which arise when a succession of individuals is involved, a situation which applies in most groups containing several layers and divisions of structure. Most of us recollect cases where complete understanding in the group was not achieved, and two amusing examples can be quoted. Bartlett[1] showed that a line drawing of an owl, when re-drawn successively by eighteen individuals after seeing a predecessor's sketch, ended up as a recognizable cat! We remember the old Army story which told of an instruction starting at one end of a line as 'Send reinforcements' and ending at the other end of the line as 'Send 3s. 4d.'. A 'grape-vine' may produce some very peculiar grapes.

These and similar examples in my managerial experience confirm the error possibility created by multi-link communications, and this possibility is intensified when we are concerned with human links. Speaking generally, human beings are much more susceptible than machine systems to cumulative linkage errors, and this makes it important to reduce the number of humans as much as possible in a communication chain. We shall consider this again, later.

If communication between a number of individuals or groups is faulty, such as was the case in the examples just quoted, at least three possibilities exist. First, the original communication was not properly defined or started on its path. Second, it developed errors as it went along, and, third, the communication linkage system was badly designed.

Let us assume that the first possibility does not arise, although it often does, which reminds us that many people misunderstand because of the obscurity of the original message. However, let us concentrate on the second possibility, which is that errors develop as the communication 'goes along'. In the examples there was considerable distortion of the original message because of the large number of intermediaries.

One intermediate step of growing importance is the 'inter-

[1] *Remembering*. F. C. Bartlett.

preting step', which translates the original message into a different language. This applies when scientists and non-scientists communicate with each other, and also where, as in Common Market discussions, English has to be translated into, say, French. In a complete communication, up and down, two translations may be required, with even greater errors possible.

Here is a linkage problem which may become more serious. It should encourage us to develop a common language more fully, or at least a greater understanding of other people's 'languages'.

Almost any experiment will convince you that the average person is relatively incapable of transmitting accurate information to a third party, and a full realization of this is vitally important to managers, who rely greatly upon the accuracy of receiving and giving through human channels. I could discuss this situation at length, but at this stage I wish only to restate what I have already said, that in almost every communication situation three things are particularly important:

(1) The original communication must be clearly defined.
(2) Particular care must be taken to ensure that progressive errors are avoided as the communication is 'passed on'.
(3) The communication linkage system must be designed to provide the most efficient method of transmission, and the most complete understanding of the original communication.

Communication for Control
If, as Miss Follett suggested, co-ordination *is* control, we have only to achieve good co-ordination or co-operation in order to achieve good control. But, whatever the theoretical possibilities, we do at present need control, even if it is exercised by a group rather than by an individual.

Put in its most simple form, the controller's job is to ensure that essential information permeates accurately and rapidly to all

N

concerned, and that he becomes aware, in the same efficient manner, of the feelings, views and performances of those with whom he wishes to establish communications.

One important reason why control is necessary is the possibility of partial breakdown of the communication system, sometimes accidentally and occasionally, let us admit, planned. The first may arise from nothing more than a routine decision to exclude a particular individual from the circulation list of, say, a document, because it was assumed that 'he wouldn't really be interested'. This is always a dangerous assumption when dealing with managers, and it makes management-by-exception, in its conventional sense, very difficult to apply, because most managers don't like to be 'excepted', or excluded from information.

The second possibility, that of deliberate exclusion, is more frequently applied than we realize, or perhaps would like. Lickert,[1] in discussing the position of a manager in his group, said that an important way for him to assess his status was, periodically, for that manager to examine where he stood in the communication network. If, for instance, there seemed to be a falling off in volume, or significance, of reports arriving on his desk, he might well conclude, not that other people were concerned with relieving him of details, but rather that the skids were deliberately being put under him!

Klein refers to this kind of situation when she discusses 'disturbances' in communication channels; she considers the question of indispensability, an important aspect in every management group, where all are indispensible but some more so than others. In the circle, Fig. 12 (page 185), if any member or link is missing it becomes a chain, and complete communication becomes much slower, although still possible. If a member or link disappears from the chain, then some members will be isolated, a situation not without significance in business. I have just said that it is important for us to realize the ease (either accidental or inspired)

[1] *Motivational Approach to Organization.* Rensis Lickert.

with which one or more people can become isolated. Consideration of this possibility may lead the controller and organizer to consider the provision of alternative networks, such as are regularly used in similar technical situations.

There are cases where one member of a group becomes the connecting link, or articulation point, between clusters of people, a situation met with, for instance, where a member of one committee is their representative on other committees, and where an organizational bottleneck can be corked up very easily. Too often, in a communication network, some can be misinformed or not informed at all. I have always given much managerial consideration to what, in the American Constitution, are referred to as 'checks and balances'. A senior manager must ensure that a main communication channel is never wholly relied upon without some alternative check, and while this may sound like a vote of no confidence in one's colleagues and subordinates, they too must utilize similar checks. In computer design, for instance, it is essential to embody self-checking devices in the programme; an organizational communication 'programme' requires even better self-checking devices, because variable humans are involved.

I shall refer again to the problem of executive isolation when I discuss leadership, which is of course another aspect of control.

The Place of Teaching Machines in Communications

I said earlier that the present strong trend towards the introduction of teaching machines may not necessarily be all to the good. Like many other managers I have been particularly interested in American TV educational developments, which have reached such a stage that they justify the term 'University of the Air'. I take some pride in the fact that as long ago as 1955, in an address to The Radio Industries Club, I strongly advocated the development of TV education. I take less pride in its subsequent slow development in this country.

It is logical to assume that if we prepare an educational programme with great skill and put it over to a large number of
students through TV or teaching machines, we are utilizing scarce
teaching skills to better advantage. But there is a considerable
difference between a student working in isolation in front of a
TV screen or teaching machine and one who sharpens his brain
on a human teacher and/or fellow students.

The teaching-machine method, including TV, involves a
closed-loop relationship between student and machine, and the
communication pattern is much too restricted to be effective for
all purposes. Some teaching-machine programmes do allow for the
possibility of personal discussions with tutors and it seems important that this opportunity should be provided in every case,
even if the subject being taught is a technical one.

I can think of no more depressing sight than a row of semi-
isolated students, each linked to his own machine and becoming
more and more proficient in the elements of, say, nuclear fission,
and less and less efficient in the problems of communicating with
fellow humans.

There is another danger, which is less realized but equally
important. Every teaching-machine method must depend on a
'programme', which has been skilfully prepared to describe the
subject, and to recapitulate at the right time, in the right way, if
a student fails to press the right button.

Every communication pattern, whether machine or human,
must be carefully designed, but an *advantage* of human links
is that the unexpected is likely to happen, despite all efforts to
ensure smooth and accurate communications. In a way we have
an analogy here to cohesion, which we shall discuss shortly,
because programmed tuition is a cohesive element, ensuring that
students conform to the best practice. But, as we will emphasize
later, managers must plan against too much cohesion and conformity, and must ensure that adequate anti-cohesive forces are
present.

Personal tuition or tutorship is capable of being programmed only to a limited extent, and its limitations are likely to create unexpected, or non-programmed, situations, which play a vital part in all learner/teacher relationships. By all means let us 'programme', but only in conjunction with a reasonable amount of 'non-programme'. Both must be present—it is the relative amounts which are important; and subject to this consideration teaching machines can play an important part in education.

Let us remember that even the more conventional forms of tuition all too frequently result in a less than desirable comprehension by the student. As a contributor to *Technology* (September 1962) said, when surveying in retrospect her B.Sc. course in chemistry: 'At the end of the course we were familiar with its subject matter, but were sure neither of its application nor its importance.'

A teaching machine is even more likely to achieve the same results.

The Time and Cost of Communication

Some would say that whatever the time and cost involved we must 'communicate' effectively. They do not necessarily realize that time is often a function of efficiency, and cost is a factor of time. A special consideration of time is essential if we are to provide the most effective communications.

I referred on page 176 to the problems raised when a drudgery factory decided to increase the number of communication links, on the assumption, too easily made, that a greater number of links within the same group of people would help communications. Let us consider Fig. 16, and quote Klein's comments on it.

Here 'we find our five and ten links respectively. Suppose that all members can receive and send messages simultaneously, and that each transmission from member to member takes one minute. How long will it take before all members are in possession of the

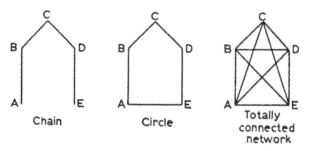

Chain   Circle   Totally connected network

Fig. 16

same information, each starting out with a different bit? In the totally connected network the time will be one minute, since only one link separates any two members. In the circle the time will be two minutes, since for each member there are two others who can be reached directly, and two to whom the neighbours have to transmit in the second minute the information they have just received. In the chain there are two members who must communicate through four links (i.e. through three other members), and though some members will possess complete information before them, four minutes have to elapse before every member of the group is completely informed.

'We may therefore say that the greater the number of links between members, the sooner all members will be equally informed, provided all members communicate through all the links at their disposal. It is also clear that the more links there are in the network, the greater is the number of members who will gain information after only one transmission.'

It is appropriate at this point to mention 'series-parallel' linkage. Every chain of command has 'delay' and 'error possibility' built into it, because a chain involves a series of links which in human terms may be faultily connected, with results as illustrated on page 192. If we consider Fig. 17, we realize quickly that a message from A to B, C, D, E not only takes much longer to reach E in a 'series' linkage, but that error possibilities are multiplied as compared with the 'parallel' linkage.

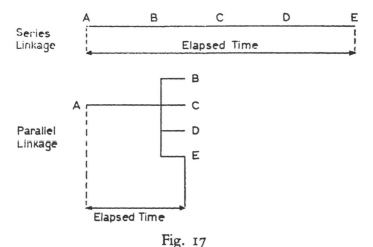

Fig. 17

It will be noticed that the series linkage is identical to the chain in Fig. 16, of which it was said earlier that it is the *longest* method of complete communication. The parallel linkage is not identical with any in Fig. 16, although it is nearest to the 'totally connected network', which provides the *shortest* possible time for complete communication.

If we reconsider what has already been said in this section, have we not produced a conflicting situation? In the drudgery factory we saw that an attempt to speed up communication through simultaneous, *parallel* distribution of statistics to upper and lower managers caused difficulties. These difficulties arose because the revised communication system appeared to take away from subordinates a previously delegated responsibility for prior consideration of certain information. But the linkage diagrams, and often our practical experience, show that simultaneous *parallel* distribution not only saves time, but, possibly, errors arising from linkage inadequacies, that is, the failure of some individuals adequately to pass on correct information. If all persons get identical information direct from the source (in our example, the drudgery factory) the errors, as well as the elapsed time, are likely to be reduced.

How, therefore, in face of these conflicting communication possibilities, should one decide which linkage system to adopt? The critical factor seems to be 'the sort of communication one desires to transmit'. There is all the difference between information which needs to go through a further digestive process, such as in the drudgery-factory case, and information which is sent out to keep as many as possible informed on current affairs. In the first case, *series* distribution may well encourage morale, reduce top managerial routine work, and train juniors. In the second case *parallel* distribution may help morale and managers by putting more people 'in the picture' more quickly.

Alternative considerations of this nature will constantly arise in the application of communication theories. They make it more difficult to apply theory too literally, yet such is the growth of communication theory that we should study more intensively its possible application to management. But let us always remember that the greater the theoretical possibilities, the more good judgement is required in their application to humans.

Many attempts are now being made to introduce mathematical precision into communication networks. Here the sociologist can learn much from engineers, although let us admit readily that there may be a difference in kind, as well as in degree, between the network of a small personal group and of a nation-wide telephone system. Haire, in *Growth of Organizations*, referring to transmission capacity and speed in various biological systems, says: 'In social organisms we cannot do much to speed the actual transmission of the nerve impulse, but we can and do develop, like the biological model, separate specialized functions for internal and external adjustments. Instead of increasing the actual transmission speed there is one thing we can do. It is a truism in communication engineering that it is always possible to trade band width for time. If a message takes x frequencies to travel in y time, you can usually use $2x$ frequencies, and by simultaneous transmittion achieve $\frac{1}{2}y$ time, . . . unable to speed up transmission, we duplicate messages and transmit simultaneously, achieving a measure of the desired time.' This is sound communication engineering, but *may* be bad management practice, as a recent example has shown.

Simplifying Communications

I make no apology for concluding this section with a further plea for simplification, particularly where it is likely to produce greater understanding between people.

Most managers would agree that management is becoming more complicated, although there would be less agreement with the statement that managers are themselves responsible for much of the complication found today. Is it not a manager's job to interpret, simplify and communicate the many modern developments around us to the rank and file of people, who feel unable to keep up with the new events, new developments and new jargon?

We frequently use today the term 'sophisticated' to describe a technical design which achieves a difficult task in a simple way. This is not, I believe, a suitable word to describe simplified management, as a sophisticated manager hardly seems likely to be in sympathy with the less sophisticated majority who constitute, generally, those who are managed.

When we 'communicate information' to people, we must establish a link *from* that person to the new knowledge we wish him to acquire. In all such cases we must surely commence at the level of understanding of the person we wish to teach, and slowly raise that level to new heights. Managers, whose level of understanding is, in general terms, higher than that of their subordinates, must first 'descend' in order to raise understanding.

If we accept this managerial responsibility we must consider every communication, whether descriptive or operative, in the light of its comprehension by the recipients as well as by its sender, who is inevitably more skilled and knowledgeable (on that particular subject) than the receivers. It is necessary, in short, to consider means of simplifying every communication.

Some Complicating Factors

A variety of complicating factors exists today. In the technical field many new ideas and hardware are crowding the scene, under, on and over the earth. Many new specialist groups have been organized, each producing its specialists, its new terms and new definitions of old terms. Some specialists have the linguistic ability to understand and be understood by other specialists, but communication between them and with laymen is becoming more rather than less difficult.

The social area is also providing its share of complication, and whether we consider world political problems, the continuing debate on the Common Market, and the student revolt in many countries it is not easy to understand the many, and often opposing forces at work.

Taken together, the effect of these many complicating factors on the layman is to confuse him, and to make him less able and *less willing* to exert himself. If he does react it is probably in a tangential negative way such as joining a protest movement or taking part in an unofficial strike.

Some Simplifying Factors

It is unfair and incorrect to assume that no attempts are being made to simplify the many new and complicated movements which exist today. My concern is that we are not doing enough. Let us remember, too, that the *early* attempts to solve a problem often result in further complication, a condition emphasized by Professor Saunders, Professor of Mechanical Engineering, London University. 'It is', he said, 'becoming increasingly apparent that the natural process of making control more complex is proceeding at a faster rate than man's steps to simplify it.' There is always a danger that in the early stages of a new development a pattern of complication tends to become built in, and for this reason alone it is at the early periods of change and innovation that we should organize our strongest 'simplifying' forces.

Let us consider a few of today's simplifying trends. In the field discussed by Saunders, that of automation and computation, there is a slow but perceptible trend towards a broader understanding of these subjects among the many specialists involved. Automation can be either a very narrow or a very wide subject, but our purpose is to ensure that among the many specialist bodies involved in it the wider implications are realized while the narrower specialist activities are being developed.

With a similar purpose in mind, the recently formed Engineering Institutions Joint Council hopes to 'bring together' more effectively a number of professional bodies, so that a common policy rather than a number of separate and differing policies emerges in the broad area of engineering.

The result of the many mergers and take-over activities in Britain during recent years may, in one way, be regarded as a 'simplifying' activity. This will be so if strong attempts are made to produce a 'simplified' organization structure and a widely accepted common purpose among the various groups being brought together.

The Common Market should provide a simplified international structure, and may reduce many of the complexities that previously existed in European relationships. Here again, this will only be achieved if deliberate and early attempts are made to build in simplification. This will not occur automatically, in fact the more compromises which are agreed between nations the more complicated things become and remain.

Whatever the organizational, social, technological and economic trends towards simplification, and the possibility of a better understanding between specialists, there remains the need to provide ordinary men and women with a more 'simplified' outlook on life, and to do this those in authority must be able to understand how 'ordinary men' can be motivated. The word 'motivation' has dubious connections, and has often been applied to narrow sectional ends; but, like many other tools or discoveries, it has good as well as bad possibilities, and it is for us, the managers particularly, to ensure that motivation is applied towards a wider acceptance of the common purpose.

In Chapter 4 I discussed some current research into man as a subjective person. Many attempts are now being made to obtain a more 'simplified' and whole picture of him through research in a variety of ways. Unfortunately these activities, in their early stages, develop the same 'complicating' tendencies as others mentioned earlier. Cybernetics, for instance, should be concerned with a simplified understanding of the whole man, and should provide a meeting ground for many different specialists and a greater opportunity for them to achieve a common purpose. But a recent publication[1] left me with the impression that whatever the ultimate goal, the early stages of cybernetic integration complicate an already complicated picture.

In other 'social' fields, various small but significant attempts are being made to simplify attitudes and responses. For instance, the new pattern of road signs now appearing on motorways is good, and certainly simplifies the problem of finding the way ahead in a faster-moving car, a condition analogous to our current earthly journey! Books like *Plain Words*, and courses such as that offered by The Institute of Directors on Communications, help to show us the advantages of simplified semantics and, from it, better understanding.

What more can be done? Let us tabulate a number of activities which can play an important part in helping to create a more simplified outlook among managers and men. Some of these

[1] *Principles of Self-Organization.*

have already been discussed, but not necessarily with a special reference to simplification.

The need for Simplification

Like most problems, a wider recognition of the problem is the first vital step which, when taken, focusses greater attention on its solution. A greater number of managers must believe in the need to simplify the complexities which appear to be an inherent part of modern social and technological developments.

A recognition of this need encourages managers to provide adequate *counter-measures* to the almost inevitable complexities which tend to become built into new developments. There should be an 'equal and opposite' built-in demand for simplification, which should start at top management level.

The Encouragement of Holism

In Chapter 4 I discussed the need to visualize 'the whole concept', whether we are concerned with a particular technical project, a group of individuals, or one single individual. Let us not delude ourselves on the difficulties involved, particularly when we apply this concept to that most complicated of all things, a human being.

But progress is now being made from many points of the circumference, and managers must spend much more effort in endeavouring to provide a common meeting point; in more scientific language, they should endeavour to integrate the many into a composite, understandable 'whole'.[1]

In the field of organization I have, in this and in an earlier book, stressed the basic purpose of organization, analysed its basic factors and principles, and 'put it together' in a new form. In doing so I may be accused of making less comprehensive and more complicated something which most managers regard as a

[1] Incidentally, a mathematically based understanding of 'integration' should surely help to achieve this.

fairly simple thing. But many existing things are not understood because they are taken for granted, and this applies to man himself. We are a long way from understanding his full significance and possibilities, and to do this we need, first, to analyse him in much greater detail, which involves greater complexity, and, *in parallel* with this, attempt to integrate the new knowledge into a new concept, which is richer and more productive because of the deeper analysis on which it is based.

How can a manager put this concept into practical effect? First, he can encourage himself and his subordinates to 'think through' a problem, as some describe it, to look at problems 'in the round', as others describe it, or to cultivate 'holism', as I describe it. Again misquoting Donne, 'no problem is an island....'

Second, a manager can take more active steps than are usually taken to ensure that when a specialist project is commenced, a 'generalist' project begins as nearly as possible in parallel with it. Every change, discovery, or action taken in a narrow area has its effect upon and is affected by the broader environment, and both must receive adequate consideration. Too often the overall picture is, as I suggested earlier, 'like a patchwork quilt, full of little unrelated bits of change'.

Simplification Mechanics

Let us descend from wider conceptions such as 'holism' to more simple things. Managers who believe in simplification can improve the mechanics in many ways, ranging from more care in dictating a memo to the title of a new committee.

We should always remember that other people cannot be expected to know what is in our mind and, as I said earlier, a good communication must be understood, and not merely sent. Let us consider the preparation of a questionnaire, which is one of today's popular exercises. How often have you, a comparatively well-educated and intelligent manager, faced a particular question, and wondered what the questioner really wanted to know? No answer has value if the question itself is ambiguous.

Consider, too, another modern technique, the use of the double negative such as 'It is not improbable . . .' Do not assume that such phrases are used only by Civil Servants; in fact, the latter are usually clear and concise—they have to be with their masters! Double negatives are often used by a person who wants to play safe and hesitates to commit himself to the more direct statement, 'It is probable'. The double negative may be valuable as an intelligence test question, but its 'double talk' has no value in a simplified communication.

Another complicating device is the bracket, which with some writers is carried to extremes. Consider, for instance, this statement in a recent article: 'The Prime Minister was (and it should be realized that the circumstances were such as to create considerable doubts in the minds of many present, which showed itself in their reactions) anxious to demonstrate that . . .' Before this article concluded, several other bracketed asides of this nature were introduced, and together they destroyed the continuity and reduced the value of the writing. Brackets should be used sparingly, and with limited enclosures.

Rhythm is as important in management as it is in dancing. Consider, for instance, the layout of business reports which show comparisons between one period and another, or refer the reader back to another report. A rhythmic sequence or pattern should be followed which allows the reader to compare or collate information more easily. For instance, each monthly report on certain subjects should discuss these subjects in the same order, using the same layout as the preceding report, so that comparisons and conclusions are more easily made.

Any systems or devices which help to clarify and simplify paper-work on a manager's desk are valuable. They may range from the use of specially coloured paper for special correspondence or reports, to the provision of better management-by-exception methods. I discussed the latter fairly thoroughly in

Chapter 3 and would again stress the great value of an 'exceptional' report or a special piece of information to a busy manager. Management accountancy has unfortunately made little progress at desk level, even if its theory is now better understood. It is rare rather than normal for an accountant to spotlight in a simple manner the special trend which he discovers from a close examination of the mass of statistics. He is in a better position than the manager to spot these trends; too often he assumes that managerial enlightenment is directly related to the volume of statistics put on his desk. The reverse is the case, and a few well-chosen indicators are usually much more effective.

One advantage derived from ordering a computer is the inducement it gives to review the company's statistical communication pattern so that the new equipment is effectively introduced. It will usually be found during this review that many practices, reports, systems and statistics are capable of simplification even without installing a computer, and this sort of exercise emphasizes the value of an occasional jolt to the group which every good manager gives. Some British companies have used our approach to the Common Market as a challenge and achieved many *indirect* advantages as well as becoming better prepared for entry into it.

Perhaps I might close this short dissertation on simplification with a comment on simplified talking. I quoted earlier a proverb which explains the value of two ears. We often say things badly and even two ears cannot understand what is said. During the writing of this chapter I heard two lessons read in church by the vicar and curate respectively. Both were worthy gentlemen with a message to deliver, but I heard every word the vicar uttered, and only a few words of the curate's effort. This, oddly enough, became an example of 'series errors' which we discussed on page 192, because when the vicar delivered his sermon he used as text a quotation given previously in the *curate's* lesson. My understanding of the sermon was lessened by my ignorance of the curate's contribution.

I am much in favour of speech training, which has proved helpful in many cases. But better delivery is fully effective only if the substance of the talk is effective, and effective speech, like charity, begins at home, with greater managerial attention to its purpose, its substance, sequence and, not to be forgotten, its length. All these, *and* better delivery, help greatly to simplify communications and create wider understanding.

Another form of activity which has helped greatly to simplify many others is Work Study. It is rather depressing that since the pioneering work of Taylor we have, until recently, regarded the factory floor as the only field for its application. Bodies such as I.C.I. and The National Productivity Council have greatly helped to widen our knowledge of this tool and spread its application into agricultural and office areas. But relatively little Work Study has yet been done in managerial fields, or even in the simplification of communications, yet its opportunities are many and its possibilities even greater. It has, for instance, great opportunities for streamlining paper-work. Modern data processing appears to create rather than to eliminate paper, and when it is realized that the cost of using a form is usually over twenty times the cost of the form itself it becomes more obvious that to eliminate the form eliminates many other costs at the same time.

The growing interest in ergonomics has a close connection with Work Study, and together they can exercise a much greater influence on managerial subjects than anything done so far. It is as easy and productive to design the best Board-room agenda for best results as to design a new machine for better performance. It is as easy and valuable to design a better personal communication network as to improve the productive flow of a cylinder block through the factory. These and many similar things can be done if managers take full advantage of experience and skill already available, but not so far used 'completely'.

o

A Final Word on Communications

A reference to the course provided by The Institute of Directors shows us that subjects like public speaking, effective writing and running meetings are all considered as part of communications. I have discussed them briefly, or not at all, in this book, because they are well documented elsewhere, and because my intention is only to draw attention to those aspects of communications which are especially concerned with organization.

The subject of communications is one of great difficulty and importance. It is one which must be studied in theoretical depth in order to understand its full implications and possibilities. And yet it is a subject which must be understood in all its *simplicity*, with a full understanding of what we want it to achieve. There is a real danger that the theoretical complexity of the subject may blur the clear image of it that managers should have, and it is with this danger in mind that I have attempted, in this short section, to emphasize only the basic elements of communications. I hope that I have enabled managers to see its purpose more clearly, and that they will regard it not as an end in itself but as an important factor in the total organization structure.

A Restatement

(1) Communication is a means to an end, and opening up channels of communication does not necessarily improve management efficiency.

(2) The 'relationships' which can be formed between various members and sub-groups of members in a group are communication links or channels. It is important to realize how many of these channels exist, and how rapidly they increase with increased membership of the group.

(3) It is important also to recognize that (2) includes two-way channels which are essential for complete communication.

(4) Technological developments are encouraging more complex communication patterns through the more frequent need to cut across chains of command and other formal patterns.

(5) The linkage diagram has, in the communication field, a value equal to the organization chart in its field. It is not advisable to combine the two.

(6) Communication for Information or Instruction is probably the most important form. It is essential to remember that feed-back, or two-way communication, must be embodied in every information-giving system. Communication channels must be designed for giving and receiving.

(7) It is necessary to ensure that information giving or instruction channels are open to and from all members of a group. It becomes relatively easy to restrict communication undesirably, either by the action of various members or by poor design of the linkage network.

(8) The most appropriate linkage network depends on the complexity of the information or instruction to be given. Frequently in management groups the co-ordinating or leadership function must be clearly exercised if errors are quickly to be corrected and integration of ideas achieved. This requires special consideration of the linkage network to be used.

(9) At times a double-link network should be used which enables mutual direct communication to be established between a manager and those subordinates two stages junior to him.

(10) The rapid development of teaching machines will require us to study their effect on linkage networks. It is not desirable to reduce 'human links' too much, and we must work out a reasonable balance between teacher-oriented instruction and teaching-machine-oriented instruction. The latter may tend to produce too much cohesion.

(11) Communication for collaboration must ensure a complete understanding between all collaborators. If the communication linkage system involves 'passing on' information, considerable errors may develop which could be avoided by selecting another form of linkage.

(12) Effective collaboration improves control, which in good feed-back style attempts still further to improve collaboration. Linkage systems play an important part in both.

(13) It is easy to exclude individuals from the collaborative network, and managers must watch carefully both accidental and deliberate attempts to do this. Checks and balances can be designed into the network which help to minimize this possibility.

(14) Communication time is important, not only because it influences the effectiveness of communication, but also because, in general, the longer the time involved, the greater the costs. These should always be considered when designing the most appropriate linkage system.

(15) The delay factor is also important, and cases arise where 'relative' time is involved. In organizational affairs the order of communication may require that some members receive information before others. The series-parallel concept may be helpful when considering the best linkage system to be used under such circumstances.

(16) While communications must involve basically a link between individuals, and therefore becomes a social problem, the growth of mathematically based communication theory will surely help us to make a better scientific approach to the subject.

(17) Good communication requires a constant attention to simplification. A good manager must be interested in every form of simplification, particularly at periods of greater change, when 'complicating' forces are greatest.

(5) FUSION (COHESION)

This is the fifth of the important factors mentioned earlier, on page 131, and the first of the three 'synergic'[1] processes observed by Bakke. I said earlier that another researcher used the word 'cohesion', and perhaps both are appropriate. However, on the assumption that semantics are important we might agree that 'fusion' represents, in popular terms, the realization of a 'solid state', which is not compatible with a dynamic group. Cohesion may be a more suitable word, and I shall use it.

Earlier, on page 171, I explained why cohesion is desirable, and how it must always overcome (but by not too great a margin) the anti-cohesion forces which invariably are present. It has been stated that every person will continue to work effectively in a group when the inducements are greater than the contributions he is asked to make. March and Simon, in their work *Organizations*, propounded a theory of organizational equilibrium which presumably is achieved when the right degree of cohesion is reached. It postulates:

'(1) An organization is a system of inter-related social behaviour of a number of people whom we shall call the participants.

'(2) Each participant and each group of participants receive inducements from the organization; in return, they make contributions to the organization.

'(3) Each participant will continue in an organization only so long as inducements offered to him are as great or greater than the contribution he is asked to make.

'(4) The contributions provided by the various groups of participants are the sources from which the organization manufactures the inducements offered to participants.

'(5) Hence, an organization is solvent and will continue in existence only so long as the contributions provide enough inducements to draw forth these contributions.'

[1] 'Synergic'—working together.

It may be desirable to study cohesion by first looking at the forces which produce the *opposite* effect, that is, the anti-cohesion forces. What are they? First, we must surely say 'the individuals making up the group'. I showed earlier that most individuals are gregarious, and *want* to become members of groups, and this desire encourages them to act in a cohesive manner. But if we believe that the individual is the basic element of every group we must also agree that every individual has his own personality and characteristics, and is therefore 'different' from other individuals. There must therefore be as many internal divisions in a group as differences between the individuals in it, and if we refer to an earlier statement on page 145 that greater strength should be applied at points of greater strain we can, by analogy, state that the anti-cohesive possibilities created by divisions can be countered by the strength of the interdivisional links (including communication links), which 'hold' different and differing individuals together.

Our first and most important exercise in group or sub-group cohesion is to achieve cohesion between all the individuals within it. Further exercises in cohesion are attempts to ensure that these individuals, or sub-groups, *acting together*, work towards the common purpose of the group.

In his admirable book *The Anatomy of Work*, Georges Friedmann made the profound observation that millions of men are 'bigger than their jobs', and it follows that frustrations are likely to be bigger than satisfactions. Let us visualize the 'group purpose' as a container within which all the individuals exist. A cohesive situation is surely achieved when all the individuals fit snugly (that is, not too loosely or tightly) together within it. Too often this container is not big enough to provide adequate scope for the individuals within it, and consequently they are cramped, and an over-cohesive situation exists. The remedy is to adjust either the container or the individuals so that members of the group are fully utilized, and reasonable cohesion is achieved.

The Cohesion Implications of Technology

A major aspect of group cohesion is to be found in the term 'division of labour', on which Friedmann has written so well and which, particularly since Taylor, has exercised a considerable influence on organizational 'divisions'. It was Frederick W. Taylor (1856–1915) who first introduced division of labour in an industrial age, although it had been practised for centuries in a variety of other forms and communities. For instance, Herodotus (484–424 B.C.) wrote that 'the practice of medicine is so divided among the Egyptians that each physician is a healer of one disease and no more. All the country is full of physicians, some of the eye, some of the teeth, some of what pertains to the belly, and some of the hidden diseases.' More recently Sargant (page 92) also referred to early medical specialization, and to the advantages it has so far brought us.

I recall many discussions during my early days as a production engineer on the technical and social implications of the subdivision of work on the factory floor, and the limitations of skill, satisfaction and opportunity this gave to workpeople, so ably illustrated by Charlie Chaplin in *Modern Times*.

Some years ago conscious and recognizable efforts were made to halt and reverse this trend, and on the factory floor *product* production lines similar to those described in my earlier book *Management Principles* (page 120) appeared with greater frequency. But however much the desire exists to call a halt to the subdivision of labour it is probable that there is an even greater tendency today to create more scientific, technological and social specialist divisions; for instance, 'office' activities are now being subdivided more intensively through the introduction of data processing.

In an era of rapid change it is inevitable that more specialist activities will emerge. It is therefore more important to make greater attempts to integrate these specialists by better organization. Today, however, despite some attempts to 'put together what has become split asunder', the splits, gaps, or divisions are more noticeable than ever before and tend to weaken cohesion.

It seems important, then, to improve cohesion by (among other ways) controlling the number of divisions produced by specialist activities. It may well be that stronger efforts to reduce specialist divisions, in laboratories, workshops and offices, and on organization charts, will achieve better cohesion. It is also possible that more attention to the *grouping* of specialist activities, like the production groups mentioned earlier, will help cohesion by strengthening the 'shape' of the cohesive lines of mutual contact. We shall group more in accordance with the purpose for which the group is formed rather than the nature of the work.

Cohesion and Conformity

I referred earlier to 'shape', which is an important aspect of cohesion. If two surfaces 'conform' then presumably they cohese better, a statement soon proved if we attempt to glue together two pieces of broken pottery. It seems to follow that the degree of understanding or the amount of conformity between individual personalities in a group is a cohesive element. Klein in *The Study of Groups* has a chapter on 'Likes and Dislikes' which can, I believe, add to our understanding if we agree that there is a close relationship between likes, dislikes and conformity. She says: 'There is a close relationship between group norms and the sentiments of group members towards one another. . . . This process of evaluation in terms of norms will patently cause some to be rejected for the same reasons that others are admired. Schachter, in *Deviation, Rejection, and Communication* (1951), for instance, took sociometric ratings in a group in which discussions had taken place. Because of the discussions the members knew something of each other's viewpoint. Members who were perceived to hold views different from one's own were rejected, those who held the same views were rated highly on the sociometric scale.

Conformity to a particular norm brings popularity from those who also subscribe to this norm.'

One interesting comment is made which is not widely appreciated. 'The ideal personality is the one you would like to be.' Members evaluate each other in terms of an ideal personality, and not so much in terms of what they actually are, or think they are. This raises aspects of leadership which are important, and will be discussed later. In recent years we have often discussed the qualities of a leader, and it seems to be agreed that sheer technical skill is not enough, although, as has been said elsewhere, this can earn respect in the group. Similarly, popularity does not make a leader; I have, for instance, seen many cases where shop stewards were elected on a popularity basis and proved hopeless as leaders. In any case, popularity is easily and quickly variable, as politicians have found. But because men become more popular when they fit into the ideal standards of the group, so, by inference, the leader fits in more than others, and is likely to be the most popular personality available. He might well be, on this reasoning, the least suitable man for the job. I'm sure there is a flaw here somewhere!

One observer found that 'the most voluble members were also the most popular, and that members who spoke very little were regularly ranked low on the sociometric scale'. Some variations of this statement are discussed, and other experimenters have said that interaction does not necessarily lead to an increase in liking. Some of us would agree! This problem of dislike is more important in top management circles than it is in, say, factory groups, where men and women may quit the group fairly easily if they dislike others, or where, as we have sometimes witnessed, certain members of a group will force a person to leave it by methods which are frequently drastic. Sending a man to Coventry is one such method.

In management circles, however, it is less easy and perhaps less desirable for the group to lose members who incur dislike;

among other things the public-relations aspect must be considered. It is therefore more important to anticipate dislikes, and to take positive steps early enough to correct the trends, many of which arise from misunderstandings and lack of full information, which the 'personal audit' mentioned on page 77 would do much to correct.

Klein deals with 'pressure on the environment', a subject of great interest to top managers, whose real worth is often only exercised when emergencies arise. I won't quote the various sociological explanations mentioned in this section, but one quotation is worth mentioning: 'When survival becomes an urgent problem for the group, the system of control tends to change. Instead of control through the mutual liking of members, quite a different, less spontaneous, control comes about. Members are induced to obey other members by the reward that the latter have at their disposal. The more control of this kind is exercised, the less members like it, and the less the controlling members are liked. This state of affairs is characteristic of highly centralized groups in which peripheral members have little opportunity for participating in the decision-making process. And indeed, by assuming that those who exercise control enjoy doing so, we may see that the more stable and centralized the group, the sooner a state of urgency will be perceived and the more power will be assumed by central members.'

This is one of the many examples where, once a situation has gone off balance, the measures taken are likely to increase the off balance rather than correct it. In control engineering circles we refer to negative and positive feed-back. The former involves a mechanism, or system, which senses a changing situation, and applies 'negative' or reversing action to correct the situation. It's like turning the steering-wheel slightly to the left when your car drifts rightwards into the centre of the road. (This applies to roads where one drives on the *left* of course.) Positive feed-back means that when you see the car drifting, you panic, and turn the car even more rightwards (and wrongwards). The exercise of negative feed-back is important to the success of any system or group, but the success is even greater when norms can be defined; in other words, when it is known which particular part of the car should ideally be in which particular left-hand part of the road, and how much swing on either side of the norm is permitted before negative feed-back is applied.

What relationship exists between these 'off balance' situations and cohesion? Surely it is that 'cohesion' must itself be achieved by reasonable balance between opposing forces. If cohesion is weakened through personal or group difficulties it may, under 'positive feed-back', weaken still more, and bring about disintegration. 'Negative feed-back' will, however, provide the right corrective measures and maintain the group in balance. The actual *degree* of balance is achieved better if cohesive 'norms' are established; in other words, when it is known how much cohesion is regarded as 'reasonable'.

When pressure on individuals increases, dislikes may arise, and some comments are made by Lippitt, Lewin and White.[1] 'The *democratic* leader encouraged interaction between the boys, the *authoritarian* leader arranged the situation so that the boys were compelled to interact with him a good deal of the time. The interchange of information between the boys would, therefore, be greater in the former than in the latter group. Moreover, in the latter group the work was not chosen by the boys, and it is therefore reasonable to assume that they were less involved in the task than were the boys in the democratically-led group. The lack of information in the autocratically-led group, and their consequent indifference to the task, makes for an inflammable situation which might easily turn into a hostile one. This is, in fact, exactly what happens. Rapid changes in the composition of sub-groups are reported in the authoritarian group, as members attempt to gain status at each other's expense; and in the end, scape-goating

[1] *Patterns of aggressive behavior in experimentally created Social climates.*

is resorted to as the only way in which the necessary feeling of superiority can be gained. It will be remembered that the auto-cratically-led groups also took no interest in, or even expressed hostility toward, the product of their labour. This is obviously another way in which the hostility, generated by the pressure of the system imposed on them, may show itself.'

Here we see the differences in group conduct betweeen demo-cratic and authoritarian leaders, and on the whole they emphasize the points made earlier. It is easy to say, as, for instance, when we advocate a committee of one (oneself), to get a job done, that authoritarian methods are more efficient. The trouble with authority, however, is that it is likely to induce positive feed-back, and therefore to exercise even more authority, until it crashes. All power corrupts; absolute power is (to some people) abso-lutely delightful.

Consider Klein's Assumption 6: 'Let us assume control by one member of the group'.[1] 'When a man is perceived to be involving the group in actions uncongenial to it, his popularity is likely to suffer . . . even when it is for the group's own good.' In *Working papers on the theory of action*, Parsons, Bales and Shils said: 'We might tentatively advance the proposition that the traditional sociometric methods of determining "leaders" are appropriate only to situations where there is no specific and well-defined instrumental task. As soon as such a task is introduced there arises a demand for the performance of the new roles which the task creates. Initially, the best-liked man may perform these roles, but as time goes on, a dissociation takes place: either (1) someone else who can perform these new roles more successfully comes to the fore, or (2) the sociometric leader becomes a task leader, and ceases to be best-liked.'

Here we see the possibility of a frequent shift of power, likes, dislikes, performances and cohesion within the group; a situation I have often seen. This possibility explains the ephemeral nature

[1] *The Study of Groups.* Josephine Klein.

of leadership, and shows that, under different conditions, different leaders may emerge and be submerged. I have seen many companies where the need for different leadership has not been perceived until too late; the early growth of a company can, for instance, require quite different individuals and group organization from those required when the same company is in a more established state. This alone makes it necessary at regular intervals for the Board to assess itself and the company organization, in the light of changing circumstances. It should be emphasized that even if internal conditions do not appear to be changing, a company lives also in an external environment, and must examine external changes too, as a basis for internal organizational change. Common Market and other 'export' problems will intensify external changes and require more attention to internal cohesion.

Finally, a full understanding of cohesion must involve reconsideration of other group factors, some of which have been discussed earlier, and some which will be discussed later. It is a difficulty that the creation of a cohesive group involves a very delicate balance between a variety of forces, most of which are variable in themselves! Individuals *want* to be in a group, but equally, at times, individuals *do not* want to be in a group. Conformity may sometimes help cohesion, but sometimes creates too much of it and produces rigidity, which is cohesion carried too far. The latter state is as bad as, and in fact often worse than, too little cohesion.

One thing seems certain: cohesive balance cannot be maintained unless the group leader exercises constant vigilance and constant adjustment of many factors. Cohesion, like its big brother, organization, is a continuing process.

A Restatement

(1) The group must always possess enough cohesive force to overcome the inevitable anti-cohesive forces which exist. Too much cohesion can, however, equal conformity, and undesirable rigidity.

(2) In studying cohesion, it is desirable first to assess the anti-cohesive forces which exist. The first of these comprises each and every individual in the group. If we regard each individual as 'different' from another, he must create a division and therefore, potentially, an anti-cohesive force. The first and most important attempt to achieve cohesion is therefore to ensure that the individuals work together.

(3) One important way of achieving greater individual satisfaction is to realize that most men are 'bigger than their jobs'. Expanding individual satisfactions, therefore, helps both individuals and overall cohesion.

(4) At a time of rapid change, such as today, there is a strong tendency to create more specialists, which, unless compensating action is taken, weakens cohesion. It becomes necessary, therefore, to 'bring together' more effectively those who are 'split asunder'. Various technical and organizational methods exist.

(5) Cohesion and conformity have a close relationship, as too much of the former may produce the latter, which can be bad for the group. Leaders have a particularly important duty to avoid creating too much cohesion, and therefore conformity. This responsibility may often have to be exercised in avoiding situations where particular members incur dislike or tend to get frozen out of discussion. The nonconformist must have special consideration.

(6) In periods of emergency the cohesive balance may be disturbed, and conformity may increase. It provides an ideal example of positive feed-back, which is an undesirable state. It is therefore particularly important to maintain reasonable cohesion at periods of stress, when power may change and become misplaced.

(7) It is desirable to modify leadership and power conditions at intervals, as different group situations and tasks emerge. The principle of continuity must ensure that at regular

intervals the Board reassesses itself and the company organization. The need to do this may arise from internal or external causes.

(8) Because of constantly changing anti-cohesive and cohesive changes, in individuals and in groups, and in external conditions, 'cohesive balance cannot be maintained unless the group leader exercises constant vigilance and constant adjustment of many factors. Cohesion, like its big brother, organization, is a continuing process.'

7

The Structure of Groups: III
Group Direction and Leadership

(6) GROUP DIRECTION

I SAID earlier that a group lives in an external environment, and must continually adapt itself to external change, such as Britain is currently trying to do in relation to Europe and the Commonwealth. In *Human Behavior in Organizations*, Argyris tells us that a complete organizational theory 'will require that the organizational and environmental studies be interrelated'. In *The Study of Groups* Josephine Klein says that 'a group has to make continuous adjustments to the environment if it is to survive. When the environment changes the group has to change also. . . .' She goes on to say: 'All the consequences that may conceivably be relevant to the change which the group faces, if it is to avert the danger to its survival, must be brought into the open, and their likelihood and relative priority evaluated. The more information is available, and the more freely it travels in the group, the better the task can be performed. The more links there are between members, the shorter the diameter is likely to be, and the more efficient the spread of information. Moreover, the more links there are, the less likely the group is to suffer from the consequences of differentiation between members. Such freedom of interaction also corrects distortions in judgement and aids the correction of errors in the group.

'We have seen in how many ways free communication in the

group is threatened. When, for instance, the pressure of the environment is suddenly so great that the problems of survival become most urgent, there may be no opportunity to canvass opinion in this free way. We have seen how consciousness of status operates against free communication. The lower-status members speak less and tend to make fewer suggestions; they influence the action process passively, by approval and disapproval "rather than by positive advocacy of a policy". Peripheral or lower-status members are less likely to learn. They tend to sit back and let the central members do their thinking for them. (This is what made it so difficult for the highly-organized star group to adjust to changing conditions when the pure colour marbles were exchanged for cloudy ones.)

'Not only differences in status, but any kind of routinization which influences members to delay in communicating information will have a bad effect. We know that groups with a leader show less equal participation than groups without a leader. The less differentiation between members, therefore, the better, but if differentiation is necessarily inevitable, it is important to stick to a routine, for peripheral members have been trained not to use their initiative. Where the organization of the group is rigid, changes in the routine of the group endanger its survival. Lastly, when there are sub-groups loosely connected with the main group the spread of information in the network is delayed. In fact, the less differentiation in the group, the better. If there are leaders in the group, they must see to it that they are sure that they are being followed by the members. They must ensure some kind of feedback.'

The inference is, clearly, that speed of adaptation to changing environment is very important, which can only be achieved if cohesion does not equal rigidity. Let us refer back to a previous discussion on adaptation, where we used the analogy of structural design.[1] Every structural designer provides for flexibility to meet

[1] *Management Principles*, page 30.

P

'winds of change', and I quoted the examples of the B.B.C. aerial at Crystal Palace, and the wing-tips of a jet airliner to illustrate this point. The structural bridge design illustrated on page 145 is an exercise in adaptation, that is, the designer builds added strength into the structure at the points where added strains are likely to occur, so that adaptation and not fracture occurs.

An organization group structure is subject to special *environmental* as well as to internal strains, and the strengthening members must be capable of quick adaptation to these external strains. For instance, a company finds an urgent need to anticipate an international trend which would, if ignored, reduce its exports considerably. So many external environmental forces bear upon a company today that an organizational 'commando' function might, with advantage, be provided, which would apply strengthening members as, when, and where required. Perhaps it could be named 'The Department of Changing Environment'![1]

One important aspect of adaptation is the need to establish standards against which to measure and apply it; that is, to provide measuring-sticks which tell managers where the group stands, and what it must do in order to achieve its plans. There are, of course, many indices available to managers who wish to know where they are, in relation to other groups, or to the national or international environment. The success of the B.I.M.'s inter-firm comparison techniques is a healthy sign, and I hope that more managers will want to know 'where they are' as an inducement to do better.

But many 'adaptive' measurements are required, and the more difficult ones are likely to be qualitative rather than quantitative, organizational rather than technical and economic.

Let us consider the problem of placing an individual into a new group, thus subjecting him, and the group, to new forces. This is a very important consideration, not only in organizational but in management selection work. I said earlier that a man failing

[1] A large American Company has recently appointed a Director of Environmental Studies.

in one group may be a success in another—and vice versa. I personally know how a conflict of norms may result in serious incompatibility.

The norms of other people, or of the group itself, can affect individuals in various ways. We all know of the pace-setter, who inspires us to emulate him; occasionally, in Union circles, he causes other group members to resent him. We recognize a personal characteristic or norm in a colleague which invokes admiration and response; we recognize the company spirit, its purpose, or its tradition, all of which are (or can be) maintained by the creation of certain norms. Altogether, there are many norms which can raise or lower the attitudes and standards of members and groups. 'Travis[1] studied the effect of a small audience on the performance of a simple hand-eye co-ordination task. The subject had to touch a spot on a moving target with a rod. He knew nothing of the standards of the audience, the audience did not communicate with the subject. It was simply present. The subject had had previous trials with his task and had reached a stage where his performance was not improving with further practice. Under the relatively mild stimulus of the audience, eighteen out of the twenty-two subjects improved on their best previous scores. If success is valued, the opportunity to demonstrate one's skill acts as a stimulus to good performance.'

The point is noted that in most cases an individual will raise his standards more frequently where he can more easily be seen to be successful. How very natural! This may have been in the minds of office managers when they threw out partitions in favour of large open offices, although the cynics would say that the main reason was to help supervision!

The setting and achievement of group norms is very important in selection and training work, and as a manager must work largely with groups, he should be selected and trained, largely, in a group environment. Some external candidates for managerial

[1] *The Effect of a Small Audience on Hand-Eye Co-ordination.* L. E. Travis.

jobs are very quick at assessing what they think the company wants, and interviewers can easily get taken in by candidates who sniff prevailing winds and alter course skilfully to suit. On the other hand, an interviewer must calculate carefully the risks involved in selecting a person whose norms, as far as they can be judged, are very dissimilar to those of the group in which he will work. It is, however, occasionally a worthwhile calculated risk, because there is a tendency today, ably documented by such books as *Organization Man*, for senior managers to seek too much conformity to established norms. The worst place to seek it is among younger managers.

Miss Klein makes a number of interesting observations on other research finds on this subject. Dashiell[1] showed that rivalry increases speed as much as an audience of onlookers does. If the performer were as much aware of his accuracy as of his speed he would improve that aspect as well. That this is a justifiable hypothesis is shown by Hurlock's[2] (1927) experiment in which an arithmetic class improved throughout the week until it was 40 per cent above the control group speed, and, unlike Dashiell's group, improved somewhat in accuracy as well. Speed the children could judge for themselves; it improved remarkably. Accuracy was brought into their situation because the results of one test were made known before the next, but because it was not so directly present in their minds at the time of performance it was rather less influential.

We are told that 'to belong to a group means to conform to its values and that to seek for membership obliges the individual to solicit approval by such conformity. The greater the individual's knowledge of the group, the more precise the direction his search for approval will take. . . . After all, what the individual wants is the appreciation of those he values; for this reason he will conform to their expectations. If they don't work

[1] *An Experimental Analysis of some Group Effects.* J. F. Dashiell.
[2] *The use of Group rivalry as an Incentive.* E. B. Hurlock.

hard, why should he? . . . The striving for success, for distinguished performance, may thus be inhibited by the need to establish membership, and the aspiring member will be careful to behave like the other members of the group. Since it is easier to conform to observed behaviour than to infer from current practices what the ideal may be, the behaviour of the new member will be regulated by the *average* performance of the group, which may or may not be the *ideal*. His ignorance will lead him to conform to the most easily observed behaviour rather than to that which is more clearly ideal, and therefore, less frequently observed. In this way, one may account for the curious way in which extremes in individual behaviour "level out" in the group, and become less marked.' Georgopoulos (1957) says that 'for the study of organizational effectiveness in large-scale organization, the group, and not the individual performer, is the proper unit of research, and analysis'. He found that the variability between groups was nearly six times as much as the variability of the workers in groups. Miltzer (1956) came to similar conclusions, and during the war I found similar wide variations between groups. It was also, incidentally, found by a post-war Allied inspection party to have existed in Germany at the same time.

One conclusion reached after all this evidence is that 'the striving for extreme scores is characteristic of men ignorant of the norms of the group, or isolated from the group'. This is well documented in sociological literature under the heading of *anomie*. 'When a man can place himself in a group and introject its values, he will be able to regulate his behaviour by what is normal for that group. He will strive to do well in the role allotted to him.'

How can we apply these conclusions to management groups? It certainly seems to point, again perhaps obviously, to several conclusions:

(1) The higher the group norms, the higher will be individual performances.

(2) Individuals tend to conform to the norms of the group.
(3) Extreme scores, performances, or attitudes are ultimately reduced more closely to the norms of the group.
(4) The larger the group, the greater the conformity, and presumably, the less chance of 'marginal' contributions by individuals.

A good deal of work has been done which draws attention to the *adverse* effects a group may have on an individual. In many cases, he can assess, and if necessary regulate, his performance by physical comparisons, and he, and the group, have the dual satisfaction of keeping pace with each other, therefore maintaining not only work norms, but morale norms too.[1] 'Sometimes, however, the physical frame of reference is inadequate and ambiguous. When this is so, the individual can perceive the situation in a number of different ways, and his perception will be much influenced by his own needs, moods and expectations. When the individual lacks knowledge of fact, and is called upon to act, he will seize whatever hints he can elicit from the environment, physical or social. Where his only source of knowledge is the opinion of others, he can use only information thus obtained, and by this means he may take for fact what is no more than concensus of opinion. In such a situation, the power of the group over the individual is most marked. Two factors, therefore, determine the influence of the groups: the amount of information the individual has at his disposal, independently of the group, and the psychological reality or pressure from the group. Many (research) workers have produced situations in which the individual's frame of reference is very inadequate. Therefore, any information which will structure the situation is likely to have a very great influence on the individual.

'Group pressure sometimes helps an individual to reach a correct solution, sometimes it confirms him in a wrong one. The influence

[1] *The Study of Groups.* Josephine Klein.

of a group may be even more marked . . . it may persuade a man to doubt the evidence of his own senses. The individual adjusts himself to the group, not only by conscious conformity, but also by inhibiting, sometimes consciously, sometimes unconsciously, his usual responses so as not to be too far removed from the average group responses. The intensity of the pressure of the group, and the depth in the level of consciousness at which this pressure is experienced, is perhaps best illustrated in an experiment by Asch[1] (1951). All but one of his subjects in a group were instructed to make deliberate mistakes in judging the relative lengths of bundles of sticks. The poor naive subject becomes more and more impressed by his inability to perceive what the others in the groups see. In the end, he tends to make the same "mistakes" as the others. There are, apparently, three types of psychological process underlying this behaviour. Some subjects really came to perceive the shorter sticks as longer. Others thought they must be subject to some kind of an optical illusion, which they sought to compensate for. Others, again, were sure that they were right, and the other members of the group were wrong, but they felt too diffident to persist in the face of such numbers. Similarly, Allport[2] (1920) reports that estimates of weights are wider in range when individuals are tested in isolation than when they are in the company of others; smells from a bottle are also apparently never quite so disgusting or quite so exquisite when they are reported on in a group.'

Perhaps there is too much emphasis here on 'poor naive subjects' who surely are never found in management circles! It does, however, put even more emphasis on the importance of group norms, and, surely, gives further support to the views I expressed earlier on the primary importance of group purpose as a norm. The higher this is set, maintained, and the more widely known it is, the higher is the performance of the individuals. It might be

[1] 'Groups, Leadership and Men'.
[2] *The Influence of the Group upon Association and Thought*. F. H. Allport.

appropriate here, once again, to say that the group purpose will defeat its own ends if it becomes too detailed, and therefore restrictive. As Robert Dubin says in *Stability of Human Organizations*: 'overspecification of an individual task, through detailed programming by the organization, may tend to support individual job change and innovations. Overspecification of a task for those performing it, implies a "best way" for carrying the task out that is organizationally determined and legitimized. . . . An obvious solution (to the individual) is restriction of output to minimum accepted levels.' I referred earlier to the overspecification of individual tasks, and Dubin's remarks emphasize that this leads to restricted output by individuals, and ultimately to a reduction in group performance.

It has been shown, in this discussion on norms, that it is all too easy for a group to inhibit a member, and vice versa. Every group should, in its basic purpose, its organization and its practice, make more, rather than less, provision and opportunity for exceptional men. The latter may well create exceptional groups, and higher norms.

Perhaps we can sum up this section on group direction by re-emphasizing the importance of rapid adaptation to a changing external environment, and the need for more comprehensive standards of performance and comparison so that the group knows where it is, and how and when it must adapt itself.

Adaptation requires a flexible structure within which must be provided the capacity quickly to meet new and unexpected strains and stresses. This can be accomplished in a variety of ways, but in view of the rapidly changing environmental conditions experienced today, specialist attention to adaptation may well be justified as a regular functional task.

In order to measure the position of a group in relation to its environment, a comprehensive set of comparisons is required. These comparisons will include those available to groups from external sources, such as financial, economic and political indices although other less tangible but equally important measurements must be made to assess a group's strength, and its rate of change. These measurements involve the setting up of a variety of 'norms', which play an important part in maintaining individual and group strength and providing an 'external' measure of group progress.

A Restatement

(1) 'A group has to make continuous adjustments to the environment if it is to survive.' In a period of rapid change, such as today, every group must constantly consider how external changes, such as the Common Market, may require it to change its structure.

(2) In particular, speed of adaptation to changing environment is important, which can be achieved better if cohesion does not equal rigidity.

(3) The ability to adjust itself to external change is increased by the group's *internal* efficiency, including those factors already discussed. It may be desirable to provide special indicators for early warning.

(4) These indicators require managers to establish standards against which they measure external and internal changes. The B.I.M. inter-firm comparisons provide one excellent example.

(5) These indicators are often considered under the heading 'Norms', and a number of interesting researches have been made in this field. In particular the following points are made.

   (a) 'The opportunity to demonstrate one's skill acts as a stimulus to good performance.' An individual will usually raise his sights where he can be seen to be successful.

   (b) The norms of a group should be known to those concerned with the selection of individuals to it. It is often worth while taking a calculated risk in selecting someone, particularly a younger manager who may not necessarily conform.

(c) It is likely that too much conformity to group norms by its members will result in lower performances.

(d) The variation between different *groups* in the performance of a certain task may vary by as much as six to one, and is much greater than the variation between individual workers under similar conditions. This emphasizes the importance of setting high group norms, and ensuring that they are widely known and regularly assessed.

(e) The larger the group, the greater the difficulty of ensuring that all members are aware of the group norms. Poor performance probably arises more from ignorance of what is expected of the individual than from any inherent disability or unwillingness on his part.

(f) The large group also encourages individuals to conform more closely to 'average' performances; output becomes restricted to 'minimum accepted levels'. This leads, in turn, to a further lowering of group performance.

(6) Finally, it is worth restating that, in order to adapt itself adequately to a changing environment, the group needs

(a) Comprehensive standards of performance and comparison, which enable it to assess itself internally and externally.

(b) A flexible structure which can quickly adapt itself to new strains and stresses.

(7) LEADERSHIP WITHIN THE GROUP (DECISION MAKING)

Here, finally, we come to leadership, which is responsible for giving dynamic co-ordinated life to the group as a whole, and ensuring that, like the automobile quoted earlier, the group moves onwards in its external environment towards a planned goal.

The term 'leadership' is one of the most used and mis-used words in our language. It is essentially a 'U' word in the Mitford vocabulary, and most of us would rather be described as a 'leader' than as (say) a successful manager. Unfortunately the term 'leadership' does not mean the same thing to all men, and there is, for instance, likely to be a wide divergence between the validity of its application to the Earl of Lucan, who led his soldiers into shot and shell during the charge of the Light Brigade, and the shop steward who leads his mates out on unofficial strike. Each could be described as a leader, but emotional overtones and class divisions prevent a wide acceptance of common characteristics in these two individuals.

Is there an agreed definition of leadership? We have a wide choice, and I will quote only a few here; but first I give you my own, which, as this is my book, seems a justifiable decision. *A leader, to me, is someone who is assessed by his followers to be one who is more often right than wrong.*

Let us consider the two characters I have just mentioned. You may wonder why I chose two such diverse examples to open this section. I have three reasons: first, there is a wide time gap between the Earl of Lucan and today's shop steward, which *might* illustrate changing concepts of leadership over the years; second, there is a considerable difference in the spheres of activity; and third, one example was 'official' and the other 'unofficial'.

'Theirs not to reason why.' I wonder whether Lucan's soldiers at Balaclava reasonably considered his decision. It was fairly certain that a situation did not exist then which prompted another General, at another time, to say that 'the men would follow their junior officers anywhere—just out of curiosity'. It is pretty certain that at least two things were dominant in the Brigade's mind at that moment of time. One was, undoubtedly, a strong sense of group tradition and pride, that long-inculcated strength which, like adrenalin injected into the bloodstream, calls up at moments of stress and strain a greater strength than that normally used by the group, and makes it temporarily stronger than the sum of its parts. There was, too, one assumes, confidence in the commander, based on personal knowledge of his qualities and of the 'rightness' of many of his previous decisions.

In a more mundane and rather more complicated way these two 'attitudes' can be present among a body of unofficial strikers, which can cause them to remain in loyal cohesion for (occasionally) long periods. They, too, are held together by a traditional bond of loyalty, in this case towards their Union, which, to large numbers of working people, is a source of hope and help more permanent than the company in which they temporarily happen to be working. The fact that their particular Union sometimes appeared to let them down served only to consolidate their loyalty to their own work (or strike) group.

What about the 'personal' leadership in an unofficial strike? In most cases the strike leader is not selected, trained, or cast for leadership, as the Earl of Lucan was in *his* setting. One forms the impression that strike leadership is expressed largely through the existence of a strong *group* cohesive force, which does not require strong 'personal' control. The leader becomes very much a 'leader among equals', and his personal acceptance by the group is directly related to the degree of support he gives to that group's traditional attitudes. This is a situation which is quite appropriate today where the 'law of the institution' plays, relatively, a greater part in total leadership. Today's leader is, on the whole, more likely to direct from 'behind', or at least to rely more upon an acceptance by the group of what he *stands* for rather than, largely, what *he is*.

Yet it would be a grave mistake to carry this argument too far. For instance, I have seen many very ordinary shop stewards, when faced by a crisis, become good leaders. At the opposite end of the scale, we witnessed, years ago, the expansion of leadership qualities in Harry S. Truman, when he was suddenly called upon to become President of the United States. Someone once said that while it is difficult to put a man into a rocket it is even more difficult to put a 'rocket' into a man. History records many cases where environmental conditions help to develop that greater internal capacity which we often call leadership.

Leadership is a continuous process, and while a 'leadership situation' may arise largely through external and impersonal causes, it is almost inevitable that personal leadership will soon be required, and be found. Differing conditions may well create changes of leadership, official *and* unofficial.

What have these two cases taught us which are worthy of more general application? I suggest four things:

(1) Leadership requires a personal element. A 'personal' leader is not always identifiable in the early stages of a situation, but such a leader will inevitably emerge. It is generally best that he should have been appropriately selected, trained and be identifiable as a leader *before* rather than after difficulties arise.

(2) The leader is likely in any given situation to be someone whose past record encourages confidence in his 'rightness'.

(3) Leadership can only be complete when the leader's decision is followed by the decisions of others to accept it. It is similar to a complete communication, in the sense that something said is only effective if it is *heard and accepted*.

(4) Every leader is reinforced by a 'group' contribution, which is compounded of many intangibles. It is the 'additive' which ensures that the whole group in a given situation becomes greater than the sum of its parts. The most effective leader maximizes personal *and* group contributions.

Let us discuss group leadership in greater detail under each of these four headings.

(1) *The 'personal' element of leadership*

In the 'Seventh Elbourne Memorial Lecture', reported in *The Manager*, January 1962, Viscount Slim said that 'leadership is a very personal thing; it is', he said, 'the projection of personality'. The aim, according to this wise and distinguished leader in various spheres, is 'to make this leadership from the top real, recognized, and effective throughout the organization. However neat the diagrams of management and communication look on paper, they will have failed if they do not do this.' His thoughts are put in their most concise form when he says that leadership means saying 'Come on', and not 'Go on'.

What is involved in 'Come on'? Surely two important requirements. First, that the leader is recognized by the majority *as a person*, and second, that at the critical periods of leadership he is *there*, and is not, like the Duke of Plaza-Toro, leading his army from behind.

Let us concentrate for a moment on the first requirements, 'to be recognized'. If leaders devote enough time to 'individual' cases and contacts, such as we discussed in Chapter 3, this, I believe, is *the* most effective form of recognition. Unfortunately, leaders today find it more convenient and often less embarrassing to be seen from a platform, recognized by a photograph, or heard over a loudspeaker. These are certainly attempts to achieve mass communication and recognition, but they are usually superficial. Real recognition requires face-to-face contact as frequently and widely as possible, and it is surprising and gratifying to realize how effectively *one* individual, having met a leader, will pass on to his colleagues the positive features of such a contact. The initial communication becomes multi-dimensional in its effect.

The second requirement, 'to be there', is more difficult to achieve, even for generals, who have long since given up leading at the head of a calvary charge. But surely this form of activity is too literal an interpretation of 'being there', and the purpose can, in most cases today, be achieved by being identified as frequently as possible with individual and group activities, such as General Montgomery did on occasions. This can be done in many ways, not least by reducing the magnetism of 'Head Office' and conducting more affairs in the branches or subsidiary units, even on the factory floor. Some companies conduct their Annual General Meeting in one of their 'working units', such as a branch factory, or a ship. Others go as far as possible to the more impersonal (and wrong) extreme by using London hotel facilities. 'Being there' means, in simple terms, being recognized around the periphery of the group as well as at the centre.

(2) *The Leader is shown to be more often right than wrong*

Being proved 'right' is not always easy, because the circumstances surrounding a particular decision are not always easy to re-create when the dust of the battle has died down. It may then be very difficult to agree on 'who decided what'.

I said earlier that many 'personal' problems remained unsolved because the *intention* was not clear, often because the 'key points' were not sufficiently brought out in discussion, and the so-called 'decisions' were not adequate or fully recognized by the person(s) with a problem. Lord Slim had something important to say which bears on this situation: 'I suppose', he said, 'dozens of operative orders have been issued in my name, but I doubt if I ever wrote one myself. . . . *But I always wrote one paragraph, usually the shortest, myself, the intention paragraph. Then there should be no mistake about what I wanted to do.*' (My italics.)

There should be no misunderstanding within the group about the leader's objective, and if this is understood by members of the group it becomes possible afterwards to evaluate the success, or otherwise, of a task. This evaluation should be discussed between the leader and his appropriate colleagues, and used as a basis for improving future decisions, and (one hopes) establishing the leader more securely as 'one who is more often right than wrong'.

(3) *Leadership involves decisions and acceptance of decisions*

I know someone whose husband is a political leader, which means that she has to sit through many speeches. She claims an ability to present to the audience a countenance which displays a rapt interest in every word spoken, while, in fact, she is not really hearing more than a few words. Her thoughts are on other things! I wonder how many spoken words are heard and understood by the average listener? I recall some years ago lecturing to the managers of a large insurance company at Oxford, and on this occasion I used a technique which involved, early in the lecture, asking individual members of the audience, *by name*, their views on a particular aspect of my subject. This ensured really first-class listening! One person, who, incidentally, I did not call on, told me afterwards that he had intended to use my lecture as an opportunity for him to sit back and think about his own lecture the following day. My technique spoilt all that!

These two examples emphasize how little of what is said may be heard. Even less may be understood. If we apply this possibility to decisions we realize readily that what tele-communication engineers call 'noise' often reduces the full impact of a leader on members of his group, with the usual unsatisfactory results.

What can we do about this situation? First, a leader must have something to say. This sounds obvious, but is not always realized. Second, he must say it in the most simple, direct manner, which is very difficult for most managers to achieve. I referred earlier, on page 206, to the need for simplifying our approach to many problems, and a good income can be made by anyone able and willing to remove the unnecessary complications from a variety of important decisions, lectures, statements, documents, etc. He will never lack opportunities.

Third, every effort should be made to ensure that there is an adequate understanding of the purpose behind the leader's decision. If the 'intention' is clear, good results are more likely to follow.

Various research workers have made what may seem the obvious point, that the 'attitude' of a leader to his subordinates influences greatly their confidence in that leader, and creates a greater interest in his requirements and goals by those subordinates. Lickert, for instance, says:[1] 'Basically, the supervision of the work group with favourable attitudes thinks of employees as human beings rather than just as persons to get the work done. Consistently, in study after study, the data shows that treating people as "human beings" rather than "cogs in a machine" is a variable highly related to the attitudes and motivation of the subordinate at every level in the organization. The extent to which the superior conveys to the subordinates a feeling of confidence in him, and an interest in his on-the-job and off-the-job problems, exercises a major influence upon the attitudes and performance goals of the subordinate.'

Lickert explains later that there is in each of us a strong need to satisfy a desire for a sense of personal worth. Each of us seeks to satisfy this desire primarily by the response we get from the people we are close to, in whom we are interested, and whose approval and support we are eager to have. 'The face-to-face groups with whom we spend the bulk of our time are, consequently, the most important to us.'

Another aspect of the leader/subordinate relationship is brought out by various researchers. Put briefly, it is that unreasonable pressure by a superior for better performance by subordinates always creates in them a low level of confidence and trust in their superior. It is easy to visualize this situation arising, and the possibility that 'positive feed-back', that is, even *more* pressure,

[1] *A Motivation Approach to a Modified Theory of Organization and Management.* Rensis Lickert.

Q

will create even *less* confidence, and usually even less response, by subordinates.

This situation has a particular significance to inter-management relationships. Top managers, by putting extra pressure on, say, foremen, may easily cause the latter to behave in a manner which produces even less satisfactory results in the long run, even if short-term improvements are achieved.

These possibilities are of fundamental importance to managers. Most of us would protest if told that we did not treat people as human beings. But many managers, through the pressure of circumstances, often must decide deliberately to adopt an organizational solution at the expense of *some* individuals. Every manager has an inescapable duty to consider the greatest good for the greatest number, but in doing this he will, if he is a good manager, endeavour to find time for personal consideration of the individual 'cogs' who may be adversely affected by these organizational changes and whose attitudes may affect the majority.

We appear to reach the conclusion that the good leader will help to create the greatest confidence in himself and his decisions if he constantly remembers two things: first, to decide what is the best overall solution for the group as a whole, and second, to take adequate time out, as we discussed in Chapter 3, for personal consideration of the 'individual' problems created.

A few words are desirable on the attitude of subordinates to the group task, goal, or objective. Many managers do not believe as fully as they should that subordinates have, or can be encouraged to have, an interest in wider company objectives beyond their own individual jobs. I have found, through long experience of joint consultation, that many subordinates, down to the shop floor level, have a real interest in company or group tasks. It flatters them when they are shown what the 'company' is trying to do, and this encourages their participation. It encourages them also to participate more enthusiastically in the group's attainment, and it stimulates constructive suggestions. The exercises required to explain company objectives to subordinates provide yet another opportunity for a manager to achieve face-to-face contact with a greater variety of people in the group and to stimulate their 'desire for a sense of personal worth'.

(4) *Personal leadership should be reinforced by organizational contributions*

We discussed earlier the need to maximize various forces, so that their 'resultant' is at its strongest. Let us consider a simple vector diagram, Fig. 18, where two forces A and B are applied, varying in amount and angle of application. The 'resultant' in terms of force *and* direction is R.

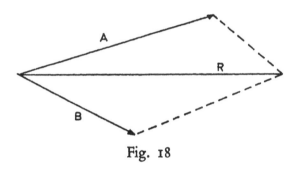

Fig. 18

We must remember that in organizational as in other spheres there are negative as well as positive forces, and in Chapter 6 we saw that the 'fusion' forces must be strong enough to counteract the tendency towards 'diffusion'; put in other words, the centripetal forces must overcome the centrifugal tendency to disintegrate the structure. The leader must understand these positive and negative forces which bear upon the group from a variety of directions, and it is this knowledge, and the ability to use it, which *adds* to the personal stature of a good leader. It is the additive which makes the exceptional man; the organizational skill which supplements the personal qualities.

There are many forces, positive and negative, which must be evaluated and allowed for in maximizing the resultant *positive* or cohesive force. It is obvious that group size, shape, structure, form, cohesion and communications, in fact all the factors listed on page 131, must be brought into the total evaluation, and play their parts in creating a satisfactory structure. It is not easy to measure these intangible forces against accepted norms, and to draw a vector diagram with anything like the precision available to engineers. This difficulty emphasizes how much research is still needed to provide leaders, or managers, with more precise tools for measuring total structural effectiveness.

Some Research Work on Leadership

In the heading to this section I included the term 'Decision Making', and it is appropriate here to emphasize the strong connection which I believe exists between the leader and the decision-maker. It seems easy to justify the statement that the greatest, and possibly the only important, function of leadership is an ability to make decisions which are more often right than wrong.

Much study has been given to 'decision-making', and later in this section I shall discuss one aspect of it more fully. I merely wish, at this point, to explain why I included the term within the broader term 'leadership', and to emphasize the relationship. Together, the terms have attracted much research attention, although it is difficult to extract from the literature much that is of *direct* value to a manager. With most research work in sociology or group dynamics one has to dig and sift fairly thoroughly through a large mound of information.

It seems important to be clear about what might be called the 'bases' of leadership, by which I mean the authority on which leadership is based. I referred on page 236 to situations where leadership was either 'personal' or 'institutional'. But another leadership 'base' is functional skill, which is discussed in *The Study of Groups* by Klein, who prefaces her remarks by defining leadership itself. She believes it is 'the ability to elicit from others a desired response'. She describes 'groups in which each member had authority; one could elicit from others the response one desired when others recognized that one knew more about the problem than they did. Such a member's authority is *functional*. He achieves it by virtue of skill in specific situations where his skill is in demand, *and it is because he is an expert* that he is given this authority.'

Later she considers how it may 'come about that this authority rests on other than functional considerations. In such groups *status* is ascribed to a man because he is that *particular* man and no other, because he is Joe himself. Joe will be able to use his authority *diffusely* in many situations; it is not specific to certain problems. In such groups, the same members tend to be always in authority.'

In examining the divorce of leadership from skill Klein attempts to show 'in each case (a) how this communication structure becomes a permanent structure, and (b) how status conditions become attached to it'. The case research studies are very interesting, and their parallels can be visualized by any manager.

Altogether, three varying group conditions are found:

(1) Groups where differentiation and therefore leadership is based on the overt use of force, or the threat of it;
(2) Groups that are differentiated by functional authority, where leadership is vested in the man recognized as best able to perform the task;
(3) Groups differentiated by status authority, where one man leads regardless of the situation in the group.

It is suggested that (1) is rarely met with in the human world; it is, however, stated that 'linear hierarchies based on overt dominance become more rare as members of groups become capable of a greater variety of activities, and as each member of the group develops his own distinctive skills'. Perhaps this might be borne in mind by those who feel (not always correctly) that 'leadership by domination' is carried too far in their own company. One feels justified in saying that the amount of domination is in inverse ratio to the development of the individuals in the group. Under-developed individuals please note!

We are really more interested in groups (2) and (3); what have researchers to tell us about them? Mary Parker Follett informed us that we are becoming a nation of experts, and 'the man who seeks to become a leader is advised to "forget your personality and learn your job". Groups of people work best when they know themselves to be skilled in recognizing the requirements—almost the logic—of the situation.' Many would say 'Amen' were it not for the fact that this sounds too much of an ideal.

In another contribution Miss Follett says: 'Select and train the best individual experts, place before them the "purpose" of the group, and the precise task to be achieved. At the same time make certain that each member knows enough of his fellow members to recognize that they are skilled in their jobs as he is in his.' It's certainly worth while trying, but something is still missing. What is it? Surely the missing requirement is control, or, in her terms, co-ordination, and Miss Klein goes on to say: 'There must be personnel who are skilled at obtaining co-ordinated effort. This is the true function of the manager, and no other kind of control can be justified.' Miss Follett herself says 'the degree of co-relation is the measure of control' and it is worth while quoting her at length: 'The contributors of the *Journal of Social Issues* (1948) in a symposium on the "Dynamics of the Discussion Group" worked and thought habitually in terms of the distribution of group functions, or roles, among the members, and not in terms of specific leadership behavior.' Thus:

'The usual procedure in studies on leadership has been to select certain personality attributes and to attempt to relate them to success or lack of success in known leaders. Implicit in most of this research is the belief that the qualitative components which make for effective leadership are invariant with respect to the situation in which the leadership function is exercised. To the extent that such studies have overlooked the fact that leadership is a complex function of many inter-dependent variables, they have not been fruitful. Leadership behavior occurs in quite a variety of situations and is determined, in no small measure, by the nature of the particular environment in which the leader perceives himself as functioning as well as by the characteristics of the person who is doing the leading.'

This says in its particular way what we have been saying in management selection circles. We are steadily retreating from the 'ideal leader', with a long list of admirable qualities, to 'the man of the particular situation', and to the recognition of a certain amount of fluidity in leadership, which will vary with the environment *and the specific task.*

But within every group *at any one time* there should be a recognized leader situation, and it seems generally, and perhaps obviously, to be agreed by researchers that groups with a leader improve more rapidly, his value particularly being in his encouragement of minorities to state their views, thereby increasing the number of solutions, and also by the way in which he can integrate new members into a group: a most important consideration in take-overs, mergers, etc., where new groupings become more frequent.

Miss Klein deals, in her Chapter 3, with a condition which I have frequently met. It is described by her as 'assumption 1, Let a routine be established in the group'. Let me quote the case of a management group, comprising the heads of various divisions, which met regularly to discuss, in theory, all matters. In practice, production matters were rarely on the agenda, because the managing director was himself a production man. Nearly always, marketing matters were lengthily (and critically) discussed, to the inner disgust of the marketing manager who, in effect, muttered: 'Why always pick on me?'

This group achieved restricted communication, with one expert on the defensive; general discussion becomes restricted, and the skill (in this case of the marketing manager) becomes implicitly questioned. His 'status' was reduced accordingly and this provided a positive feed-back which still further reduced his status, and achieved an out-of-balance situation.

To quote again: 'Once a man's status becomes generalized, his ability to elicit the response he desires is less closely bound up with technical skill. At the same time his position in the communication structure has been fixed.' This seems to point to the desirability of qualities other than technical skill if leadership is to be maintained. It reminds one of the many failures of leadership where promotion was made on technical competence. The latter may temporarily, and in certain circumstances, be enough, but it is rarely satisfactory over long periods.

Perhaps the next of Miss Klein's assumptions—'Let us assume likes and dislikes in the group'—is apposite to our discussion, because there are many such situations in higher business circles. Perhaps we shouldn't make progress unless we have conflict! Newcomb and Bales[1] point out that some group members get shut off from communication, first, because they suffer, for one reason or another, from reduced status, and second, because 'autistic mechanisms' may operate against them. Bluntly, when they say something, other people don't listen; a situation we discussed earlier.

The problem of the group member who says little is met by all managers. Researchers have said that such people are generally of lower status, which makes me feel that as a somewhat garrulous speaker I must, by implication, be of very high status, which I doubt. Other descriptions of me have been used! But the quiet man is a problem, particularly when we realize that research findings often show him to be of low status, and less informed than others *because* he is excluded from the full communication treatment.

[1] *Artistic Hostility and Social Reality.* T. M. Newcomb. *Channels of Communication in Small Groups.* R. F. Bales.

In several such cases, I, when acting as a chairman, have taken considerable measures to correct this situation. It is possible to encourage the low-status person to speak, to open up items on the agenda, to take over sub-groups, and the like. It's a worthwhile effort. Incidentally, this problem may be related to the chairman himself. Klein says 'a quiet man has less control over the group', a statement which may be difficult to accept when one considers Mr. (now Lord) Attlee. A convention exists which says, in effect, that 'Chairmen shall be seen and not heard', and as a chairman, one tries not to be too dogmatic, but to allow others full expression. But research tells us that the chairman shouldn't be as quiet as all that; in fact, should lead in discussion, as part of his total leadership. A most interesting variant on this is put forward by Carl Rogers in *Client Centred Therapy*: 'Some counsellors—usually those with little specific training, have supposed that the counsellor's role was merely to be passive and to adopt a laissez-faire policy . . . He is more inclined to listen than to guide. He tries to avoid imposing his own evaluations upon the client. He finds that a number of his clents gain help for themselves. He feels that his faith in his client's capacity is best exhibited by a passivity which involves a minimum of activity and of emotional reaction on his part. He tries "to stay out of his client's way". This misconception of the approach has led to considerable failure in counselling—and for good reasons. In the first place, the passivity and seeming lack of interest or involvement is experienced by the client as a rejection, since indifference is in no real way the same as acceptance. In the second place, a laissez-faire attitude does not in any way indicate to the client that he is regarded as a person of worth . . . Many clients will leave both disappointed in their failure to receive help and disgusted with the counsellor for having nothing to offer.'

Miss Klein sums up by saying:[1] 'It is not really important whether the leader is appointed or has emerged from the group,

[1] *The Study of Groups.*

provided this function is fulfilled. He will be characterized by the great number of requests he makes for opinions or expressions of feeling and the amount of encouragement and agreement he shows.' I wonder how many managers would pass that test?

One last comment on her Chapter 3 is worth while, dealing as it does with competitive situations. British businesses have often been accused of laxity in facing competition, and I, for one, am convinced that a greater amount of competitive spirit should be built into every business and every Board room. Broadly, Follett seems to imply that a *co-operative* condition between skilled individuals is enough, but one must recognize that high stress conditions can be brought about where co-operation gets thrown out of the window. In all such cases, the obvious need is to avoid co-operation collapsing to a stage where it is 'every man for himself'. Like the Guards, good team-work involves long and good training, based on a good tradition or purpose, and there is much skill in creating internal competition, and yet maintaining optimum communication, co-operation, and leadership under stress. The better organized the group, the less the number of highly stressed situations, although when they occur they show up the basic strength of the organization and the managers. It is sometimes worth creating a storm in order to see how the boat sails; it is worth even more to be sure that when this happens she will sail at all!

The Place of Stress in Organization

The word 'stress' has many varying connotations, one of the latest being the term 'executive stress'. It seems to be agreed among a greater number of people, including some doctors, that this is bad, and must be avoided.

Like all things, stress is good up to a point, and *bodily* health at least seems to be the better for a reasonable amount of exercise stress. I am sure that mental health is similarly improved, and the problem is to stretch, stress, or strain without, in engineering terms, exceeding the elastic limit.

The leader should, I believe, create and maintain reasonably stressed conditions, and much skill is required to do this without permanent harm to the group and the individuals. In a paper given to the Royal Society of Arts[1] I suggested two 'components' of stress which in combination could be applied to almost every situation in every group. The first component is based on Newton's third law of motion—'to every action there is an equal and opposite reaction', and the second component may be stated as 'Life is Movement'. Those interested will no doubt read the paper in full (it is quite short), but briefly it attempts to create an analogy between the 'life' of an organizational group and a simple pendulum. In both there must be an energizing force, whether it be manager or mainspring. In both there must be a vibrationary rhythm which is compounded of repeated action and reaction.

Management, or leadership, to be effective, must create reactions, or challenges to itself within the organization. These challenges provide stress conditions, but if the vibrationary system is under proper control the stresses will themselves be under control and never allow the system to reach a 'critical period'.

Herbst, in his exploration of a coal-mining group,[2] has many interesting things to say about stress. Most of his book is hard going to a practising manager, and its application to wider groups is difficult. But he attempts to show the relationship between group stress and productivity. He says, for instance, that 'if the amount of opposition between the group and its environment becomes too low, this can become just as much a threat to the group as when stress becomes excessive'. It is obviously necessary to create conditions which make the group as a whole fight for its existence as a viable entity.

Herbst is more concerned here, and elsewhere in his book, with

[1] Cantor Lectures, 1962. *Journal of the R.S.A.*, January 1963.
[2] *Autonomous Group Functioning.* P. G. Herbst.

group attitudes. I am convinced also that each *individual* within the group requires somewhat similar conditions in order to give of his best, and this problem is one which will repay much more research than has yet been made.

I have frequently seen situations where clear leadership was unrecognized and this may become a more frequent situation as companies become more widely dispersed, and the overall pattern of the Company and its central management become blurred. An experiment is described[1] where members of three groups were asked if their groups had a leader. These three networks are shown in Fig. 19.

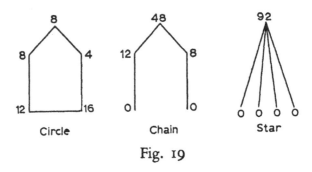

Fig. 19

'The figures stand for the percentage of responses which indicate a leader by position in the network. As is to be expected, the circle members don't know, and their guesses are pretty equally distributed among all positions. The central members of the chain and star are frequently, and the peripheral members never, perceived to be in a leadership position.' Christie, Macy and Luce in 1952 also submitted evidence that a central member of the chain network deduces from the number and type of messages he gets that he must be in the central position. In the Heise and Miller experiment[2] networks in which the centralities of all members are equal did not encourage the emergence of this

[1] Bavelas 1952.
[2] Page 186.

(leadership) function. In network 3 (my Fig. 13), A is the most central member and the natural co-ordinator. Accordingly, network 3 is more rapid and accurate than network 1.

It is interesting to compare these results with the popular concept of 'management-by-exception', which assumes that leaders are to be protected from routine, and therefore presumably from too many contacts and communications. They should be withdrawn from, rather than be at, busy crossroads in the network, although we showed earlier that if they become too withdrawn, leadership may become blurred. But the leadership function is exercised in a variety of ways, and 'management-by-exception' can be reconciled with a leadership which is *active* in group discussions and co-ordination and therefore recognizable. We discussed this earlier, and this further example suggests again that management-by-exception is a convention which has varying meanings, some of which oppose others. It should never become Management-by-Remoteness.

Another interesting aspect of the diagrams just quoted is the extent to which they emphasize an earlier point, that is, the comparative *isolation* of certain executives, particularly when they are at the end of a communication channel. One way of reducing the feeling of isolation felt by someone living at the bottom end of a cul-de-sac is to extend the road into another street, thereby providing alternative methods of coming and going. Similar possibilities apply to blind-end (occasionally dead-end) organizational streets, and one of several ways is to encourage the greater use of cross-co-ordination. If you refer again to the 'chain' in Fig. 19 you will see that there is a 'leader' position and two dead-ends at O and O. These two individuals are akin to what Americans describe as 'low men on totem poles'! But draw a line across the base and you achieve the circle, with a quite different pattern of linkage, communication and response.

Briefly, organizational dead-ends should be minimized, and cross-channels used, not only to improve co-ordination, but to ensure that 'the members are more strongly motivated to perform their task with zest'. Perhaps illustrations of this nature may more strongly motivate managers towards appreciating the importance of linkage diagrams as an aid to better leadership.

Decision Making

Constantly, in discussions on organization, and particularly leadership, we find it necessary to consider decision-making. One of my favourite slogans is 'out of debate must come decision', and an ability to achieve this is a characteristic of leadership.

Many opinion polls have been held in industry, and highest on the list of desirable qualities required by subordinates in a boss is, invariably, 'the ability to make a quick, firm decision'. Terms like 'joint discussion' and 'communication' infer that discussion is enough, but as a sales friend is fond of saying, 'there's only one really worthwhile exercise—it's signing on the dotted line'. That is decision.

Let us consider two types of tasks.[1] 'The task may be such that when a course of action is proposed it is so obviously the correct procedure that members cannot but agree. The problem is solved as soon as communication and evaluation have led to a full understanding. The major phase has been that of adaptation. The first proposal of action is at once followed by agreement. Decision-making is not difficult in those circumstances. This may happen in such tasks as mechanical puzzles—'how can we make the bell ring?'—in crossword puzzles, and in other problems with demonstrably correct solutions. Where there is *no* demonstrable solution, it will take longer to come to a conclusion, unless members share a frame of reference to such an extent that certain things seem more or less self-evident to them. Although there is no demonstrable proof of the existence of God, a group of Christians would at once agree that he does exist. The more similar the members' frames of reference are, the less time it will

[1] *The Study of Groups.* Josephine Klein.

take for a group to come to a decision, even when problems with no demonstrable solution are in question. Thus the length of time devoted to decision-making is a fair indication of the degree to which a group shares a frame of reference, provided that 'all members share the decision-making process. In the group that has existed for some time, and in which interaction has been general, this condition is likely to come about.'

If members do not share a frame of reference, or do not have similar norms, greater leadership must be exercised, and they must be induced to co-operate and mutually decide, even if they aren't very willing to do so. This, as we know, is often very difficult. But in a good group, where there is considerable interaction, there is also a second means of control—friendship. 'The first sign of a withdrawal of friendship, or of interaction . . . controls the behaviour of members.' An important varient of this situation occurs when, as in many management groups, sub-groups exist, often on a permanent basis. The effect of isolation brought about by a withdrawal of friendship does not affect so much those who are also members of a sub-group. It may, indeed, cause the sub-group to close its ranks and form a clique, in somewhat similar fashion to the Union members mentioned earlier.

This raises an opportunity to refer again to the value and the dangers of sub-groups. I believe thoroughly in the appointment of sub-groups to perform specific tasks, and almost as much skill is required to form these as the parent group itself. There is however a greater tendency in sub-groups for members to be chosen largely because of their special skills (in finance, production, etc.), and 'status through skill' is, as we have already said, a satisfactory temporary condition. It is rarely advisable, however, to form a sub-group on the basis that it must contain 'one of everything'. Some departments or members claim membership of a sub-group as a matter of right, some are put on to watch others, and so on. Generally, two rules should be observed:

(1) Each member has some specific knowledge which is likely to contribute substantially to the solution.

(2) The sub-group should disband after its initial job is done, unless strong reason exists for its continuance.

Every group leader should take particular care to see that sub-group activities do not produce cliques, 'fixed' decisions, or restricted communications within, or without, the main group.

Two other quotations from a research paper in this field are worth noting, even if, again, they underline the obvious. Maier[1] said: 'Experimental evidence on group decisions thus far indicates that a solution worked out by a group is more acceptable to the group than one imposed on the group by authority.' And again: 'Experiments show that a leader, if skilled and possessing ideas, can conduct a discussion so as to obtain a quality of problem-solving superior to that of a group working with a less skilled leader, and without collective ideas. Further, he can obtain a higher degree of acceptance than an unskilled person.'

Lickert, in a discussion on decision-making, says:[2] 'Interestingly, the tighter the control in an organization, in the sense that decisions are made at the top and orders flow down, the greater tends to be the hostility between subordinates. In autocratic organizations, subordinates fight for power and status. Consequently, the greater extent to which the president makes the decisions, the greater is the probability that competition, hostility, and conflict will exist between his subordinates.'

An interesting discussion on decision-making took place[3] at a conference of social scientists and managers. This centred largely around two basic types, (a) programmed and (b) non-programmed decisions. The 'programmed' decision-area is increasing, both numerically and in relative complexity of prob-

[1] *The Quality of Group Decisions as Influenced by the Discussion Leader.* N. R. F. Maier.

[2] *Motivational Approach to Organization.* Rensis Lickert.

[3] The Acton Society Trust. May 1960.

lem, largely because of the current trend towards more sophisticated control systems and computation equipment. A typical example of the latter is the computer, which is being programmed to make many decisions of an ever more complex nature, although it is always important to remember that these machines are programmed by, and for, the use of people.

The 'non-programmed' decision may become relatively less numerically (this is difficult to assess), but relatively greater in importance. It is the manager's vital task to take over where the 'machine' leaves off.

How is this trend likely to affect organization? I mentioned earlier that technical communication and administrative links will encourage us to cut across conventional organizational patterns much more in future. These links will carry a greater number of programmed decisions and relieve some of the routine in decision-making. But this will only increase the importance of personal non-programmed and *non-programmable* decisions.

An increase in 'programmed decisions' will underline the need for greater flexibility in the organization. Two examples, one an analogy and the other an actual case, illustrate my point. The first concerns the organizational flexibility of a good football team,[1] where informal interchange of roles can often be seen at its best. The second case is where a cheque-signing machine, an important part of the 'system', broke down when salaries were due, and appropriate directors were absent. Instead of an organizational and managerial breakdown, four executives were found whose individual authorities to sign cheques up to a certain amount provided, collectively, the total sum required! In both examples, a basic plan existed, but it was supplemented by personal qualities which came into force when the 'programme' failed.

Each significant programmed decision, or systems control point, should be tabulated, and organizational and personal substitutes should be available, who (or which) will, in emer-

[1] Continental teams have taught us a great deal.

R

gencies, take over the machine and make decisions in the good, old-fashioned way. It could be said that these flexible emergency actions are themselves part of the basic 'programme'. This is true to a point, but they usually require the people involved to exercise greater initiative and flexibility of choice than is necessary (or desirable) in the 'programmed' area.

I have just discussed two important groups of decisions, programmed and non-programmed decisions. I emphasized that an increase in the former will increase the importance of the latter, which is the sort of 'decision' we are discussing in this chapter. It is interesting here to compare ourselves with the Americans, who, on the whole, have progressed faster than we have in the field of programmed decisions. Cameron Hawley, well known as author of *Executive Suite* and other management novels (I nearly said fiction!), said at the A.M.A. Midwinter Personnel Conference, 1960, that European firms are found to be more efficient in overhead control than their American counterparts. One American top executive, asked why his suite of executives was so large, said: '—I'm not at all certain that I could get away with it as far as our organization is concerned. Our second-level executives have all been brought up in a different school. *They just haven't been trained to take over* in the same way that these European boys have.' Now 'taking over' means 'taking over decisions', and current American discussions and fears of 'conformity' may well support Hawley's quotation, and the feeling that there is too much emphasis in the U.S.A. on the 'programmed' decision and relatively not enough on the non-programmed variety, and the managerial qualities required to make them.

To some extent the rapid development in the U.S.A. of teaching machines has a connection with decision-making. Teaching methods are now, in a widening variety of activities, becoming orientated towards 'learner-centred' education, rather than 'teacher-centred'. This means that a 'programme' is prepared for a course of instruction in a given subject, and the learner, in conjunction with a teaching machine, decides when he wishes to proceed to the next stage of instruction. If he presses the wrong button he is told by the machine where he went wrong, and given a chance to proceed *correctly* to the next stage. By trial and error he eventually completes the programme.

I have referred on page 195 to the advantages inherent in this method of tuition, although there are some disadvantages too. There is no complete analogy between the 'programmed decision' discussed in this chapter and the decision of a learner to press a certain button in a programmed sequence of tuition, but there is a possibility that the widespread use of teaching programmes will lead to a more willing acceptance of 'programmed decisions', and (possibly) less willingness and ability to make the non-programmed type. This suggests that in their present form teaching machines are of little direct help in *management* education.

Decisions, to many managers, are largely 'playable by ear', that is, they are greatly determined by the feel of the situation. Let us hope that in a substantial number of cases this will always be so, because no machine or system is ever likely to be invented which will take over from human beings that special ability to synthesize the many variables in a complex management situation and, *after balancing them, come down on the appropriate side with a right decision.*

But if scientific and technological developments are to justify their cost they must provide better means of helping people to use more fully their own special God-given qualities on the more important 'man-sized' jobs. In production parlance we can use the term 'roughing cut' to describe the preliminary work on a component and the 'finishing cut' to complete the job. In management terms, the roughing cut looks like being performed more effectively today by the use of techniques such as management games, operational research and P.E.R.T.,[1] aided by data

[1] Programme Evaluation and Review Technique.

processing equipment of ever greater scope. This is the area of the programmed decision. But the latter, having made its greater contribution, now provides the manager with his preparation work more efficiently done, and with, consequently, a better, 'man-sized' opportunity to apply a finishing cut and make a non-programmed decision.

Before closing this short section on decision-making I wish to return again to company purpose. Readers of this and my other books will have no doubts about the value I place on the need for senior managers to define company purpose, and to modify it in the light of changing internal and external circumstances.

I believe that many senior managers deliberately seek to escape the responsibility of *deciding* what is the company purpose. Selznick[1] has said that 'once an organization becomes a going concern with many forces working to keep it alive, the people who run it readily escape the task of defining its purpose'. How true of organization, and possibly of individuals too. Most of us put off the difficult task of answering the question 'Where are we going?' We are usually content to 'go on going on' until something forces us to re-assess our progress.

Good managers must be like good navigators, who not only have an objective, but constantly need to check their progress towards it.

A Restatement
    (1) Leadership has many meanings. My own definition of a leader is someone who is assessed by his followers to be one who is more often right than wrong.
    (2) Many applications of leadership are not easily recognized as leadership situations.
    (3) Four elements of leadership were isolated:
        (a) Leadership requires a 'personal' element. Such a person should preferably be recognized and trained before, rather than after, difficulties arise.

    [1] *Leadership in Administration.* Philip Selznick.

(b) An acceptable leader is one whose past record encourages others to have confidence in his 'rightness'.

(c) Leadership can only be complete when the decision is followed by the decision of others to accept it.

(d) Every leader's contribution can be reinforced by a 'group' contribution.

(4) There is a close connection between leadership and decision-making. The leader's primary skill is an ability to make decisions which are more often right than wrong.

(5) Researches in leadership have attempted to isolate the 'authorities' on which leadership can be based. The following seem important:

(a) *Functional skill.* The leader derives his authority 'by virtue of skill in specific situations where his skill is in demand'.

(b) *Personal Status.* The leader is acceptable because he is 'that particular man'. Such a leader can use his authority *diffusely* in many situations.

(c) *The overt use of force.* It is suggested that this form of authority is rarely met with, and becomes more rare as other members of the group develop. 'Leadership by domination' is encouraged when there is underdevelopment of group members.

(6) If we combine (3)a, b and c with (5)a, b and c we seem to arrive at the following 'authorities' on which a leadership situation can be based:

(a) *Personal Status.* The leader is accepted because of group confidence in him. This may be based on long experience of him and the success of his past performances.

(b) *Functional Status.* A particular situation requires the use of special skill in order to solve it. The leader in such a situation can be one who is widely known to possess a high amount of this special skill.

(c) *Domination Status.* At certain periods 'leadership by force' will be accepted. It is rarely found, and if it does not wreck the group it tends to disappear in favour of other 'authorities' as members of the group become more developed.

(d) *Group Status.* This can be exercised because 'the group itself' has high leadership status, arising from its past achievements. A 'personal' leader may not at such a time be evident, although he will quickly emerge. His leadership opportunities are greater because he can exercise the accepted authority of his group in addition to his personal qualities.

(7) The quality of leadership can almost always be improved by increasing the contributions of all members of the group. Many situations arise where particular individuals are 'frozen out', are discouraged from contributing, or require encouragement to contribute. The leader must correct these conditions, and the use of linkage diagrams will often help him to design a better pattern of communications.

(8) The inference from (7) is that leadership and chairmanship qualities are synonymous. The chairman, it is suggested, should not desirably be one who is 'seen and not heard', but should actively promote full discussion, request opinions, and achieve common acceptance of decisions.

(9) Decision-making, which is intimately involved in leadership/management activities, varies in difficulty as the group situation itself varies. Two different situations are envisaged.

(a) Members share a frame of reference. In a group of Christians there would be general agreement on the existence of God. A decision is made quickly.

(b) Members do not share a frame of reference, or they may possess widely varying norms. In this situation decision-making is more difficult and leadership more important.

(10) Situation (9)b raises problems of considerable importance. A leader can 'impose' a decision in such circumstances and the implied withdrawal of personal approval of the anti-conformists by conformist colleagues is one; this can be a powerful weapon. A more positive way is to persevere with *all* the 'authorities' of leadership (6)a to d with a realization that cohesion, while important, must not be so completely achieved as to equal conformity. Good leaders should encourage a group membership whose norms are varied and variable, and ensure full participation by all members, even at the expense of time. Leaders should remember that a decision, to be complete, must be fully acceptable.

(11) Two principal 'types' of decision are recogizable:

    (a) *The programmed decision*, which is becoming increasingly delegated to machines, or other non-human forms. There are, of course, human forms, such as the greater delegation of authority and responsibility to subordinates.

    (b) *The non-programmed decision*, which is the more important category, and which it is necessary for a manager to make after full consideration has been given to the supporting evidence, and the 'programmed' assistance.

(12) The development of management is intimately associated with an ability to make better non-programmed decisions. This can be done if we develop fully the many management 'aides' now becoming available in the form of machines and systems, and if we encourage a more intensive development of management selection and training.

8

Some Organization Principles

WE HAVE dissected the organization structure and discussed many aspects of it. Various pieces of research have been quoted which individually may have clarified a particular problem, but collectively may have contributed little to a synoptic understanding of the whole structure.

In an earlier book, *Management Principles*, I said that few organization principles have, so far, been accepted and widely applied by managers. My approach in that book was to examine some of the 'conventions' in this field, as a basis for investigating more fully the principles which exist. It might then be possible to compare conventions and principles.

Where will a manager find a set of principles to help him design an organization structure? One of the latest and most comprehensive books[1] to appear summarizes in Appendix I the contribution of a number of pioneers, and in particular describes the various steps taken by Urwick to modernize his own 'set' of principles. It is hardly necessary to take my readers through these steps (they should read Brech's book), but it is noticeable, and understandable, how Urwick draws upon other researchers, particularly Mary Parker Follett. Reproduced in the Appendix are Urwick's ten principles.

It is interesting to compare Urwick's later principles with

[1] *Organization—The Framework of Management.* E. F. L. Brech.

264

those advanced in recent years by other students of organization. In *Principles of Management* (1948) M. A. Cameron presented his own principles of organization, which have been summarized by Brech—see Appendix, page 307. Brech also refers to the discussion which followed, some years ago, a paper by W. D. Brown[1] which includes his (Brech's) comments made at the time on these principles. In Brech's words, 'only the principles concerned with the formal outline of organization (set 1) are principles in the true sense of the term, and of these only some are truly so'. These latter may be listed in Brown's own words—see Appendix.

In one of the latest American books[2] Allen does not commit himself to a list of formal organizational principles. He does, however, quote those adopted by the Atlantic Refining Company (his page 298) and presumably in doing so thinks they are pretty good. For the sake of comparison with the three sets of principles just mentioned, please see Appendix.

A glossary of terms is attached to the 'Atlantic' principles which I shall not quote, although some of them differ considerably from what early researchers, or even I, would assume they mean. In every definition we face the problem of words, and what they mean, and this problem will become more difficult as more specialists invent more new words. Definition is an essential prelude to a statement of principles, to avoid what Weaver calls 'semantic noise'.

I will attempt a reconciliation between these sets of principles, again stressing that I will use Urwick's principles as a starting point, without necessarily, at this stage, assuming they are right or comprehensive. Let us consider Fig. 1.

Urwick (1)   *The Principle of Objective*
          Key term—'The purpose'.
Cameron (1)   *Appropriateness*
          Key term—'The common end'.

[1] *Manchester Monograph on Higher Management, No. 6.* W. D. Brown.
[2] *Management and Organization.* Louis A. Allen.

Brown   No appropriate reference.
Atlantic (1)   *Objectives*
                 Key term—'The objectives'.
COMMENT:
Three of the four sets of principles stress what I have called,
earlier, 'the purpose' of the group.

Urwick (2)   *The Principle of Specialization*
                 Key term—'Every member confined . . . to per-
                 formance of a single function'.
Cameron (2)   *Specialization*
                 Key term—'Specialists—concentrating on a nar-
                 row section of activity'.
Brown   No direct reference.
Atlantic   No direct reference.
COMMENT:
Urwick's 'principle' is obviously considered unnecessary by
two of the four authorities. I find this principle difficult to
interpret. It can be applied in the literal sense of one-person-
one-function, or specialism, which may be easy to apply to
machinists, inspectors, or even chief accountants. But how do
we apply it to the manager whose span of control includes a
variety of specialists? What is a manager a specialist in? It is
not enough to state that he performs the function of a manager.
If we look at Atlantic IID we see more clearly the need for
specialist *groupings* to be homogeneous, which is more understandable as a principle.

Urwick (3)   *The Principle of Co-ordination.*
                 Key term—'Organizing facilitates co-ordination:
                 Unity of Effort'.
Cameron (6)   *Co-ordination*
                 Key term—'The framework constructed with the
                 need for co-operation constantly in mind'.

Brown	No direct reference.
Atlantic	No direct reference.

COMMENT:

Both Brown and Atlantic mention co-ordination and co-operation, but in a less direct sense than Urwick and Cameron. One forms the impression that if the group is organized as Brown and Atlantic specify, then co-operation and co-ordination will naturally emerge as products of the environment. These approaches are fundamentally different, and I feel that Urwick and Cameron are more correct in raising the basic requirement of co-ordination to 'principle' level.

Urwick (4)	*The Principle of Authority* Key term—'Supreme authority rests somewhere' and there should be a 'clear line of authority from the supreme authority to every individual in the group'.
Cameron (4)	*Clearness* Key term—'A clear line of authority'.
Brown (a)	Key term—'One chief executive in every organization'.
Atlantic	Several indirect references to responsibility and authority, but nowhere stated that there shall be a 'clear line of authority'.

COMMENT:

All authorities here, except one, recognize the principle of a clear line of authority, which infers the existence of *one* top executive. Urwick's own phrasing is clear and concise, and it seems that a rather complex organization having, say, three joint managing directors and one full-time chairman would still be acceptable in the light of Urwick's principle, and, indeed, to other authorities also. Perhaps this is as it should be, because a principle should be independent of particular titles such as Managing Director, which often inaccurately describes the real job. The full-time chairman, acting as chief executive, may say, with truth, that although he calls himself chairman, and his three chief subordinates joint managing directors, his organization still satisfies the principles we are discussing. As an organizer I agree, but those who depart from 'convention' should make certain that all concerned know why and how. I remember the case of a certain large corporation which invited Union and public criticism by the way it changed the executive relationships between its chairman and managing director without adequate *outside* explanation. It is not enough, in these days of public relationships and responsibilities, to say that *you* know what you are doing; others must realize, too, that if your organization departs from convention, there should be a reasonable explanation of the extent of and reasons for the difference.

Urwick (5)	*The Principle of Responsibility* Key term—'Absolute responsibility of superior for acts of subordinate'.
Cameron	No direct reference.
Brown	No direct reference.
Atlantic	No direct reference.

COMMENT:

Atlantic states (IIIB) that 'Authority and responsibility must correspond', and all the authorities, apart from Urwick, appear to include responsibility and authority in one statement or principle. Only Urwick separates lines of authority (Urwick's 4) and responsibility (Urwick's 5), and the close relationship between the two (Urwick's 7).

Urwick (6)	*The Principle of Definition* Key term—'Content, authority, responsibility, relationship of each position to other positions, defined in writing and published'.

Cameron (4)   *Clearness*
               Key term—'Clear line of authority—clearly defined functions for each post'.

Brown (b)   Key term—'Responsibility of each executive explained in general terms to each member'.

(d)   Key term—'Functional authority clearly explained to everyone'.

Atlantic (IIIA) Key term—'Definitions of authority and responsibility shall be clear and precise'.

COMMENT:

The general intent is obviously to define clearly and explain widely. There is room for wide interpretation of the term 'define clearly', and I have an instinctive regard for Brown's phrase 'general terms'. However, all authorities realize the great importance of definition and dissemination, and if this principle alone became more widely practised, greater progress in organizational understanding would result.

Urwick (7)   *The Principle of Correspondence*
               Key term—'In every position, the responsibility and authority should correspond'.

Cameron (4)   *Clearness*
               There is an indirect reference to lines of authority and clearly defined functions. These could also be described as responsibilities.

Brown (a)   There is a reference to the responsibility . . . and complete authority of the chief executives only.

Atlantic (3)   Key term—'Responsibilities and authorities must be defined and their inter-relationship established'.

COMMENT:

Refer back to my comment on Urwick (5).

Urwick (8)   *The Span of Control*[1]
               Key term—'No person should supervise more than

[1] See earlier (pages 158 onwards) for a discussion on the span of control.

five or six direct subordinates whose work inter-locks'.

Cameron (5) **Span of Supervision**
Key term—'In all higher ranks the number personally supervised by one man must be limited to a maximum of six'.

Brown (c) Key term—'The span of control of a line executive limited to those with whom he can maintain frequent contact, and amongst whom he can maintain co-operation'.

Atlantic (V) *Supervision*
Key term—'An executive should not have reporting to him directly more than five or six subordinates whose duties overlap or are inter-related'.

COMMENT:
The magic numbers 'five to six' appear frequently, and some would say that they are too precise to be embodied in an organizational principle. One trouble, however, is that purely *qualitative* statements such as Brown's can be interpreted in very wide *quantitative* terms. I know chief executives who have at least fifteen subordinates reporting to them, and would claim that they satisfy Brown's conditions.

Urwick (9) *The Principle of Balance*
Key term—'The various units of an organization should be kept in balance'.

Cameron (3) *Balance*
Key term—'A good organization is well balanced'.

Brown No reference.

Atlantic (IIIA) An indirect reference is made to the possibility that unclear definitions lead to 'Warping of organization'.

COMMENT:
It might be useful, in discussing the worthwhileness of this

principle, to consider balance in its mechanical sense. If we put too much weight on one side of a ship, plane, bicycle or see-saw, we create obvious strains and movements. We do not so obviously and immediately see the strains when we unbalance a group of people, but the strains (and stresses) will emerge in due course. I referred on page 247 to the state of unbalance created in a certain group where the sales manager felt that too much pressure was being exerted on him. Other cases come to mind, where a state of unbalance, and corresponding strain, was created between head office and the rest of the organization. I have seen, among other cases, a feeling develop in an export division that it is being neglected in favour of other divisions.

Balance is never perfect, and we really never wish it to be perfect, as a small amount of movement or flexibility is necessary for materials and men. But reasonable balance is essential to a good organization, and its achievement calls for considerable study by top managers, and an occasional re-balancing of the organization in the light of personal or other developments.

Urwick (10)	*The Principle of Continuity*
	Key term—'Reorganization is a continuous process'
Cameron	No reference.
Brown	No reference.
Atlantic (IVE)	There is a reference to the need for providing qualified replacements for all positions.

COMMENT:

It is surprising to find a lack of unanimity on the importance of continuity. I agree with Urwick that the principle of continuity is important, and at regular intervals, indeed whenever there is a change of even one personality, there should be a review of the organization structure and the personalities in it. Too many organizations have become out-of-date or unbalanced through failure to observe this principle.

A Summing-Up

Again using Urwick's principles as the master-list, we find that out of the ten quoted, only four appear, in more or less the same wording, to be commonly accepted by *all*. These are:

Urwick (1). The Principle of the Objective.
Urwick (6). The Principle of Definition.
Urwick (7). The Principle of Correspondence.
Urwick (8). The Span of Control.

Put briefly, all regard as basic structural requirements: (a) the existence of a company purpose, (b) the reasonable definition and dissemination of jobs, (c) the close relationship between authority and responsibility, and (d) the limitation of managerial spans of control. Perhaps if we satisfied only these principles we should do very well, although I would like particularly to commend Urwick's Principle No. 9—The Principle of Balance. It is becoming more important as the number of specialists increases.

I would like to refer again to the 'conventions' discussed in an earlier book, *Management Principles*. These conventions are neither comprehensive nor fully accepted, but they do represent a good selection of the organizational views held by a majority of managers. Some are recognizable as reasonably identical with *some* of the 'principles' we have just been discussing.

An examination shows this degree of reconciliation:

Convention 2. There should be only one executive head.
Urwick 4.   The Principle of Authority.

Convention 5. The Span of Control should be limited.
Urwick 8.   The Span of Control.

Convention 8. An organization chart should exist.

Urwick 6.   The principle of Definition.

Convention 9. Management succession should be assured.
Urwick 10.   The Principle of Continuity.

Convention 11. No responsibility without authority.
Urwick 7. The Principle of Correspondence.

It will be seen that only conventions 5, 8 and 11 correspond to the four *common* principles isolated on page 272.

The Moral Authority in Organization

Frequently, in this and a previous book, I have stressed the importance of 'company purpose' as a basis for organizational effort. Is it necessary to include within the essential principles of organization one which encourages managers to lay an adequate moral foundation for subsequent tasks? How many company 'purposes' include a written intention to satisfy well-recognized *moral* requirements; do not most of us take these requirements for granted when we specify 'company purpose' in a variety of other, and usually more technical, terms? Most of us regard ourselves as decent people, working in a decent company. Most of us are, and do! But as technological complexities increase there is a stronger need for us to remind ourselves that we must *organize* ourselves deliberately to be reminded of personal and moral issues which might otherwise tend to be pushed aside or forgotten in the heat of our other problems.

Such a reminder, to be effective, must be built into the organization, and may well justify the adoption of a managerial principle such as—

The Principle of Moral Responsibility

How should we consider the implementation of this principle? First, let us quote Lepawsky.[1] 'An organization', he says, 'can be sketched and charted just as the human body can be physically depicted', and his inference was that this concept of structural form was the easiest, and to many organizers the only, problem

[1] *Administration. The Art and Science of Organization and Management.* Albert Lepawsky.

S

of organization. This attitude, to him and others such as Golembi-ewski,[1] is inadequate, as it leaves out the moral fibre which must be interwoven into the structure. 'Organization, in this sense, becomes more akin to psychiatry than skeletology.'

When we consider the moral responsibility of organization more fully we seem to be led directly back to the satisfaction of the individual within any and every organizational situation. In Chapters 3 and 4 I attempted to show the key role of the individual in his group and how he, internally within himself, and externally his own group, have identical objectives, that is, the growth of the individual. This objective must always include attention to moral issues.

It is worth reproducing Golembiewski's chart which analyses these moral issues in a clear fashion.

BEHAVIORAL CONDITIONS ASSOCIATED WITH HIGH OUTPUT CONSISTENT WITH JUDAEO-CHRISTIAN VALUES WHICH SHOULD GUIDE MAN-TO-MAN RELATIONS IN ORGANIZATIONS

Values Guiding Man-to-Man Relations	*Conditions Associated with High Output*
1. work must be psychologically acceptable, generally non-threatening	1. congruence of personality and job requirements 1a. compatibility of personalities of work-unit members
2. work must allow man to develop his faculties	2. job enlargement 2a. job rotation 2b. training, on and off the job 2c. decentralization
3. the task must allow the individual room for self-determination	3. job enlargement 3a. general supervision 3b. wide span of control
4. the worker must influence the environment within which he works	4. group decision making 4a. peer representation in promotion 4b. self-choice of work-unit members 4c. decentralization
5. the formal organization must not be the sole and final arbiter of behavior	5. decentralization 5a. group decision making

[1] *Organization as a Moral Problem.* Robert T. Golembiewski.

On the left he states the moral 'values' which must be sought if we are to provide the individuals with adequate personal satisfaction. On the right he suggests a variety of techniques or organizational conditions which will encourage the attainment of these values. A study of the right-hand 'conditions' will show us a variety of requirements, which in my book are treated either as structural elements (decentralization, decision-making, etc.) or principles of organization (span of control). Because these requirements are woven into the organizational fabric by me and by other exponents of organization does not invalidate the basic thesis that, permeating organization as a whole is a moral purpose which is more likely to be remembered and implemented if it is accepted as an essential principle.

The Application of Principles

Are a relatively few commonly accepted principles enough to help a manager build a sound organization structure? They certainly go some way towards clarifying the approach to organization among good managers; they would, if carefully considered and applied, help greatly that very large group of managers who rarely think at all about principles.

The first part of this chapter has been devoted to an examination of organization principles. How are they to be applied, and what connection do they have with the structural factors discussed earlier?

Rarely does a manager or organizer face an organizational task with a blank piece of paper. Usually he is concerned with an existing company or group which requires to change itself, or be changed by circumstances. It is not therefore *organization* but *reorganization* which is the most frequent task of the organizer, and I propose therefore assuming, in the following exercise, the need to reorganize a certain group, and the desirability of making a scientific approach to the problem. This means, in my interpretation, a seven-step consideration such as was outlined earlier.

In discussing each of these steps I will refer appropriately to those structural factors and 'principles' that particularly arise.

Step (1). Define the Objective

I was much interested in the reviews of my recent book on organization, *Management Principles*, in which I stressed, at an early stage, the great importance of a clear objective. Several reviewers suggested that the early part of my book, in which I defined organization and discussed its basic components, was less interesting than the second part, in which I discussed managerial conventions.

To some extent this reaction was expected, certainly by my publisher, who suggested at our earlier discussions that most practising managers were interested not so much in a scientific approach to organization, but rather to its application. For this reason it was finally decided to write two books, the second being devoted to a more detailed analysis of organization, which would be more likely to attract younger, and more theoretically educated, managers than those who were looking only for its practical application.

As a manager who has, on occasion, been praised for 'practical application' I am the last person to denigrate its value. But I made it clear earlier in this book that organization requires a deeper study than it has already received, and this, to be successful, *must* include a greater understanding of its purpose, its principles, its basic elements, as well as its skilful application. It is with 'purpose' that we are concerned in Step (1) when we consider 'Define the Objective'.

During the writing of this chapter a major reorganization of government was announced. One commentator truly remarked that unless a modified national 'purpose' was made known to the nation we could not be expected to understand or even support the many and miscellaneous personal changes made by the Prime Minister. 'If the Conservative Party has a strategy for the nation it is not apparent.' Prior to any such reorganization the 'purpose' behind it must surely be clearly known and communicated to those involved, whether they be ministers, managers or rank and file. *The Times* suggested that most members of the wavering electorate were 'looking for a change'. But 'change' is hardly an objective, although few would deny its importance. It is surely *changing for what purpose* that the Prime Minister and every reorganizer must be clear about and must ensure that others understand, also.

In business life there are many objectives which individually, or in combination, may be the 'purpose' of a reorganization. There may be, for instance, a need to establish in the public eye a stronger financial status, or a better product range. There may be the need to erase from the public mind some internal personal recriminations, and to re-create a respectable image. There may, of course, be a need to restore profitability! *It is vitally important for every reorganizer to reach agreement with the top management group on the objective(s) before starting to investigate the organization.*

Step (2). *Investigate the Facts*

In organizational as in other spheres, facts are sacred and difficult to obtain. There are obvious facts, hidden facts, and, more difficult than these, facts which are not easily accepted as facts even when they are carefully demonstrated.

In this last category is the *actual* state of the organization which in most groups differs from that picture, or chart of it, which is in the minds of senior managers. Perhaps the term 'working to rule' explains this difference in easily understood terms. It is often stated, probably with truth, that a public organization such as British Railways would, if its employees 'worked to rule', seize up completely. Over many years the formally laid-down channels of communication and procedures have been 'unofficially' streamlined, and a reversion to the 'formal rules' would involve serious losses in efficiency.

This state of affairs is to be found in many companies, although breaking the rules is not always accompanied by *an increase* in efficiency. I remember, for instance, a well-known paint company which during reorganization brought about by the introduction of a new data-processing system, found that the 'short cuts' which had unofficially accumulated over the years had also weakened greatly the quality control standards that were presumed to exist.

I recall another company which took over a competitor and became, in the process, a larger unit. After the first two years of integration it became obvious that serious inefficiencies had become built into the new structure, and a review of one important department revealed that *six* layers of management had been created *on paper* between the managing director and the senior factory managers. This was a bad organizational situation, and it was not surprising to find, on deeper analysis, that *in practice* four layers were in operation. I am sure that many similar examples could be uncovered.

These cases illustrate the tendency for organizational 'facts' to drift away from what was originally agreed. When, therefore, the organizer reaches Step (2) of his scientific approach his first duty is to prepare two statements or charts. The first demonstrates how, according to the managers, the group is presumed to operate. The second shows how it actually does operate. Many surprised faces are seen after a comparison of the two is made.

At this stage it is again necessary to reach agreement among the senior managers concerned on the 'facts' as they are uncovered. This is always more difficult than it should be, as few managers like to admit that so many off-beat practices have developed, particularly when they suddenly appear to explain deficiencies in production, profits, etc., which had previously been unexplainable. But this agreement, difficult though it may be to obtain, is essential if the next logical step is to be effectively made. Taking responsible executives with him step by step is an important part of the organizer's job, because in more than most activities organization is very concerned with the past, the present and the future of senior people.

It is at this stage of the scientific approach that the structural factors listed on page 131 and the principles on page 272 can be brought into consideration. It is possible to prepare a matrix such as Fig. 20 and to use this as an *aide-mémoire* when investigating the facts which will be considered more fully at Step (3). More about this later.

An Organization Matrix

	Size	Shape	Internal Structure	Communi-cation	Cohesion	Group Direction	Leadership
The Principle of the Objective							
The Principle of Definition							
The Principle of Correspondence							
The Span of Control			✓				
The Principle of Balance							

Fig. 20

Step (3). *Analyse the Facts*

Like other analytical studies, this is best done in comparative solitude, and without too much external pressure to report conclusions. Let the organizer be warned against a first impression that the whole place needs a thorough reorganization, and also against the desire to impose a 'one best way'. We should remember that many forms of organizations work, and our job is to make as few, rather than as many, changes as possible to achieve the objective. It must be remembered too that when investigating the facts we are investigating individuals as well as structures, and every organizational change is likely to involve, perhaps seriously, one or more individuals. The 'law of the situation' must be applied, and we cannot start to reorganize from scratch, but from where, for better or worse, the group actually is at the moment. A colleague has described some of the more important 'facts' in the following slightly facetious terms:

'(1) "The main thread and individual weighting".
The main functions (Sales, Production, Design, etc.) may be identified. Depending on the purpose and needs of the organization, one of these can be defined as "the main thread" to which in the particular organization the others in effect provide the service. At the same time individuals responsible for these functions have "weight" as defined formally by level, and/or informally by personality. Ideally there should be a precise correlation between these factors. Unbalance in this respect has an obvious significance.

'(2) "Positive and negative currents".
Some individuals by their character and personality are centres from which activities flow, others are mainly "receivers". A chart depicting the apparent directions of these currents is very revealing.

'(3) "Completely or partly immovable objects".
This is primarily a small company feature, although I imagine it occurs in larger organizations. People are "immovable" who hold their position by reason of some circumstance extraneous to the precise needs of the organization. Owners, and uncles, aunts, and nephews of owners are examples. There is not much future in projecting an optimum chart of organization which envisages the removal of "an immovable object". In extreme cases one might have to indicate that the problem of such terms could be insoluble. Certainly it will involve a series of stages.

'(4) "The caste system".
These are the informal patterns of grouping in an organization. These may be based on internal circumstances such

as special areas of skill or knowledge, or on external circumstances such as social classifications, religious, or other
affiliations. The "caste" systems carry tremendous unofficial
weight in an organization. Some of these one may hardly
expect to identify in a brief preliminary survey, although
observations may indicate their probable existence.

'(5) "Limpets — barnacles — chameleons — scene shifters —
anarchists".

This is a very useful individual classification if it is extended
over the chart of organization. Limpets are people who
abhor change of any sort in principle and change in their
position or duties is virtually impossible. Barnacles cling
tenaciously to existing situations but are capable of being
moved. Chameleons turn whichever way the wind blows
and will adapt whatever action circumstances demand to
avoid undue disturbance. Scene shifters are people who tend
to like change and who on the whole need change from
time to time: they can be counted on to produce a climate
of change almost involuntarily, over a period of time.
Anarchists are the people who are always in battle and whose
containment in any situation presents continuous problems. One of the things that has struck me over the last
twelve months is that since change is inevitably taking
place in an organization, people in the latter end of this
scale—tiresome as they sometimes are—tend to be very
much less tiresome in the long run than people in the static
end of the scale. In fact, if one is thinking in terms of
management development, whilst it is extremely difficult
to define potential in the individual, it is probable that
adaptability to change is a key requirement. Some of our
difficulties in fact may be due to the questionable high
value that has been put in industry on loyalty, by
which has sometimes been meant the quality of "staying
put".'

There is much to be said for this analysis. In one form or another, the reader will already have recognized the relationship between these 'facts' and various situations already discussed in this book.

We can now use our matrix Fig. 20 more fully. First, we can compare each 'principle' with the actual condition prevailing in the group. Second, we can analyse the actual organization structure and consider our findings in relation to those desirable features which should be present if principles and structural requirements are properly applied. It is possible, when these two investigations are completed, to place our comments in the matrix squares at appropriate co-ordinate positions so that special attention is drawn to those problems which arise where a particular 'principle' has a special relation to a particular 'factor'.

Let us consider such a possibility. Investigation has shown that the top span of control appears to be much greater than the 'principle' lays down. An investigation into the group's communications shows up a serious lack of understanding between the senior managers concerned. Here, therefore, seems to be a situation where the *relationship* between the two problems needs special consideration, and may result in a change in one or the other, or both. A suitable reminder in the appropriate 'co-ordinate square' is indicated for more detailed investigation and possible modification. It will almost always be found that such a relationship involves alternative solutions rather than 'one best way'. This provides both a difficulty and an opportunity in organizational affairs.

Step (4). *Establish Principles or Laws*

Here we return again to the various conventions, experiments and principles relating to groups and structures which we have been discussing in recent chapters. With this assorted, and often contradictory, bagful of possibilities, how *can* our investigator proceed?

Perhaps the value of a scientific approach is not necessarily judged by the number of principles or laws we can apply to a given situation, design or structure, but by the amount of analytical consideration given to the problem. We should, in my view, take a great organizational step forward if we always went through the analytical exercises I have described. Already we have defined the objective, established the facts of the situation, and reached agreement on both. We are therefore well on the road to a better organizational solution.

I hope that readers will not take these comments too literally, and assume that, having reached this stage, no further consideration of organizational conventions and principles is necessary. Far from it. An analysis of the facts (Step (2)) will probably have shown up a number of weaknesses which may have contributed to the company's difficulties, and need modification in a reorganization exercise. The next step is obviously to eliminate these weaknesses in the future organization and it is here that diagrammatic aids are so important. I find that where various structures are superimposed on each other, the use of transparent paper is invaluable in deciding how the existing structure can be redesigned with the least number of structural and personal changes. This exercise is carried out with a constant eye on previously exposed weaknesses, and the constant use of structural considerations and principles as a check-list against proposed solutions.

Does it matter very much whether we use more rather than less structural factors and principles for this purpose? The whole review would probably not take more than a few hours, which is a small time to devote to the design of a structure which is presumed to last for years. Even the slightly contradictory and ambiguous nature of some of the principles I have quoted should do no harm—in fact, they may cause a manager to think through the differences more intensively.

For these broad reasons I am not in this book attempting a further reconciliation of the various principles and conventions,

or attempting to produce an integrated short list of basic statements. Already, on page 272, I have isolated at least four or five
commonly accepted principles, and I said that 'if we achieved
these requirements we should do very well'.

Perhaps I might encourage some of my readers to attempt a
more detailed correlation between conventions, principles and
research results than I am prepared to do here. There is much to
be done, but let me say again that if every manager actively concerned with organization and reorganization went as carefully
along the organizational road as we have already gone, great
improvements would take place, and organizational structures
would be better designed.

Step (5). Validate and Apply

We are now at the first stage of application, where we should
realize that to know what to do with knowledge is as important
as gaining that knowledge.

Organizational changes can be wholesale or retail, widely,
narrowly, slowly, or quickly applied, and the choice depends
on the circumstances. There are times when major surgery is
better than dieting; generally, however, it is better to avoid
immediate drastic change but rather to prepare a plan for intro-
ducing improvements on a reasonable scale of change and time.

It is important, when planning an extended reorganization,
to make certain that an unsettled atmosphere is avoided over a
long period. One is reminded of the tongue-tied lieutenant
drilling troops, who were marching dutifully towards the cliff
top. The sergeant, unable to stand it any longer, finally blurted
out: 'For God's sake, say something, sir, if only good-bye.'
Individuals within a reorganization scheme are entitled to reasonably specific and prompt information about their futures, even,
and perhaps more so, if it involves saying good-bye!

Therefore let us have a plan, and publicize it with a time-table
of changes. Preferably, these organizational changes should start

at the top levels and work downwards, for at least two reasons: one, top managers should always give a lead; and two, if new jobs are created, the senior men should have the opportunity of participating in their subordinate changes.

I have often helped to plan large-scale reorganizations of plant or factory activities. There is great skill and much satisfaction to be gained from the wholesale changeover of a large department during a week-end of hectic change. But I do not recommend similar wholesale changes in *organization* unless drastic conditions prevail. It is obvious to all when a machine or a conveyor is not working; it is not so obvious when a managerial function or communication channel is not working, and for this reason we should make very sure that some managers are taking the strain while others are moving into new positions. Using again the analogy between structural and organizational engineering, we know how necessary it is for the structural engineer to make sure that certain 'members' take the strain while others are being moved out from or into position. Organizational changes require the same consideration, and for this reason alone major, sweeping, 'all change' movements are generally to be avoided. It is often better to make pilot experiments and changes, validate them, and proceed in similar planned steps towards the final, agreed solution.

Let me return for a moment to the wording of Step (5). Validate and Apply. Bearing in mind earlier comments it is worth considering how the proposed changes are best carried out. The manager responsible for making these changes is often in a dilemma arising from two opposing requirements. First, he probably wishes to complete his organizational changes as quickly as possible so that the revised group may settle down to achieve its new purpose. Second, he may well find that 'wholesale' reorganization creates more drastic personal problems than he is prepared to tolerate or risk.

As I have emphasized frequently, organization primarily concerns people, and it is in his management of personal problems that a manager is most severely tested and judged. I believe that certain 'basic' considerations apply fairly widely in such circumstances, and the following points seem to be worth special attention:

(1) The need to reorganize a part of the group should encourage senior managers to carry out a broader review of the organization, and to consider the desirability at this time of making other changes which may previously have been deferred 'until a more appropriate date'. Patchwork consideration of the organization is rarely desirable, although its application may be programmed over a period of time.

(2) Interim changes which leave the individuals involved in doubt about their future are bad. Decisions concerning 'people' should be stated as clearly as possible, and should endeavour to avoid the possibility later on of any individual saying that he had been misled or misinformed.

(3) A senior manager in the wrong job is likely to create personal and job problems far beyond his own personal area.

(4) Personal readjustments or retirements which arise from essential organizational changes should always be treated generously. If a company achieves its long-term objective more quickly because of more drastically applied personal changes it should be willing to pay more heavily for that accommodation.

When reorganization is being planned it will be found that a balance must be struck between 'doing it all at once' and reorganizing in stages. For reasons previously stated, the latter is more likely to be adopted, and this makes it necessary to prepare yet another organization chart. Let us assume that when Step (1) was commenced, an organization chart of the group existed. At the completion of Step (1), when the *actual* state of the organization became known, as compared with the assumed state on the existing organization chart, it became possible to draw a new factual chart which we will call Chart 2.

Now, at our first stage or *reorganization* we find that it is desirable to draw Chart 3, which illustrates only an interim situation, but does represent changes which lead *towards* the final solution, and which take account of the personalities already in the group.

We are now ready to consider

Step (6). Apply Widely

The period of time considered reasonable to persevere with the interim reorganization (Chart 3) depends on many circumstances. It can provide valuable evidence which may or may not modify the final solution which it is proposed to apply in Step (6). But interim situations should be recognized as such by all concerned, and it is better not to delay the final reorganization any longer than is absolutely necessary. This warning is given because there is nearly always a tendency in organizational affairs for interim solutions to jell into permanency, particularly when (as is frequently the case) difficult personal problems are involved. It is right that we should be reluctant to make final decisions which may terminate, or otherwise drastically affect, individuals, but managers are paid to do just this and to do it properly.

It is hardly necessary to state that at this stage it is desirable to introduce organization Chart No. 4 which illustrates the final stage of reorganization. In practice it is desirable to design Chart 4 at about the same time as Chart 3, so that the latter can logically lead on to the former. Chart 4 may not, before and during the interim stage, be widely publicized, but it must be known to exist and to be the final objective, particularly to those individuals who are considerably affected by the changes. It should not be forgotten that there is no finality in organizational affairs. Let me remind you again of Principle of Continuity: 'Reorganization is a continuous process'. It is necessary to allow a reasonable period of time for the 'final' reorganization to validate itself and as 'people' are involved, a reasonable time for personal readjustments is necessary; this is rarely less than six months.

But managers should be watching trends very carefully during this validation period, although it is wise to remember that 'breathing down the necks' of newly appointed subordinates is bad. Once managers have been appointed they must be allowed, reasonably, to make, and correct, their own errors. Even so, many finishing touches may be desirable, and evidence once again collected which, when the next period of reorganization is considered desirable, will be available for consideration.

The Application of 'Principles' to Centralization/De-centralization Problems

In an earlier book I discussed centralization and de-centralization at some length, as they intimately affect and are affected by organizational tasks. It is worth stressing again that the managers of a large group, controlling a mixture of centralized and de-centralized activities should be even more concerned to examine and regularly re-examine it in the light of the organizational factors and principles we have discussed in this book. The attitude of managers in centralized or de-centralized groups should be similar in kind, and different only in size of application.

Finally, it might be appropriate, in concluding this discussion on principles, to quote an early pioneer, Henri Fayol, who said: 'Without principles, we are working in the dark and in chaos; without experience and judgement we are still working under great difficulties, even with the best of principles. The principle is the lighthouse, which enables us to get our bearings, but it can only help those who know the way to the port.'

9

Group Dynamics—An Overall View

THIS TERM has emerged in recent years[1] to describe the internal and external movements of a group of individuals. It is, I believe, a good term, because it focusses attention on the dynamic nature and purpose of a group; without adequate 'dynamics' a group, whether it is a family or a company, withers and often dies.

It may seem too ambitious a project to compress an overall view of group dynamics into a few pages, particularly bearing in mind that an authoritative collection of theory and research findings edited by Cartwright and Zander runs to over 800 pages. Perhaps readers will be encouraged by my short summary to read more fully. It is a fascinating field.

In my earlier book *Management Principles* I quoted Brech as saying that the dynamic concept of organization is outmoded. My definition of organization, however, includes 'the ability to act as one body', which involves the maintenance of dynamic life in that body, and this 'is provided by a combination of personal, internal groups and external environmental forces; only when these are maximized is "the ability to act as one body" at its strongest'.

In previous chapters I have attempted to show how a manager can maximize the forces at his disposal. The first and most significant

[1] It was originally used by Kurt Lewin just after the last war.

of these forces is exerted by effectively utilizing every individual member of the group. It is not always easy for a manager to visualize his group as a number of individual people; it is usually easier and more convenient to consider the individuals collectively as a group. But at regular intervals it is desirable to separate out what the organizer has put together, and to consider each and every individual within one's span of control as a potentially greater force than he is at present. The yearly assessment of individuals by managers, carried out usually for a salary review, is useful but it rarely goes far enough to cover the exercises I have in mind.

I have long wondered why management accountants have not yet seriously endeavoured to treat each individual in a group as a capital asset, and annually to value him for inclusion in the company's balance sheet! Perhaps the reason is obvious, and is that few senior managers are prepared, first, to analyse themselves, or their senior colleagues, to the extent of deciding their current net worth to the company, what rate of depreciation should be applied, and when and how they should be 'written off'!

Perhaps this possibility is too remote for serious consideration, and perhaps, too, many of us would say that, such is the wide scale of human valuations and variations, it is an impossible task. I must agree that it is very difficult to assess the financial value of, say, an Einstein or a Churchill. But it is not difficult to work towards this form of assessment, and more care and time should be spent by managers in endeavouring to assess, with all the best tools available, what is the present *and the future* value of those individuals for whom they are responsible. In each and every individual in the group is a potential force, which, in the right circumstances, can be put to use more effectively than was previously thought possible.

One of the most important managerial beliefs is that *every member of one's group is capable of better things than that person has so far achieved. If one does not possess this belief, one is surely not a manager*. To have this faith in members of his group is a rare managerial quality, and he who believes it, and shows that he believes it, will more often than not find proof of its truth.

Therefore, in considering his group's dynamic content, a manager must consider, first, how best he can maximize the personal value of each and every individual, not only by increasing individual contributions, but ensuring that the *resultant* increase is in line with the group's objectives; in other words, individual strengths are applied in the right direction. A more powerful missile without better guidance is a menace. I am reminded of a manager who, with a satisfactory gleam in his eye, said to me recently: 'We've got a pretty good bunch of chaps now, all pointing more or less the same way.' This is, indeed, high praise. There is satisfaction in helping to increase an individual's stature as a person. There is even greater satisfaction in ensuring that his added stature is applied fully to group objectives.

The second of the three forces needed to maintain dynamic life in the group is created by effective design of the group structure. Every group, whether it contains a collection of individuals, an assembly of component parts, or an association of chemical compounds, is a *potential* force. In its static state it generally has little value, and it justifies itself only when it is put into motion in order to achieve the objective for which it was designed.

In Chapter 5 I said that a group structure comprised seven interrelated factors and a complicated mixture of internal weaknesses and strengths. Weaknesses are present because of the inevitable tendency of every dynamic group to disintegrate, usually along the lines of least resistance to strains. Strengths can be built in, first, by exploiting the natural tendency of most individuals in the group to work towards cohesion; second, by a careful design of the internal structure, which involves attention to factors such as group size, shape, internal structure, cohesion, communication and leadership. Each of these must be 'designed' as a discrete part of the whole group. But even this is not enough and the main assembly, i.e. the group, must also be well designed as a composite whole.

We find therefore that *three* separate, but obviously related, design skills are necessary to create the most effective group structure. There is a *selection skill* which is exercised in choosing individuals who will best contribute to group purpose. There is a *component design skill* which is exercised in considering how best each of the seven factors on page 131 is to be designed. There is, finally, an *assembly design skill*, which involves considering the individuals, the components and the principles, and making whatever personal and special adjustments are necessary to ensure that a composite dynamic group emerges.

It is desirable here to make the point that an organizational group, like its engineering namesake, requires continuous adjustments if it is to go on functioning satisfactorily. The group will inevitably face personal, structural and environmental changes which, to be successfully accommodated, must, as far as possible, be anticipated. The better the original design, the less drastic these subsequent changes are likely to be, and the easier it should be to accommodate change. The organizer should bear in mind a fundamental point which every good engineering designer remembers—that is, to provide for 'design stretch'. We are all familiar with products whose official designation may be, for instance, 'Tank Mark I'. The tank may, after several planned design changes, be designated 'Tank Mark V', at which stage its original design has probably been stretched to the desirable limit, and a basically new design is needed.

Every organizational group should have built into it a flexibility to accommodate changes in those factors or principles which are most likely to be affected by subsequent group requirements. Each group must decide its own particular rate of change, but having done so it should design the group structure in a form best able to accommodate 'stretch'.

The third of the forces necessary to maintain dynamic group life is that which keeps the group 'in orbit', that is, moving in effective relationship to its external environment. Just as no individual can be sustained without group relationships, so no group can exist without its 'external' relationships, some of which are imposed on the group, like foreign competition, while others are created by the possibility that the group may impose itself on others while proceeding along its chosen path.

As with a missile or a satellite, it is not enough to create a brilliantly designed group assembly structure. Success comes only when it is launched and continues on a planned external path. Group dynamics must include a consideration of where, how and when the dynamic force is exerted in order to keep the group in effective motion.

The Forces of Dynamic Life

In this book I have attempted in logical order to discuss 'the personal, internal group, and external environmental forces' which provide dynamic life. Let us now, in retrospect, pull them together in one final attempt to show their separate significances and their collective strength.

The 'Personal' Skill

I discussed at some length the individual as a single, subjective person, and I emphasized that the first, and perhaps the greatest, group strength is provided by the 'personal' qualities within it. I emphasized also that the greatest *potential* strength within a group is contained within these same persons, on the assumption that every person possesses a capacity not yet fully utilized. To understand individual persons we must be able to understand any one person, and this raises issues and problems of great importance to society and to practising managers.

Our understanding of any one man's capabilities is still slight, particularly when we endeavour to assess his managerial qualities.

Research work in the field of man's 'personal' qualities must inevitably commence with a full understanding of his physiological and psychological state, which is still far from realization. In the meantime, however, knowledge is slowly becoming available to managers from these specialist fields which, even if incomplete and occasionally dangerous, does at least indicate the scope for further study and, in particular, the need for some authoritative body like the D.S.I.R. to ensure that new knowledge uncovered by other specialists is translated into managerial terms, and made more widely available to researching and practising managers.

It is essential that this new knowledge is made available in the form of qualitative and quantitative norms or standards of measurement against which particular individuals may be judged, not only to assist in their placement within a group but to help in understanding more fully the many personal problems which arise in every group.

This leads us directly to another aspect of the individual person which I discussed at some length and for which managers are directly responsible. A fuller realization of the importance of the individual in maximizing group effectiveness must lead managers towards a greater interest in 'personal' problems, and in no part of his job is a manager judged more critically than by the manner in which he treats individual persons. A realization of this involves him in finding adequate time for these personal cases, and I suggested many ways in which this time could be effectively used.

In discussing the individual, I emphasized particularly the need to consider the 'whole man'. This raises questions of great philosophic, technical and social importance, and many managers will feel that this concept of the whole man is beyond their capabilities and indeed their responsibilities. But who, in our community, has more responsibility than a manager for creating an environment where men and women may achieve satisfaction? The working environment, despite today's shorter hours of work, still occupies most gainfully employed people for a major part of their waking life, and in it they must earn the money and achieve the ambitions which help greatly to sustain them and their families for the remaining part of their lives.

Within this working environment are to be found in concentrated form all those forces (social, organizational, technical, etc.) which are met with in the outside world, and within it, too, their impact on the individual is likely to be at its strongest. For these reasons a manager must surely, among all in authority, clearly understand the whole man and attempt fully to develop him and his group for mutual satisfactions.

Managers must themselves achieve the status of 'whole men' before they are capable of leading others, and one important modern dilemma facing us is how to bridge the gap which today exists between the arts and sciences, or, in human terms, between those many people (often in high authority) who see in science and technology a danger to human values, and those others (an increasing number) who believe that only a full understanding and utilization of science and technology can increase personal well-being. The whole man must be a bridge-builder, with even more concern for synthesis than analysis.

I may perhaps have given the impression that this 'gap' is today being closed more deliberately by scientists and technologists than by so-called humanists. It is among the former that one appears to find stronger attempts to devise organic and social mechanisms which will integrate the many new specialisms into a more comprehensible 'whole'. Examples of this are numerous and among others I mention three important integrating activities: first, the development of the Engineering Institutions Joint Council which was recently set up to bring together more effectively the institutions concerned primarily with engineering; secondly, the British Conference on Automation and Computation (B.C.A.C.), which attempted to integrate groups and institutions of many different kinds, and thirdly the influence which new specialisms, such as cybernetics and ergonomics, are having upon the integration of many different specialisms.

There is, too, a significantly greater use by scientists and technologists of words which until recently were 'social' in their significance. I referred particularly to the two words 'control' and 'communication', and although there are obvious dangers in the semantic misunderstandings which may arise when words and terms achieve a more complicated definition, I believe that a compensating advantage will emerge when more people are encouraged by this trend to consider definitions and their significance more deeply and widely. The wider definitions and uses will help to bridge the gap.

Inevitably, future attempts to bridge the gap will encourage a scientific approach to the problems involved. Whether approached from the 'humanist' or social side of the gap, or from the scientific side, there will be a considerable increase in 'social research', which will attract to itself an increasing number of humanists who have so far opposed (if anything) the development of science and technology. Whether in the foreseeable future this will largely reduce the considerable differences which now exist in education and inclination between humanists and scientists is a difficult question to answer. I see, at *present*, a stronger desire among scientists to understand the 'human' aspects of their specialisms than I see among 'humanists' to understand science. There must never develop a one-way traffic system over the bridge, but both the 'scientific specialist' and 'humanist specialist' must develop a broader understanding of his own chosen field, and a fuller understanding of the other fellow's contribution. There must be a more highly developed common market of ideas, methods, techniques and tools, and from this a greater understanding of the whole man and a more effective development of group mechanics.

The Group Skill

Let us now reconsider the relationship between groups of individuals and the generation of dynamic force. To understand the whole man fully we must realize the importance of group activity and the fact that no one individual can live a full life except in association with others. He sustains, and is sustained by, a group. Organization, which helps to define the group, has many definitions, although it is basically, as Barker suggested, a tool or instrument which serves the individuals and the group within which they exist. Its aim is to help all the individuals attain a common purpose, and, with it, greater personal satisfactions.

At this stage we must again emphasize the 'dynamic' nature of organization and therefore its close association with the subject of this chapter, Group Dynamics. A tool such as organization is effective only if effectively used, and my own definition assumes that it is in continuous use and not merely available or quiescent. This is a most important concept, and I believe that many failures in business arise because managers fail to realize the necessity for an *actual* rather than a *potential* dynamic content within the group's organization structure.

I suggested, after an analysis of various definitions, that seven structural factors existed within this comprehensive definition of the organization structure. These are:

(1) Size.
(2) Shape.
(3) Internal Structure.
(4) Communications.
(5) Cohesion.
(6) Group Direction.
(7) Leadership.

In considering these factors we observed that they vary in concept. For instance, cohesion and leadership may appropriately be described as personal concepts; the others, size, shape, internal structure and (possibly) communications, as functional concepts, which are capable of graphic or diagrammatic representation. In this respect the design of a group structure is analogous to an engineering assembly, where one meets not only with the problem of designing the best component (personal) parts, but designing also the best operating (functional) capacity into the complete assembly (group).

Functional capacity is the real objective of a designer, whether he is an engineer or a manager, and I sympathize with those who say that if a company appears to function well it does not matter how it is organized or whether it offends every management principle. As with golf, 'it's not how, but how many, that counts'! If a group *functions* well it becomes difficult to accept the statement that its individuals are unsatisfactory, its 'factors' or principles poor, or its assembly imperfect. In organizational affairs, as I suggested in *Management Principles*, functional satisfaction is often achieved by some very odd people and organizational groups, and this is the most important reason why a scientific approach to organization is so difficult for so many managers to accept. They say, with some truth: 'See how well we manage by guesswork and by God'!

There is today a greater interest in good aesthetic design, that is, an ability to look right as well as function correctly. The 'good design' is to me a combination of both, and, translating this view into organizational terms, I look with suspicion at any organization structure which 'looks wrong' even if I am told that it functions well. It is certainly true that the odd bad golf-stroke comes off just as the occasional untidy-looking organization structure functions well. But the better the skill in golf and management the more consistent the dividends. If I had the skill at golf to ring the hole with my approach shots, I would have a better chance to hole out in fewer strokes. Analogous skill in management gives analogous results.

It is difficult to summarize the many individual experiments and conclusions discussed under each of the seven structural factors. It may be more convenient, first, to consider whether they may be sub-grouped into a smaller number of complementary elements, and from this to discuss *relationships* rather than factors. Certainly, if we are to persevere with our attempts to understand more fully the 'whole problem', we must spend as much time on relationships as on the factors involved in these relationships.

I suggested earlier that cohesion and leadership could more appropriately be described as *personal factors*. By this I mean that success in achieving them depends more upon the qualities of the group leaders than upon the skill of subordinates, although this does not mean that 'everything depends on the group leaders'. It does, ultimately, but the principal actors must depend greatly on their supporting cast. Continuing with this analogy, I do not find it difficult to visualize the acceptance by top managers of a special personal responsibility for the two factors cohesion and leadership, and a delegated responsibility for other factors, even if, in the final analysis, top managers must be responsible for every element of the business.

A most important relationship exists between cohesion and leadership, which is contained in the word 'conformity'. I said earlier that I preferred cohesion to fusion, because the latter connoted 'a "solid state" which is not compatible with group dynamics'. Cohesion is not an absolute condition, and a variety of cohesive states can exist within a main group. This is, too, a constantly changing cohesive pattern.

In discussing leadership we found that here too was a need for a constantly changing organizational pattern as leadership requirements changed. Taken together, we see in cohesion and leadership the need to apply the Principle of Continuity, that is, 'the need to consider reorganization as a continuing process'. It is a major responsibility of top managers constantly to assess the cohesive and leadership conditions needed by the group, and to take early action.

Can the remaining five factors be logically grouped for synoptic consideration? I suggested earlier that 'they are functional' concepts which can be delegated more successfully to others for preparation of the groundwork; these factors, in order of discussion, are Size, Shape, Internal Structure, Communications and Group Direction, and at this stage we might with advantage remind ourselves of the third of the skills required to maintain Group Dynamics.

Assembly Design Skill

This is a special responsibility of top managers and it produces, when the various elements are 'put together', a 'composite dynamic group'.

In organizational as in other business affairs there is a great need to delegate as much as possible to the programmed areas or, in other words, to those who do the groundwork more thoroughly. Each of the five factors has considerable possibilitie, in this direction, not only within itself but in combination with other sub-groups. Each can draw upon mechanical or other analogies as a contribution to its own solution; each can use graphical or mathematic aids; each can involve statistical exercises. Each also involves a consideration of the principles of organization isolated on page 272. Together, these details can be studied by subordinates and given consideration and decision by top managers, who are now ready to apply the final skill needed to put the whole thing together.

It is possible to make an analogy between organizational and engineering design skill. It is disturbing to find many mechanical designs which fail to reach the high purpose of those who originally conceived them. Somewhere along the road someone lost sight of the original purpose, failed to design the individual components well, or failed to put the components together into a functional, aesthetically satisfying whole.

When customers purchase complete assemblies they rarely

study, at first, the 'components'. For instance, in purchasing a new car we are usually impressed first by the aesthetic considerations and the overall specification. All too often afterwards various components fail with depressing regularity, and our attitude to the complete design is conditioned accordingly. What is the right approach towards the complete design? It is perhaps asking too much that a prospective purchaser should examine its ability to satisfy each of three basic requirements, its overall purpose, the quality of its components, and the skill in which they are assembled together. One thing is certain; he should pay more attention to the second and third requirements than he usually does. If this happens many designers will be challenged more directly than they are today to produce a better overall job.

If something goes wrong when we 'assemble' people into a group it is usually more convenient to blame one or more individuals *in* the group than those who are responsible for assembling the group. Perhaps the fault may be individual as well as organizational, but the latter must always receive its share of attention. It often reveals that the 'fault' is in a more senior person than the particular subordinate who ostensibly 'failed'. ·

When a senior manager assembles all the components he is exercising a considerable design skill. He must ensure that the elements or components are themselves appropriately designed, not for general but for special application to the particular design for which he is responsible. It is now that he must realize the full implications of a scientific approach, which is not to produce a universal truth but *to provide an organization structure best fitted to the particular purpose in the circumstances which exist.* This special task is particularly relevant to the problem of management selection, where the primary purpose is to find a manager best likely to achieve a particular task in a particular set of circumstances, rather than to select a 'universal manager'.

Reconsidering the problem of Group Dynamics as a whole, I am increasingly impressed by its similarity in many ways to the problem of creating the best design of almost any complex functioning product. Both are concerned with the creation of a complex unit which must, in functioning, achieve the planned objective. Both contain a widely varied collection of individual parts, each of which must be specially made (or selected) so that it can be relied upon for individual strength and collective 'fit'.

Both need special attention to assembly, in terms of overall shape, size, control, etc., and both require functional ability, where all the individual parts and factors are co-ordinated into a dynamic whole.

Both designs should accommodate as much stretch as possible to allow for changing demands and conditions. Both, finally, need a special additional (managerial) skill in making the adjustments necessary for smooth continuous running.

I wonder how many engineering designers would feel themselves able to cope with Group Dynamics?

Can we state more precisely those special design and assembly skills which managers must possess to put together most effectively the 'elements' available? Most of these skills have already been discussed in one form or another, but let us draw them together. Managers need:

(1) A scientific approach, which ensures that every important problem can withstand a step-by-step examination, ranging from a knowledge of the 'facts' to a validating conclusion.

(2) A consideration of the principles of organization and *how much divergence from them is to be authorized—and why.*

(3) A full realization of the importance of the linking media between elements. To illustrate this I will repeat an earlier statement that automation was born when the importance of the 'link' between two or more machines was fully realized. It was not enough to realize the importance of the two machines, or elements. It was their relationship

and how this should be designed which produced a complete group.

'Putting together' several elements, which differ in kind as well as degree from each other, is a much more difficult task, and the linking media are many and varied, although, as suggested earlier, cohesion and leadership play a key part in this task.

(4) A special consideration of the Principle of Balance. This principle is not considered essential by all the authorities quoted, but I said earlier on page 270 that its importance is growing as specialization increases. Let us examine the opportunity for giving special design consideration to each of the separate or discrete parts which make up the total structure. In technical fields we are increasingly dividing the total assembly structure into a greater number of separate components in order to achieve the best design. Consider, for instance, a relay assembly which comprises a variety of components of different metals and specifications. Some components require the electrical considerations to be paramount, while in others mechanical characteristics are more important. Each part is specially designed for its job, and together all unite into a more effective relay than was possible with less choice of specialist parts.

Much the same is possible in a group structure. Each *person* is selected more carefully for his particular job, and together all are fitted effectively into a well-designed group. Just as there is an increasing variety of special materials available to the engineering designer so there is an increasing number of specialists available to the organizer and manager. We can expect, therefore, that the trend of organization structional design is towards a greater number of specialist 'divisions'.

Will this cause a greater weakness or strength of the

component structure? The answer clearly is that each is possible, depending greatly on how we design the divisional links. If the divisional patterns are designed to use specialist skills fully; if the divisional links overlap rather than underlap; if the *inter*-communication aspects are borne in mind, then we shall develop greater strength by the greater use of specialists, and the greater sub-division of the structure. The cynic may well say that there are many 'ifs' in this programme, and I must agree that the present trend towards greater specialization is a weakening rather than a strengthening force. Perhaps a fuller realization of this will encourage us to examine organizational divisions more carefully.

(5) A reconsideration of the 'growth' factors (page 126) which were used as a basis for preparing the organizational groundwork. Two important things depend on the accuracy of these predictions. One, the validity of the whole organizational programme, which can only be as good as the basic information fed into its preparation. Two, the amount and direction of design stretch that should be provided to allow for growth. An important element of growth is the possibility and, usually, the desirability of 'personal' changes, and top managers must have a full up-to-date knowledge of personal growth requirements before completing the final assembly of the organization structure. At this final stage, therefore, a special top management responsibility is to ensure that adequate room for organizational stretch is provided, that the direction of stretch is known, and that the individuals involved can match the requirements.

(6) Finally, and emerging directly from a consideration of (5), there is a special need to ensure that the complete design encourages, in various ways, the 'exceptional' consideration of individuals and personal problems which we dis-

cussed in Chapter 3. The best mechanical design has built into it a lubrication system and a number of checks which indicate, directly or indirectly, whether the system is under control. When the assembly achieves dynamic movement it needs constant vigilance to ensure that its internal movements are working and lubricated as planned and that, externally, the whole group is on its desired path. It is at this stage that the top manager achieves his final objective, and I finish this book.

U

Appendix

ATLANTIC PRINCIPLES

Objectives

I. *The objectives* of the enterprise must be defined.
   A. Organization must distinguish between the principal and auxiliary objectives of administration in order to permit concentration of administrative efforts on the principal objective.
   B. The organization should be built around the main functions of the business and not around an individual or group of individuals.

II. *Distribution of Functions*
   The proper distribution of functions is a primary objective of organization planning.
   A. Auxiliary functions which do not contribute directly to the main task and are performed mainly for one unit should be assigned to that unit. Assignment of such functions to another unit might result in ineffective performance since the unit primarily served would have no direct authority over the execution of the auxiliary functions.
   B. Functions should be allocated so as to avoid duplicated or overlapping functions, the neglect of essential functions, and the over-emphasis of subsidiary functions.
   C. The organization structure should be kept as simple and economical as possible. Increasing the complexity of the organization structure augments expense and makes effective co-ordination more difficult.

    D. The functions assigned to an organizational unit should be as homogeneous as practicable. Inherent nature of the work and similarity in technical knowledge or skills required are two of several criteria useful in determining homogeneity.

    E. Responsibilities are better performed by individuals than by groups. Individuals act while groups debate. Action depends upon decision, and decisions are made most expeditiously by individuals who represent a single source of accountability.

III. *Responsibility and Authority*

Responsibilities and authorities must be defined and their inter-relationship established.

    A. Definitions of responsibility and authority should be clear and precise. Failure to establish and implement such definitions leads to confusion, misunderstanding, and the warping of organization according to personalities.

    B. Authority and responsibility must correspond. To hold an individual accountable for activity of any kind without assigning him the necessary authority to discharge the responsibility is unsatisfactory and inequitable.

    C. Authority to take or initiate action should be so placed as to permit the great bulk of routine decisions to be made at lower levels, with only exceptional matters to be decided by higher levels.

IV. *Delegation*

Delegation is an essential feature of sound organization.

    A. No organization can function effectively without delegation. Lack of courage to delegate properly and of knowledge of how to delegate is one of the most general causes of failure in organization.

B. Organization must distinguish between planning, doing and controlling as phases of administration, and, of these three, doing is the most adaptable to delegation.

C. Less important duties should be delegated and those of greater importance reserved.

D. The chain of delegation should be as short as practicable. The longer the chain, the more time is consumed in reaching decisions and the greater the cost in reduced effectiveness and unproductively employed manpower.

E. Means should be provided for furnishing qualified replacements for all positions. Delegation of authority and responsibility is an effective means of training and testing personnel for higher levels of supervision.

V. *Supervision*

There are limits on the supervisor.

A. An executive should not have reporting to him, directly, more than five (or at the most six) subordinate executives whose duties overlap or are inter-related.

B. Supervision of an individual should be exercised only by one immediate superior.

VI. *Control*

Increased delegation necessitates increased control.

A. Provision must be made for adequate control. Since an executive does not relinquish accountability upon delegation, means must be provided for keeping him informed concerning the manner of performance of the responsibilities he has delegated.

URWICK'S PRINCIPLES

(1) *The Principle of the Objective*

Every organization and every part of the organization must be an expression of *the purpose* of the undertaking concerned or it is meaningless and therefore redundant.

(2) *The Principle of Specialization*

The activities of every member of any organized group should be confined, as far as possible, to the performance of a single function.

(3) *The Principle of Co-ordination*

The purpose of organizing *per se*, as distinguished from the purpose of the undertaking, is to facilitate co-ordination; unity of effort.

(4) *The Principle of Authority*

In every organized group the supreme authority must rest somewhere. There should be a clear line of authority from the supreme authority to every individual in the group.

(5) *The Principle of Responsibility*

The responsibility of the superior for the acts of his subordinate is absolute.

(6) *The Principle of Definition*

The content of each position, both the duties involved, the authority and responsibility contemplated and the relationships with other positions, should be clearly defined in writing and published to all concerned.

(7) *The Principle of Correspondence*

In every position the responsibility and the authority should correspond.

(8) *The Span of Control*

No person should supervise more than five, or at the most six, direct subordinates whose work interlocks.

(9) *The Principle of Balance*

It is essential that the various units of organization should be kept in balance.

(10) *The Principle of Continuity*
Reorganization is a continuous process; in every under-taking specific provision should be made for it.

CAMERON'S PRINCIPLES

(1) *Appropriateness*
The organization chosen must be appropriate to *the common end.*

(2) *Specialization*
Each undertaking is forced to employ an increasing number of highly qualified specialists, each concentrating on a narrow sector of activity.

(3) *Balance*
A good organization is always well balanced; it will provide for all functions in proportion to their relative importance in achieving the common end.

(4) *Clearness*
This means having:
(a) a clear line of authority, and
(b) clearly defined functions for each post, so that each person in the undertaking knows exactly for what he is responsible.

(5) *Span of Supervision*
In all the higher ranks of management and administration the number of men personally supervised by one man must be limited, probably to a maximum of six.

(6) *Co-ordination*
To be specified wherever possible in the framework of organization and the framework to be constructed with the need for co-operation constantly in mind.

(7) *Control*
In the sense of checking, this must be independent to be effective.

(8) *Research*
A principle to be applied to organization itself.

(9) *Flexibility*
This is a dynamic principle which is almost impossible to draft into the static framework of organization.

BROWN'S PRINCIPLES

(a) There shall be one chief executive in every organization who shall be responsible for carrying out the policy of its policy-making body. He shall be a full-time worker in the organization and shall have complete authority to take any action consistent with the policy he is implementing.

(b) The responsibility of each executive shall be explained in general terms to every member of the organization.

(c) The span of control of a 'line executive' shall be limited to the number of people with whom he can maintain frequent contact, and amongst whom he can maintain co-operation. He shall grant the right of frequent access to those immediately responsible to him.

(d) The functional authority of all those carrying responsibility for special functions shall be clearly explained to everyone in the organization.

(e) Specialists or functional managers shall, within the span of their special knowledge, have the right to prescribe to executive managers on methods and techniques. They shall have the right to appeal to the executive manager to whom they are themselves responsible, to endorse their prescriptions with executive authority, if those to whom their prescriptions are given fail to carry them out.

(f) No man shall be executively responsible to more than one person.

(g) No man shall give orders to anyone except those who are his immediate subordinates.

Index

317

For Product Safety Concerns and Information please contact our EU representative GPSR@taylorandfrancis.com Taylor & Francis Verlag GmbH, Kaufingerstraße 24, 80331 München, Germany

Printed and bound by CPI Group (UK) Ltd, Croydon, CR0 4YY

08/05/2025

01864324-0001